Preface

When Commodore Wilbert E. Longfellow started the Life Saving Service of the American Red Cross in 1914, his primary objective was to organize local volunteers into lifesaving corps to supervise local bathing areas. By training outstanding lifesavers from each corps to teach swimming, the Commodore continued his program of "waterproofing America." Through his innumerable talks and public demonstrations, he made America aware of the need for water safety education. The immediate results of this education were an increase in the popularity of aquatic activities and a significant decline in the national drowning rate.

Since 1914, the Red Cross has continued to expand on the Commodore's innovations by publishing textbooks and instructors' manuals on swimming and water safety. These publications are revised periodically to introduce new skills, and materials and programs have been expanded to include areas of interest relating to aquatics safety.

The public began to recognize the American Red Cross as a leading authority in water safety. With this recognition, however, also came a tendency for people to take certain aspects of the Red Cross water safety program for granted. They began to look at course titles and often misunderstood their purpose. To the public, the holder of a lifesaving certificate became a qualified lifeguard without additional training. Students enrolled in lifesaving courses because public opinion and state legislation established such courses as the main criteria for employment as a lifeguard.

Authorities in the field agree that a gap exists between the skills learned in a lifesaving course and the specific training required to carry out the responsibilities of a lifeguard effectively. Certain factors must be considered when training an individual as a lifeguard:

- The amount and type of training required of a lifeguard vary from one area of the country and from one facility to another. Emphasis must be given to the type of facility, the environment, the weather, and other factors. Training courses may vary in length from a few hours to more than one hundred hours, not including in-service training once a lifeguard is employed.

- Training prerequisites for positions vary greatly. Current certifications in first aid and cardiopulmonary resuscitation (CPR) are required by many organizations that employ lifeguards. Additional training in pool chemistry, filtration systems, or the use of small craft is a requirement in some areas.

It would be difficult for any organization to develop a textbook and program for training lifeguards that would meet the needs of all lifeguards and all aquatic facilities. The several national organizations that are concerned with the education and training of lifeguards must develop and maintain skill and training levels that are commensurate with the needs of their respective programs and facilities. The purpose of this text is to focus attention on the skills and knowledge required for an individual to properly assume the responsibilities of a lifeguard at a swimming pool or a protected (nonsurf) open-water beach. Students using this book should previously have completed training in lifesaving, first aid, and cardiopulmonary resuscitation (CPR). Learning the information in these courses is a necessary step to becoming a lifeguard. This book emphasizes that additional training will be needed at the aquatic facility where the individual will be working.

This text is a guide for lifeguards, instructors, and administrators of aquatic facilities, for establishing a system of lifeguard selection and training.

Acknowledgments

The American Red Cross wishes to thank the following Safety Services volunteers and professional staff for their significant contributions of time and materials to the development of this publication:

Fredrick F. Andres, Ph.D., Associate Professor, Department of Exercise Science and Physical Education, the University of Toledo; William Carl Berry, Supervisor, Aquatics, Grossmont Union High School District, El Cajon, California; Douglas G. D'Arnall, Marine Safety Captain, City of Huntington Beach, California, and Past Chairman, Council for National Cooperation in Aquatics; James Gorman, Director, Safety Services, American Red Cross, Greater Cleveland Chapter, Cleveland, Ohio; Ralph L. Johnson, Associate Professor, Director of Aquatics, Indiana University of Pennsylvania, Indiana, Pennsylvania; James C. Langridge, Director, Health and Safety Services, Boy Scouts of America, Irving, Texas; John Malatak, Director, Safety Services, American Red Cross, Nashville Area Chapter, Nashville, Tennessee; Joseph Pecoraro, Supervisor of Beaches and Pools, Chicago Parks District, Chicago, Illinois; Ed Petterson, Aquatics Facilities Director, County of Los Angeles, Parks and Recreation Department, Los Angeles, California; Frank Pia, Supervising Chief Lifeguard, New York City Department of Parks and Recreation; Miss Beatrice A. Pyle, Associate Professor, Department of Health, Physical Education, and Recreation, Miami University, Oxford, Ohio; and Allen Wagner, Director of Aquatics, Health and Physical Education Chairman, East Allegheny High School, North Versailles, Pennsylvania.

Special gratitude and acknowledgments are extended to the volunteers and professional staff from the following American Red Cross chapters who participated in the field tests of the materials for the lifeguard training program: Albany Area Chapter, Albany, New York; American Red Cross of Massachusetts Bay, Boston, Massachusetts; American Red Cross in Greater New York, New York, New York; Pittsburgh-Allegheny County Chapter, Pittsburgh, Pennsylvania; and San Diego County Chapter, San Diego, California.

The Red Cross expresses deep appreciation to the staff of the Epilepsy Foundation of America for their assistance in providing technical review and advice regarding the procedures for dealing with epileptic seizures in an aquatic environment.

Deep appreciation is extended to Richard Guy for his patience and talent in developing the illustrations.

Special gratitude is also extended to the following Safety Services staff members at national headquarters for their significant assistance in the development of this publication: Cliff E. Lundberg, Director, Safety Services; Orin Myers, Director, Water Safety Program; Ray Miller, Director, Small Craft Program; Don Sleeper, Assistant Director, First Aid Program; Linda W. Marable, Safety Specialist, First Aid Program; and Thomas C. Werts, Assistant Director, Water Safety Program, who had the major responsibility for the development of this textbook.

Contents

Chapter 1

PHILOSOPHY OF
LIFEGUARD TRAINING

During the past two decades, aquatics has become one of America's largest recreations. The number of residential, private, and public pools; health spas; state parks; campgrounds; and public beaches has increased steadily. More people are engaging in activities in, on, under, and around the water. All this increase has created a demand for people properly trained to guard these activities.

WHAT IS A LIFEGUARD?

Depending on whom you ask, the answers to this question will be many and varied. For example, a lifeguard may be considered to be —
- A supervisor who sits in a stand watching people in and around the water in order to assist anyone in trouble.
- A disciplinarian who enforces rules and regulations.
- A public relations person who promotes the facility.
- A maintenance person who helps to maintain a clean and safe facility.
- A janitor who cleans the snack bar area, locker rooms, and grounds once or twice a day.
- A teacher who gives swimming lessons.
- A babysitter who operates a safe place where parents can drop the kids off for the day.
- A person trained in first aid.

- A swim coach who trains the team and organizes meets.

The truth is, a lifeguard may perform all of these roles, to some degree. The extent of the job depends on many factors: the governing body of an aquatic facility, its manager, the number of people who use it, and the number of lifeguards on duty at the same time. The fact is that lifeguarding is no longer just a summer job. It has become a career for many persons.

Historically, the major requirement for a lifeguard was the possession of a current Red Cross Senior or Advanced Lifesaving certificate or an equivalent certification. In many cases, unfortunately, the individual who is hired is given little or no on-the-job training to develop lifeguard skills and knowledge. Organizations such as the American Red Cross, the Boy Scouts of America, the Young Men's Christian Association (YMCA), the Council for National Cooperation in Aquatics, the United States Lifesaving Association, and the Aquatic Council of the American Alliance of Health, Physical Education, Recreation, and Dance (AAHPERD) are striving to educate the public and the owners, operators, and managers of aquatic facilities regarding the difference between lifesaving and lifeguarding.

For years, the lifesaving course emphasized personal safety: how to prevent accidents and how to protect yourself in emergencies. People were also taught how to rescue others. The emphasis has been on extending an object such as a towel or pole or on throwing a flotation device to the person. If neither of these methods was successful, the individual was taught to use some sort of boat to reach the person in trouble. The point has been that the potential rescuer's main concern was personal safety. The rescuer was taught to enter the water **only as a last resort** to make a swimming rescue. The lifesaving course was never intended to be a complete lifeguard training course.

Red Cross philosophy is different for the lifeguard training course. Lifeguard candidates are taught that their primary concern is the safety of others. Professional and volunteer lifeguards at private and public aquatic facilities understand that they are responsible for providing the safest possible conditions for the patrons.

The attitude that a lifeguard needs only lifesaving training is a misconception. The ability to recognize a hazardous situation and to prevent an accident or further injury is vital to lifeguards. They must be able to supervise bathers, minimize dangers, educate patrons to safety, enforce rules and regulations, render assistance, prepare records and reports, and perform whatever additional administrative duties are required. The position of lifeguard has become one of authority and responsibility.

Over the years, state laws and local ordinances have set standards for the quality of water, specifications of facility equipment, and the construction of facilities. Staff members at many aquatic facilities have been required to take technical training in subjects such as the operation of filtration systems and basic water chemistry.

Laws and ordinances governing sanitation and equipment were continually updated to reflect changes and improvements. In contrast, the requirement for an individual to become a lifeguard remained the same: possess a current lifesaving certificate. In 1974, the Red Cross included information on the job of a lifeguard in the Advanced Lifesaving course. However, this information was intended for informational purposes only. The lifesaving course was still not intended to train lifeguards. Qualifications of lifeguards in modern rescue techniques, first aid, and CPR were still left to the interpretation of individual facility management.

The training needs of lifeguards at most aquatic facilities are not being met through the Advanced Lifesaving course. Therefore, the additional skills needed by lifeguards have been identified. Two separate courses, Advanced Lifesaving and Lifeguard Training, are now being offered. The need for a lifesaving course will continue in local communities. Parents will need to be trained to improve the safety around residential pools. Individuals involved in aquatic activities will still need to be taught how to deal with emergencies. This involves protecting and saving themselves as well as assisting others.

The lifeguard program focuses on the training of individuals who have a lifesaving, first aid, and CPR background. It deals with the additional skills and knowledge required by individuals to develop effective lifeguard systems at swimming pools and at nonsurf, open-water beaches. These facilities need trained persons who can recognize and eliminate or minimize potentially dangerous situations. These individuals must know how to establish and carry out emergency plans for specific facilities, as well as how to educate the public on its role in promoting a safe facility.

The Red Cross does not intend to provide an all-inclusive lifeguard training program. As previously mentioned, it would be too difficult for any one organization to train lifeguards for all types of aquatic facilities. Lifeguards must become familiar with the characteristics of the facility where they are working. They must continually train in order to maintain a high degree of physical and mental alertness. They must understand the importance of maintaining current certifications in lifesaving, first aid, and CPR. They should also seek out and participate in additional training programs that relate to their duties and responsibilities, such as pool operations and other areas that may not be contained in programs developed by national organizations.

Chapter 2

REQUIREMENTS AND
RESPONSIBILITIES
OF THE LIFEGUARD

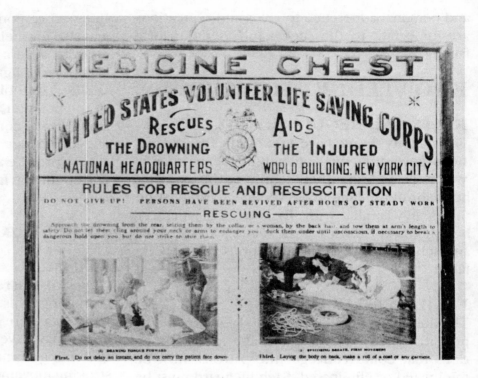

The primary responsibility of the lifeguard is to provide for the safety of the patrons utilizing the facility. Although many view this as the ability to make a swimming rescue of a drowning person, the principles of preventive lifeguarding should be foremost in the mind of the lifeguard. The knowledge of rescue skills and the ability to perform them are essential. However, the knowledge and skills of how to prevent accidents from occurring are of even greater importance.

The management of each facility should establish regulations that must be met by all lifeguards. Many of these regulations will be in accordance with state and local ordinances such as requirements for age, physical fitness, and certification in lifesaving, first aid, and CPR. There are, however, many additional characteristics and qualities that are needed by lifeguards to function effectively. These are discussed in the remainder of this chapter.

PERSONAL CHARACTERISTICS

RELIABILITY

The lifeguard should arrive for work on time and assume the responsibilities of the position. The individual should willingly accept assignments and show initiative in making constructive suggestions toward better facility operations.

EMOTIONAL STABILITY

Every individual reacts differently to stress situations. The lifeguard must have the ability to make sound decisions when dealing with difficult situations and must be able to make decisions that conform to the policies of the facility. In an aquatic facility, decisions that are made by the lifeguard may affect the total staff of the facility.

TACT AND JUDGMENT

A lifeguard must be able to gain the respect and cooperation of the public. The enforcement of rules and regulations must be standardized. The lifeguard must be courteous to patrons, but unnecessary conversations must be avoided.

PHYSICAL FITNESS

A high level of fitness is required of lifeguards at all times. Speed, strength, endurance, and flexibility are vital attributes in a rescue. Lifeguards should be required to participate in all in-service training programs. These programs should include practice of swimming, rescue, and first aid skills. Where needed, weight training and exercise programs may be included.

POSITIVE ATTITUDE

The lifeguard must understand his or her responsibilities to the employer as well as to the public. Cooperation with other guards in team efforts and personal adherence to rules and regulations are important to the successful operation of a facility.

KNOWLEDGE REQUIRED

RULES AND REGULATIONS
Each facility should have a set of rules and regulations governing the conduct of the patrons as well as an additional set identifying the expected behavior of the lifeguards. The lifeguard must be thoroughly familiar with all of the rules and must be able to explain clearly the reasons for the rules and subsequent disciplinary actions that may be taken.

FACILITY CHARACTERISTICS
The lifeguard must have knowledge of known or potentially hazardous areas of the facility. Situations that could endanger the patrons must be minimized or eliminated. Each lifeguard must be thoroughly familiar with all emergency situations that may occur at the facility and with any follow-up procedures that are required.

CHAIN OF COMMAND
Lifeguards should be aware of the operational procedures for the facility as well as the "chain of command" (Appendix A) and the positions of the lifeguards within that structure. The names, titles, and responsibilities of all staff should be part of the job orientation. Each position in the chain of command should have clearly defined responsibilities. These responsibilities may vary from one facility to another.

ADDITIONAL DUTIES
Depending on their experience, their position in the chain of command, and the needs of the facility, lifeguards may be given additional responsibilities. These may include maintenance, instruction, or coaching duties. There should be no doubt about the job responsibilities, the work schedule, or other duties that may be required of lifeguards. However, at no time should these additional duties interfere with the lifeguard's primary responsibility: the safety of the patrons.

LEGAL RESPONSIBILITIES
Lifeguards must be aware of the legal implications of their job. All lifeguards must realize that they are responsible for actions taken by them and also for their failure to act properly. Individuals who accept the position of a lifeguard also accept an obligation to the owner of the aquatic facility. That obligation is to fulfill all of the duties of the position, to participate in all training sessions, and to continually update all personal skills and knowledge. Lifeguards also accept an obligation to provide as safe a facility as possible for the patrons of that facility.

PERSONAL SKILLS

SWIMMING AND LIFESAVING
Lifeguards are required to possess a high level of swimming skills. Swimming endurance and swimming speed are equally important. Since the lifeguard may have to support the victim during a swimming rescue, it may be necessary to modify stroking movements while swimming. The size of the victim and the conditions of the victim and the water will require a well-conditioned lifeguard with a variety of skills.

Skills learned in a lifesaving course are the minimum that should be required for a lifeguard position. This does not mean that they should be the only skills required. Lifeguards must be aware of the conditions in the facility that will have an effect on the performance of lifesaving skills. The depth and clarity of the water, the movement of the water either by wind, current, or mechanical means (wave pools), and other conditions at the aquatic facility will be determining factors in how the lifeguards adapt lifesaving skills to rescue situations.

USE OF EQUIPMENT
Rescue equipment has become more standardized over the years, and many state and local ordinances clearly define minimum standards concerning such equipment. The types or styles of equipment used at a facility will be determined by the needs and budgetary limitations of the facility. Rescue equipment also includes first aid equipment that should be available. Lifeguards must ensure that all rescue equipment is in good condition and must be skilled in its use. A more detailed discussion of rescue equipment is in Chapter 7, "Equipment."

Lifeguards may be given additional off-duty responsibilities involving the maintenance of the sanitation, filtration, and communications equipment. They must be familiar with the use and condition of this equipment, since it has a direct influence on the safe and efficient operation of the facility. Poor maintenance and care of equipment cannot and should not be tolerated.

FIRST AID

First aid certification should be required of all lifeguards. The level of training should depend on the specific types of injuries that may occur at the facility. Red Cross Standard First Aid is a recommended minimum. In many facilities, the rescuer may have to begin artificial respiration with the victim in deep water. The use of flotation devices by the rescuer helps keep the victim's mouth and nose out of the water and allows the lifeguard to inflate the victim's lungs without water getting into the air passages. More information on this subject is found in Chapter 9, "Water Rescues and Special Situations." However, the limited information about first aid in this book will not qualify someone to become proficient or certified in administering first aid.

CARDIOPULMONARY RESUSCITATION (CPR)

All lifeguards should be trained and certified in CPR, which is the combination of artificial respiration and manual artificial circulation that is recommended for use in cases of cardiac arrest. **CPR should be administered only by persons currently certified in CPR.** It requires special supplemental training in the recognition of cardiac arrest and in the performance of CPR. Instruction includes practice in performing CPR individually or as part of a team, on adult or infant manikins. Annual retraining is required by the American Red Cross.

RESPONSIBILITIES

The primary responsibility of lifeguards is to ensure the safety of patrons. This includes accident prevention in the water and on the surrounding pool deck or beach area and the rescue and care of accident victims. The following items are some of the most common responsibilities of lifeguards.

PRIMARY RESPONSIBILITIES

- To prevent accidents and minimize or eliminate hazardous situations

  All activities in an assigned area including the pool deck area or beach as well as the water should be properly supervised. A lifeguard must never leave an assigned area until being properly relieved. The area should be kept clean, and a system should be established to ensure that all gates and doors are locked and that all patrons have left when the facility has been closed.

- To respond quickly to all emergency situations in the water

  Using the proper procedures and techniques, the lifeguard must be able to assist anyone in distress or rescue anyone in a drowning situation. The lifeguard must constantly scan the assigned area and be able to recognize patrons who are in need of assistance.

- To administer any emergency first aid needed by the victim of an accident

  Staying within the limits of their training, lifeguards must be able to provide the initial emergency care necessary to sustain life and to maintain life support until qualified medical personnel arrive.

- To communicate with other lifeguards and facility staff the need for additional assistance or equipment

  In emergency situations, the lifeguard must be able to summon support personnel and relay similar requests from other lifeguards.

SECONDARY RESPONSIBILITIES

- To observe and enforce all rules and regulations of the facility

  The lifeguard must obey the same set of rules as the patrons as well as those rules that are specifically for the facility staff. The lifeguard should never drink, smoke, eat, read, or listen to the radio while on duty. Nothing should distract the lifeguard from the proper supervision of the patrons.

- To educate the patrons and inform them of the purpose of and need for rules and regulations

Lifeguards should educate the patrons to safety practices by providing talks and demonstrations.

- To assist parents or family members in locating a missing child or relative

  Procedures for conducting a search for missing persons should be established at all aquatic facilities. While consideration must be given to the needs and apprehension of parents and family members, the continued supervision and safety of other patrons using the facility must be ensured.

- To complete all required records and reports on schedule and to submit them to the proper person or office

  Repair of damaged or defective equipment, budget recommendations, and personnel policies depend on records being kept and processed in the proper manner.

- To carry out all additional duties assigned by the supervisor

  Each facility may assign the off-duty lifeguard to assist in teaching swimming classes, to be the swim coach, or to supervise other staff members. Maintenance duties may also be assigned, such as cleaning the shower or locker room, picking up litter, backwashing the filters, maintaining the proper chemical balance of the water, vacuuming the pool, and handling lost and found articles.

- To conduct oneself in a professional manner

  The lifeguard is the representative of the aquatic facility who has day-to-day contact with the patrons. The public's attitude and respect for the total organization will be greatly affected by the actions and conduct of the lifeguard.

As lifeguards move up within the chain of command, their responsibilities will increase. An assistant head lifeguard may have more supervisory responsibilities or may be responsible for specific inspections of equipment. A head lifeguard will be responsible for the performance of all the lifeguards. The training and evaluation of the lifeguards, as well as the scheduling of activities, are other examples of responsibilities that may be assigned to the head lifeguard.

All lifeguards must be thoroughly familiar with the responsibilities assigned to them. These responsibilities must be explained before employment and should be a component of the lifeguard manual for every facility. Although the responsibilities of a lifeguard are many and varied, facility managers, supervisors, and lifeguards must clearly understand that **the responsibility for providing for the safety of the patrons cannot be allowed to take a secondary position to any other duties.**

Chapter 3

SELECTION AND TRAINING

The proper training of lifeguards is not something that can be accomplished on a one-time basis. It is an ongoing process, beginning with taking any prerequisite courses for the job and continuing throughout the duration of employment as a lifeguard. Training begins with the development of a working knowledge of lifesaving and personal safety skills. It continues with certification in first aid and cardiopulmonary resuscitation (CPR). Beyond these skills and knowledge is training specific to the aquatic facility where the lifeguard is employed. This training includes an orientation to facility hazards, methods of operation, organizational structure, and other subjects pertinent to that facility. Training continues after lifeguards are employed: physical training, discussions and demonstrations of emergency action plans, and training in other job responsibilities.

This chapter deals with the selection and training of lifeguards from preemployment through in-service training. It will serve as a guide for managers and owners in planning and initiating full training programs that will meet the needs of their respective facilities.

PREEMPLOYMENT REQUIREMENTS

PHYSICAL EXAMINATION

All lifeguard candidates should submit the results of a medical examination by a licensed physician certifying that they are able to perform the duties of a lifeguard. This examination should be required before employment each season or on a periodic basis. Owners and managers of aquatic facilities, who are responsible for hiring lifeguards, should be aware of all state and local requirements that pertain to the physical qualifications for lifeguards, for example, some states require a minimum vision ability, such as 20/40 uncorrected vision ability in each eye, corrected to 20/20.

LIFESAVING TRAINING

Owners and managers of aquatic facilities should be knowledgeable about all state and local agency requirements for the training of lifeguards. Some agencies use a statement such as "Lifeguards must have a current American Red Cross Advanced Lifesaving certificate or equivalent training." The responsibility of determining the equivalency of the lifesaving training is that of the governing agency. All potential lifeguards at pools and non-surf beaches must show evidence of having current lifesaving/lifeguard training from a certifying organization such as the American Red Cross, the YMCA, or the Boy Scouts of America before being hired.

The screening tests for the employment of lifeguard candidates should be conducted, if possible, for all candidates at one time. Alternate dates should be set for those candidates who are unable to attend the primary testing session. Testing should include both written (objective questions) and practical tests to determine each candidate's knowledge and skill abilities. The tests should be adjusted for the facility where they will be given. For example, an entry into a swimming pool may differ from an entry into a lake. Also, the removal of a victim from the water will differ from one facility to another. The tests should be scored and the results marked on the candidate's application.

SWIMMING SKILLS

All lifeguard candidates should be tested on their respective overall swimming ability, speed, and endurance. They will need strength and stamina to swim to a victim, to support the victim in deep water, and, if necessary, to bring the victim to safety. Therefore, all candidates should be tested on their swimming skills in two categories: (1) swimming alone, to simulate the swim to a victim, and (2) swimming while supporting a 10-pound diving brick, to simulate carrying a victim. The candidates should perform each event at an all-out pace, and their condition should be observed after each event. All candidates should be judged on the speed and efficiency of their swimming strokes during these tests, since they have a direct bearing on the amount of energy that is expended. The swims should be timed, and the results should be posted on the candidate's application.

Some examples of swimming events and times that may be used for qualifying are as follows:
- 50-yard freestyle in less than 36 seconds
- 500-yard freestyle in less than 10 minutes
- 200-yard freestyle in less than 3 minutes
- 50-yard sidestroke supporting 10-pound brick in less than 1 minute 10 seconds
- 50-yard elementary backstroke supporting 10-pound brick in less than 1 minute 20 seconds
- 2 minutes treading water supporting 10-pound brick on a pass-fail basis
- 25-yard sidestroke supporting victim on a pass-fail basis

Obviously, all of these events do not and will not apply to every aquatic facility. For example, a 500-yard swim need not be part of a screening test for a person who will be a lifeguard at a pool

with a maximum length of from 20 to 25 yards. Consideration should also be given to the use of a 10-pound diving brick to simulate carrying a victim. This would provide standardization to the test events.

FIRST AID

Lifeguards should have a thorough working knowledge of first aid to be able to properly assist victims of accidents. Such knowledge should be required of lifeguards by individual facilities even if it is not required by state or local agencies. Lifeguard candidates should show evidence of holding a current Red Cross Standard First Aid certificate. A review of the skills and knowledge in a Standard First Aid course should be part of the training given to lifeguards during their orientation or during the initial sessions of their in-service training.

A test of first aid should be given and should include knowledge and skills. Practical situations should be set up to test the lifeguard on the handling and care of victims in the types of accidents that could occur at the facility. Examples are—

- A child who runs, falls on a concrete deck, and suffers abrasions on the legs and arms.
- A drowning victim who needs to be resuscitated.
- A man who has hit the diving board during a dive and has suffered a dislocated shoulder.
- A woman who is suffering from heat stroke.

Many situations can be devised relating to different types of accidents and injuries that have happened at the facility. The candidates should be tested only on the skills that are contained in the minimum required first aid course. For example, if the minimum requirement is the American Red Cross Standard First Aid certificate, the candidates should not be tested and graded on their knowledge and handling of an emergency childbirth, since this is part of an advanced first aid course.

CARDIOPULMONARY RESUSCITATION (CPR)

All lifeguards should be required to be certified in CPR. It may not be feasible, however, to **require** CPR training as a prerequisite for employment, since some areas of the country offer limited amounts of CPR training. In areas where candidates are not certified before being employed, CPR must be included as part of the orientation and the in-service training program for all aquatic facilities. A certified course conducted by the American Red Cross or other certifying agency should be scheduled as soon as possible. It should include procedures for CPR and management of an obstructed airway for adult and infant victims. Periodic refresher training should be conducted throughout the operational season of the facility.

SMALL CRAFT SKILLS

At camp waterfronts and at open-water, nonsurf areas, lifeguards should be trained in the use of small craft as rescue boats. If small craft skills are not a prerequisite for employment, training and certification should be included as part of the orientation and the in-service training program. A Red Cross boating safety course dealing with the appropriate craft should be the minimum requirement.

ORIENTATION

Once lifeguards have been hired, it is the responsibility of the owner and manager of an aquatic facility to ensure that all of their lifeguards receive a seasonal orientation to their job and to the facility. Periodic reviews of these subjects should also be part of the in-service training program.

It must be remembered that lifeguards are under constant observation by management, other lifeguards, and the public. The actions or reactions of the lifeguards have a direct bearing on the attitudes of these groups. Therefore, lifeguards must fully understand and carry out the obligations they have accepted.

A training manual should be issued to all lifeguards as part of their orientation. They should be required to sign for the manual, indicating receipt of all the material. The manual should contain the following informational items: copies of the job description of a lifeguard; policies, procedures, rules, regulations, and methods of enforcement; responsibilities; emergency plans; samples of records used at the facility; a list of emergency telephone numbers; and the chain of command. It is the responsibility of the person supervising the lifeguards to update all of the material contained in the training manual. It is

the lifeguard's responsibility to ensure that the manual contains all of the required material

The following subjects should be included as part of a lifeguard's orientation to the aquatic facility. Recurrent lifeguards (those who have worked at the facility before) should be given an orientation at the beginning of each season or whenever there is a change in any of the information.

MANAGEMENT

All lifeguards should be thoroughly familiar with the chain of command for their facility (refer to Appendix A for various chain of command structures). Lifeguards should also know where they fit into that structure, who their supervisor is, and what their personal responsibilities are. Individuals who are in supervisory positions (e.g., head lifeguard or assistant head lifeguard) must also know the responsibilities of those lifeguards that they supervise. Each position in the chain of command must be clearly defined, since lines of authority can be confusing in larger organizations and facilities (Appendix A). For example, an aquatic director may have responsibilities for supervising both a pool manager and a head swimming instructor. A lifeguard may have duties as both a lifeguard and a swimming instructor. In this latter case, the lifeguard may be supervised by both the pool manager and the head swimming instructor. The lifeguard must clearly understand the lines of authority in these situations.

Communications through the chain of command must be explained to, and clearly understood by, the lifeguards. They should know (1) to whom they are responsible and from whom to take orders, (2) who to go to with specific problems or general requests, and (3) who to go to with complaints, problems, or suggestions.

OPERATION OF FACILITY

Each staff member should be assigned to a specific job during an orientation. Any reassignments should be made by the manager or the supervisor. To help with the development of a lifeguard's maturity, each new lifeguard, if possible, should be assigned to work with someone who has a good background and practical experience in being a lifeguard.

It should be the responsibility of the head lifeguard or the manager to make up all schedules for the facility. A daily schedule of activities such as free swims, instructional courses, and swim team practices should be posted so that everyone entering the facility knows what areas of the facility will be open or closed during various hours of the day. The schedule of the work hours for the lifeguards, including breaks, should be posted in the office and in the guard room. Any changes or substitutions must be cleared with the manager or the head lifeguard before being made on the schedule.

The logistical operation of the facility is everyone's responsibility. The safe and smooth operation of an aquatic facility depends on the actions and conduct of its staff. Lifeguards, locker room attendants, and other staff members should watch for any improper use of the utilities, such as showers left running, lights left on, or misuse of the telephone. Each of these situations can have a significant bearing on the operational budget of an aquatic facility, including equipment purchases, future raises, or maintenance.

It must be clearly understood that at no time should any additional responsibilities take priority over the lifeguard's main responsibility: the safety of the patrons. However, there may be times when a lifeguard who is off duty must accept assigned responsibility for the care and maintenance of the facility and its equipment. If so, the cleanliness of the area and the operation of the filtration system should be part of an orientation for all lifeguards. There should be an operational manual available that outlines this information in detail.

RULES AND REGULATIONS
Part of the orientation for lifeguards must cover the rules and regulations of the facility. Methods of enforcement should be clarified so that all lifeguards use standard procedures when enforcing the rules. Rules that apply to the patrons should be thoroughly explained to the lifeguards, as well as rules that apply to the lifeguards themselves. Rules governing the conduct of the lifeguards include the wearing of a proper uniform, daily opening and closing routines, and restrictions of personal habits such as smoking and drinking. It should be explained that lifeguards will be evalu-

ated on their adherence to all rules that apply to them. Further information on rules and regulations can be found in Chapter 4, "Preventive Lifeguarding."

PREVENTIVE LIFEGUARDING
The orientation to an aquatic facility should help to familiarize lifeguards with the hazardous areas of the facility. Knowing where accidents are likely to happen can determine where lifeguards should be stationed, when they should be rotated, or how they visibly scan their respective areas of responsibility. The orientation should also include the discussion of subjects such as procedures to follow for stormy weather, currents and tides, and the clarity and possible pollution of the water.

RECORDS AND REPORTS
An orientation for lifeguards should include a complete explanation of all of the records and reports for which they will be responsible. An explanation of the need for accurate and on-time records and reports will help them to understand the need to exercise care in filling out and submitting reports. Accurate and complete reports are necessary for the smooth operation of the facility. Records and reports are discussed more fully in Chapter 6, "Records and Reports."

LEGAL RESPONSIBILITIES
In order to cover this subject properly, this session should be conducted by the legal counsel for the facility. This should ensure that there is no misinformation provided and that all lifeguards receive the same information.

EMERGENCY PROCEDURES
Every staff member of an aquatic facility should be familiar with the emergency action plans for the facility. This includes the types of emergencies that may happen as well as what the lifeguards' individual responsibilities will be at the time of the emergency. Lifeguards should be trained to take action steps both as a primary rescuer and as a back-up rescuer. They should know what must be done whether they are on duty or on a rest break.

IN-SERVICE TRAINING

In-service training is the responsibility of management. Regularly scheduled sessions to review aspects of lifeguard principles and practices should be mandatory for all lifeguards to attend. The individual lifeguard should review and exercise skills regularly if an in-service training program is not established by the facility management.

One factor that makes the lifeguard different from the lifesaver is the higher degree of technical skills and knowledge required of lifeguards. This ability is dependent upon the individual lifeguard's level of total fitness. Mental alertness and physical conditioning must be maintained and, when needed, improved. The ability to react quickly and correctly will develop and improve with experience and proper training.

The following items are best dealt with at the locations where the lifeguards will be facing them on a daily basis. Therefore, each in-service training program should be tailored to meet the needs of the facility. Some examples of these items are as follows:

- Swimming pool lifeguards may need to become knowledgeable about pool filtration and the maintenance of the correct chemical balance.
- Lifeguards at beaches will need more information about the configurations of currents, about the conditions of the bottom, and about search and recovery operations.
- Lifeguards must be aware of, and know how to deal with, hazardous areas such as blind spots, slippery decks or docks, and drop-offs.
- Times and distances for swimming events, for example, will be determined by the size of the facility and its structure.

The scheduling of training sessions will be based on the hours of operation of the facility and the availability of the staff. In an outdoor facility, the weather will have a bearing on the activities to be covered and on the length of each session. The scheduling of sessions, subjects, and events will also be determined by such things as—

- Size of facility.
- Number of lifeguards employed.
- Number of lifeguards on duty at any one time.
- Amounts and types of equipment available.
- Facility budget.

- Types of incidents encountered and their frequency.

Competition between lifeguards of a facility or between lifeguards of different facilities helps to enhance skill and knowledge. If the competition is open to the public for viewing, it can increase public awareness of the responsibilities and rigorous training demanded of lifeguards. Competition can also help to promote the "team approach" to lifeguarding.

Training sessions involving lifeguards and emergency medical technicians (EMTs) or area rescue squad personnel should be scheduled whenever possible. It will be these personnel to whom the lifeguards will be turning over the responsibility for the care of some accident victims. Therefore, cooperative training sessions will make for a smoother transition in the handling of accident victims in actual emergencies.

PHYSICAL TRAINING AND CONDITIONING

Although the specific fitness requirements for lifeguards differ with location, in general, it is only the level of fitness and skills that differs. Both swimming pool and waterfront lifeguards must possess a basic level of physical fitness in order to perform their duties.

Experienced lifeguards know that fitness, which is the result of physical conditioning, is required to effect a rapid and efficient rescue. Physical conditioning for lifeguards has two phases. Emphasis must be placed on (1) general conditioning followed by (2) training to meet the specific requirements of the job.

General conditioning focuses upon the development of the cardiovascular system, muscular strength, endurance, and flexibility. These factors form the fitness foundation for lifeguard training.

Specific conditioning for water rescues should involve swimming events and rescue situations. Speed and endurance swimming events can simulate approaching a victim. Intervals of treading water and towing diving bricks can develop endurance and strength, especially in the leg muscles, which are used to support both victim and lifeguard.

Other skills required for lifeguarding may be similarly practiced. Shallow- and deep-water assists, paddling a canoe or rowing a boat, and paddling a rescue board are skills that should be part of the training program.

Each physical conditioning session should be started by gradually increasing the tempo of exercise (warm-up). Suddenly entering into strenuous exercise without this warm-up period may lead to a muscle pull or other related injury. Following the training session, a gradual cool-down is also recommended. This procedure permits a slow return of body processes to the normal, preexercise state. The cool-down period helps prevent the pooling of blood in the arms and legs, which may cause dizziness and fainting.

Developing physical fitness demands individual time and effort. Researchers have found that fitness can be retained by exercising as little as two days per week. A fitness program can be easily integrated into the lifeguards' weekly work schedule. Workouts should be a combination of conditioning exercises and job-related skills. Races, timed tests, and other motivational devices will help to ease the monotony of these sessions. In addition, competition may stimulate interest in achieving higher levels of performance among the lifeguards.

FITNESS TESTING

Objective fitness testing is probably the most precise way of determining the qualifications of lifeguards for employment and the effectiveness of a physical conditioning program. Although no

TABLE 3-1

SUGGESTED PERFORMANCE STANDARDS FOR LIFEGUARDS

TEST ITEM	LEVEL OF PERFORMANCE IN MINUTES AND SECONDS	
	POOL	OPEN-WATER BEACH
1. Recovering 10-pound object in 10 feet of water with 30-foot approach	0:09.5	0:08.0
2. Towing 10-pound object 50 yards with inverted breaststroke kick	1:20.0	1:10.0
3. Towing 10-pound object 50 yards with scissors kick	1:10.0	0:60.0
4. Swimming 50 yards freestyle	0:33.5	0:30.0
5. Swimming 500 yards/American crawl	10:00.0	8:30.0
6. Treading water 2 minutes supporting 10-pound object with both hands	P	P

P = Pass or fail, no time requirement.

exact information is available regarding the amount of fitness required for lifeguards, experience has pointed out several determinants of success. In particular, tests of swimming speed and endurance, as well as tests of the ability to handle the rare struggling victim, seem to have much support as reliable determinants.

The values of timed tests are several. First, timed tests are objective and remove the lifeguard examiner from having to rely solely upon experience in evaluating potential guards. Second, these tests give the lifeguards meaningful feedback about their capacity to handle emergency situations. Last, they give a new meaning to conditioning. The goal is a tangible number expressed in minutes, seconds, and tenths of seconds, by which success can be measured. Throughout the lifeguarding season, retesting can be used to determine who needs emphasis on conditioning more often as well as to provide evidence about a guard's suitability for employment should the question arise.

Modern lifeguarding is a difficult and demanding profession that requires a diversity of skills. Physical fitness for lifeguarding is one aspect that can be objectively evaluated. Timed tests of swimming and rescue ability represent the best indicators presently available for determining a potential lifeguard's capabilities. In addition, they serve as guidelines by which training and conditioning can be judged for appropriateness.

Table 3-1 lists suggested tests and performance standards that may be useful in evaluating lifeguards. Specific modifications in these test items and times may be required for some aquatic facilities.

SUGGESTED IN-SERVICE TRAINING CURRICULUM

The information that follows deals with the skills that could be or should be included in in-service training programs. Some of these skills may not be applicable or may need to be modified for different facilities.

SWIMMING EVENTS
The following events are designed to test the overall swimming ability of the lifeguards, who should swim at an all-out pace during each event.

Run-Swim-Run
Leave lifeguard stand, run 100 yards along beach, enter water, swim out 25 yards, turn and swim 50 yards parallel to shore, swim back to shore, then run 50 yards along beach back to lifeguard stand.

Run-Swim-Run
Leave lifeguard stand, run 50 yards, enter water, swim 50 yards, leave water, run 50 yards back to lifeguard stand.

500-Yard Swim
Swim 100 yards out from beach, turn and swim 300 yards parallel to shore, then turn and swim 100 yards back to beach.

Buoy Race
Run 50 yards, enter water with rescue buoy, swim 50 yards to victim, then swim 50 yards back to safety towing victim. Victim's height and weight should be proportionate to lifeguard's.

Swim and Recover Object
Swim 25 to 50 yards, surface dive to depth of 10 feet, and recover 10-pound brick. It may be necessary to make more than one dive in murky water. A variation of this drill would be to recover two objects during one dive.

Enter Water and Underwater Swim
Dive into clear, deep water to depth of 10 feet and swim underwater 25 yards. Entry should be feet first if water is murky. In swimming pools with diving wells no deeper than 10 feet, entry should be made feet first.

LIFESAVING EVENTS
These events are designed to simulate a one-rescuer/one-victim situation. The following events should be combined and varied. For example: jump into shallow water, approach victim from rear, execute single-armpit level-off, and maintain control of victim in single-armpit assist.

Entries
- Jumping and diving into deep water — minimum depth of nine feet:
    From guard stand or guard tower — jumping only
    From deck or dock
- Jumping and diving into shallow water (minimum depth of four feet) from height no more than 18 inches above surface of water. All dives must be long, shallow dives. Diving into shal-

low water (four feet or less) by untrained divers, from side of pool or dock, should be prohibited. Entries should be done from standing, stationary position and also with running approach:

> From deck or dock
> From shore

Approaches
- Victim on surface — active:
  > Front
  > Rear
- Victim on surface — passive:
  > Front
  > Rear

Level-offs
- Chin
- Single armpit
- Double armpit

Carries
Distances should be length of pool or at least 50 yards at beaches.
- Cross-chest
- Cross-chest control hold for active victim
- Single-armpit assist
- Double-armpit assist

Defenses
- Block
- Block and carry
- Block and turn

Releases and Escapes
- Front headhold (Should be practiced with and without body scissors.)
- Rear headhold (Should be practiced with and without body scissors.)

Removal From Water
The victim should be positioned for artificial respiration, after being removed from the water in each of the following situations.

- Pool:
  > Shallow water
  > Deep water

- Beach:
  > Shallow water
  > Drag to beach
  > Pack-back carry

Artificial Respiration in Water
- Without aids:
  > Shallow water
  > a. Away from wall
  > b. Holding on to wall
  > Deep water
  > a. Away from wall — four quick breaths only
  > b. Holding on to wall
- With aids:
  > Using swim fins for support
  > Flotation supports: rescue buoy, rescue tube, ring buoy, and so on
  > Rescue board
  > Rescue boat

USE OF RESCUE EQUIPMENT
Rescue equipment will vary with local needs.
- Reaching poles and/or shepherd's crook
- Heaving line and/or jug with heaving line attached
- Ring buoy
- Rescue tube:
  > Conscious victim
  > Unconscious victim
- Rescue buoy (can):
  > Conscious victim
  > Unconscious victim
- Lines and reels
- Rescue board
- Mask, fins, and snorkel
- Additional equipment, as needed: grappling irons, poles, and lines

RESCUE-BOAT OPERATIONS
Lifeguards should train in the type of craft used as a rescue boat at their facility.
- Launching boat
- Approaching victim
- Contacting and assisting victim

FIRST AID
The content of the American Red Cross Standard First Aid course should be the minimum requirement for all lifeguards. Additional training should be given in areas of specific needs, for example, pool lifeguards getting additional information on chemical poisoning. Camp-waterfront lifeguards may need extra training in the care of accident victims who may have to wait for a longer period of time for the arrival of a rescue squad because of delays in response times in isolated areas. The review of knowledge and first aid skills should

include —
- Artificial respiration

    Mouth-to-mouth and mouth-to-nose:

    Adult victim

    Infant victim

    Mechanical methods (Use the equipment that is currently utilized at the facility. If the training group is made up of guards from different facilities, attempts should be made to familiarize all lifeguards with the types of equipment that are common to all of the facilities.)

    Foreign body obstruction of the airway:

    Conscious adult victim

    Unconscious adult victim

    Infant victim
- Control of bleeding
- Care for shock
- Splinting and bandaging

CARDIOPULMONARY RESUSCITATION (CPR)

This practice must be performed on manikins.
- One rescuer — adult and infant victims
- Two rescuers — adult victim

DEALING WITH BACK AND NECK INJURIES

    Shallow water
- Deep water

PHYSICAL TRAINING AND CONDITIONING
- Warm-up
- Flexibility exercises
- Strength training
- Speed play

PREVENTIVE LIFEGUARDING
- Recognition of hazardous areas and how to minimize or eliminate them
- Rules and regulations:

    Objectives

    Methods of enforcement
- Public relations

EMERGENCY PROCEDURES

Emergency action plans can never be rehearsed enough. Each type of accident and emergency will have its own set of rules to follow. Situations should be varied each time there is a training session. The numbers and locations of the victims in the facility, the types of accidents, and the locations of lifeguards are just a few of the methods of changing procedural guidelines. The following are areas that should be concentrated on each time there is a training session:
- Victim recognition:

    Distress situations

    Drowning situations
- Individual assignments
- Emergency calls and signals
- Back-up systems
- Records and reports

LEGAL ASPECTS

The liability aspects of a lifeguard's job should be discussed. Ideally, a legal adviser who is knowledgeable in this area of liability should conduct these sessions.

MAINTENANCE TRAINING

If the management of the aquatic facility has assigned maintenance duties to the lifeguards, these duties should be part of the in-service training program. The following are some of the more common maintenance duties requiring special training:
- Filtration systems

    Depending on the type of system, methods of backwashing or cleaning the filters must be reviewed.
- Pool chemistry

    The safe handling of chemicals must be reviewed, as well as how to handle emergencies involving chemicals — for example, a chlorine gas leak. One part of this training that must be practiced is the proper donning and testing of a self-contained breathing apparatus. All facility staff should know the location of this equipment.

RECORDING IN-SERVICE TRAINING

Records of training sessions should be maintained, with evaluations and test results recorded for all staff members. The minutes of all meetings should be posted in the guard room. An in-service training log may be used for this purpose and should contain the following information:
- Date of training session
- Subject(s) covered
- Name(s) of instructor(s)
- Names of lifeguards in attendance
- Length (time) of session
- Individual times and distances, if applicable
- Name(s) of lifeguard(s) absent

Chapter 4

PREVENTIVE
LIFEGUARDING

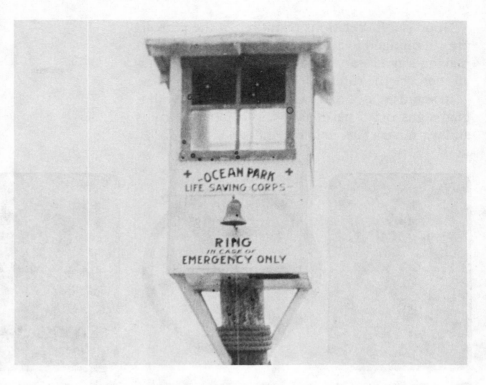

The duties and responsibilities of lifeguards will vary from one facility to another. The most important responsibility will always be to prevent accidents in, on, and around the water. Prevention will decrease the number of rescues that lifeguards will have to make. Lifeguards must be aware of what is going on at all times in their assigned area of responsibility. They acquire this awareness through training and experience. Inexperienced lifeguards will have to be trained as thoroughly as possible in order to be able to recognize and properly handle varied situations.

RULES AND REGULATIONS

The prevention of accidents can best be accomplished through the initial and continuing education of the lifeguards and patrons of the facility. The very basic education for the lifeguards usually occurs during their training in lifesaving. Courses such as Red Cross Lifeguard Training provide lifeguard candidates with the basic knowledge required by individuals who will be responsible for protecting others in an aquatic environment. These courses are designed to provide information about the general areas of lifeguarding and to suggest additional training for specific facilities that can be carried out once the individual is employed or agrees to work at a facility. Further education is the responsibility of the facility management. All rules and regulations must be thoroughly explained, understood, and posted, so that the lifeguards can interpret and enforce them and, in turn, continually educate the patrons. Rules and regulations are necessary and should be presented positively.

Signs that simply read "Walk" are a positive approach to preventing potentially dangerous situations. Verbal or pictorial signs such as "No Running" exemplify the negative approach. Some examples of behavior to be encouraged or discouraged using the positive approach whenever possible are as follows:
- Behavior to be encouraged
   Showering with soap
   Wearing proper swim attire
   Showing concern for the safety of others
   Checking the area in front of the diving board before diving
   Allowing only one person at a time on the diving board
- Behavior to be discouraged
   Running, pushing, horseplay
   Leaving shoes on the deck
   Smoking in the pool area
   Diving from the side in less than five feet of water
   Bouncing more than once on the diving board
   Attempting fancy dives without proper training

Good public relations result when the patrons are encouraged to act in positive ways rather than making it necessary for the lifeguards to continually enforce the rules.

In some areas it may be necessary to have bilingual signs or to have pictures to indicate rules and warnings (Figs. 4-1, 4-2, and 4-3).

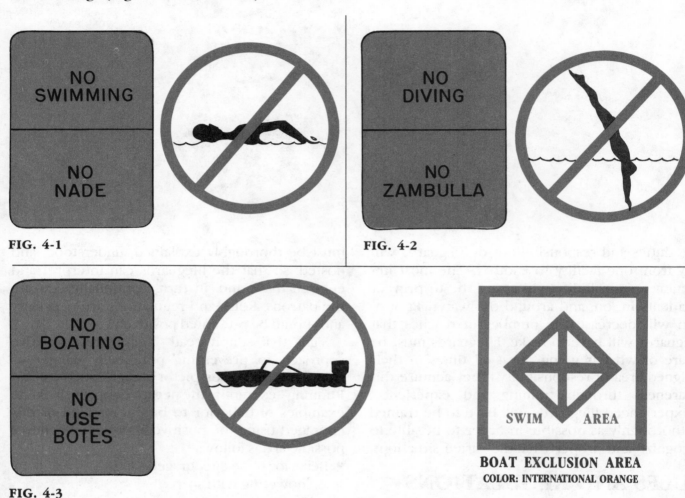

FIG. 4-1

FIG. 4-2

FIG. 4-3

BOAT EXCLUSION AREA
COLOR: INTERNATIONAL ORANGE

Depth and distance markings may need to be posted in metric form as well as in feet and yards.

A set of general rules will provide the patrons with guidelines for their conduct and will help them to enjoy the facility without endangering themselves or others. These rules should be posted in plain view at the entrance to the facility, and also within the facility, so that they may be easily seen and read and referred to by both the patrons and the lifeguards. The suggested list that follows contains some of the more common rules for patrons using an aquatic facility. These rules can be adapted to individual facilities.

PERSONAL CONDUCT

Examples of the many rules that frequently deal with the conduct of the patrons are —
- Patrons are allowed in the swimming areas only when a lifeguard is on duty.
- Horseplay, such as running, splashing, shoving, or ducking, is not permitted.
- Swimming is allowed only in designated areas.
- Diving is allowed only in designated areas.
- Sunbathing is allowed only in designated areas away from the side of the pool.
- Glass containers or metal objects are allowed only in designated areas.

- Throwing of objects, such as baseballs or rocks, is not allowed.
- Alcoholic beverages or illegal drugs are not allowed.
- Profanity, improper behavior, intoxication, and vulgar remarks are prohibited.
- Bicycles are not allowed in the facility.
- Disrobing is allowed only in locker rooms.
- Swimming after dark or when the facility is closed is prohibited.
- Fishing in or near swimming areas is prohibited.

Adult supervision may be required for all non-swimmers and children under a specific age set by the facility. The height and/or swimming ability of an individual will assist the lifeguard in making decisions on this rule. Some facilities may have restrictions on the use of suntan lotion or may require bathing caps.

USE OF EQUIPMENT

Rules should be set governing or identifying the proper use of the following equipment:
- Masks, fins, snorkels, or scuba equipment
- Artificial flotation devices such as inflatable air mattresses, rubber balls, inner tubes, or water wings (Flotation devices used during instructional periods do not, or may not, fall into this category.)
- Pool ladders (no horseplay, one person at a time on ladder)
- Lifelines (no sitting or hanging on lifelines)
- Docks and rafts (no swimming under docks or rafts)
- Lifeguard stands or towers (no climbing on stands or towers)
- Emergency equipment (to be used by lifeguards only)
- Small craft, surfboards, and rescue boards (not to be used in swimming areas)
- Diving boards:
    Only one person allowed on board at a time.
    Boards should be mounted by ladder only.
    Diver must wait for previous diver to move to poolside ladder.
    Diver must make one bounce only.
    Diver must dive straight out.
    After diving, diver must swim to designated ladder.
    Swimming in diving area not allowed.
    Hanging on to board not allowed.
    Divers must dive only in designated diving areas.

- Small craft (All persons using small craft must wear a proper fitting PFD.)
- Small craft equipment (All small craft equipment such as oars, paddles, or sails must be returned to the proper storage area after use.)

LOCAL ORDINANCES

The following are examples of rules established by regulating bodies such as local health, police, and fire departments:
- Showers are to be taken before entering the water and after the use of the rest rooms.
- Bathing caps may be required.
- Persons with open sores or rashes are not allowed in the facility.
- Spitting, spouting water, or blowing the nose in the water is prohibited.
- Chewing gum in the water is prohibited.
- Food, drinks, and smoking are permitted only in designated areas.
- Pets are not allowed in the facility.
- Street shoes and street clothing are not allowed in the deck area.
- Only the maximum designated number of patrons are allowed in the facility at any one time.
- Appropriate bathing attire must be worn (swimsuits, cut-offs, shorts).
- First aid equipment is to be used only by qualified (authorized) personnel.

Additional rules may be established by the facility management, such as allowing only members or their guests to use the facility.

ENFORCEMENT OF RULES

Methods of dealing with discipline problems have been a subject of great concern to lifeguards and the management personnel of aquatic facilities for a long time. The patrons who come to a facility have, in most instances, paid to use the facility either through membership fees or general admission fees. Some patrons feel that this gives them the right to do just about anything they want to do. They do not stop to think what the results of their actions might be, such as injury to themselves or to another person, or perhaps to a small child who is injured while attempting to imitate their actions. Lifeguards, through their training and experience, must be aware of actions that may result in an injury and must know why rules must be enforced. Their concern must be for the safety of everyone in the facility, no matter what certain individuals may think.

While enforcing rules, lifeguards should briefly explain the reasons for the rules whenever it is possible. Pointing out the dangers of a certain act and its potential consequences may prevent many patrons, especially children, from repeating the same act. Lifeguards must be consistent, fair, and equal in all of their disciplinary actions. There should be no favorites who are allowed to break the rules with no disciplinary action taken. There is no need to apologize for enforcing a rule; however, a positive attitude is a must. A great amount of respect can be earned for the rules, for the lifeguards, and for the facility management if the lifeguards are firm and not rude to patrons when enforcing rules. Saying, "Sir, it is against the rules to do that. Please stop." is an example of a firm, positive statement.

The enforcement of rules is meant to help to establish correct attitudes of safety among patrons. It is not meant to be degrading or to be viewed as punishment. Many people who violate rules at the facility may be unaware that a specific rule exists. The reinforcement of positive behavior can be established by the lifeguards, by first stopping the improper action and then informing the individuals of the rules or regulations.

Methods of enforcing rules may be determined by the age of the person who breaks the rules. A way of handling children is to have them sit out of the water for a certain amount of time. However, this type of action may be improper on a cold or windy day. At times, it may be better to have children read all of the rules and then explain them to a lifeguard who is not on duty at the time. Another problem in dealing with children is the attitude of their parents. The lifeguard should call on the head lifeguard or the pool manager to explain any action that has been taken if there is a problem with a parent. Lifeguards should not get into a discussion or an argument with a parent while on duty.

Teenagers and adults want to be treated as mature individuals. A simple correction and an explanation of the rules should suffice. The head lifeguard or the pool manager should be called in to deal with the situation if the individual continues to violate the rules. Expulsion from the area should be the final course of action when enforcing the rules. The police may need to be called if there is any further resistance by a patron.

Each facility should have a standardized procedure to be followed in the event that it becomes necessary to eject someone from the facility. This procedure should be posted in plain view to enable all patrons to see it. The procedure should contain specific reasons for an ejection, the steps that are to be followed by the lifeguard and the management personnel, and the involvement of law enforcement personnel, if necessary. Any action should be recorded in the facility's log book. There should be a standardized management policy for dealing with refunds or the prorating of fees, if an admission fee is charged.

FACILITY CAPACITIES

Each facility should have an established figure for the maximum number of patrons who are allowed to use the facility at any one time. This maximum capacity limit should allow these patrons to thoroughly enjoy the facility and at the same time allow for the maximum degree of proper supervision by the facility staff. Capacity limits are often established by a department of health, either at the state or the local level, which uses ratios or formulas to determine these capacities. However, it is very difficult, if not impossible, for any regulatory agency to establish a formula that applies to all facilities, because of the differences between facilities. Some of these differences are as follows:

- Sizes and configurations of the swimming area: length and width; rectangular, L-shaped, U-shaped, Z-shaped, or H-shaped areas; and separate pools or areas for diving, swimming, wading, and for very young children

- Water conditions: amount of surface area for shallow- and deep-water areas, clear versus cloudy or murky water, currents and tides that can move bathers, and tides or other conditions that can cause changes in depth of water

- Lifeguard's ability to see patrons: size of area, and amount of glare from sun or from indoor lights

- Nonswimming areas: size and locations of space for pool deck, dock, beach, or grassy areas.

The management of a facility is expected to comply with the capacity limits that are established by the regulatory agency that has jurisdiction over that facility. However, if there are no such limits established, or if there is a desire to make changes in these limits, the facility staff should or must work closely with the appropriate regulatory agency. An aquatic facility may set capacity limits that are lower than those established by a regulatory agency, but it may not exceed them. The entire staff of the facility must be knowledgeable about the capacity limits and must be fully aware of the procedures that must be followed to comply with the prescribed limits.

Regulatory agencies and facility management should consider the following factors when establishing capacity limits for a facility and when determining the correct lifeguard-to-patron ratios for that facility:

- Patron capacity

All areas of the facility should be dealt with separately when establishing maximum capacities. The areas for diving, swimming, and wading will each have a different concentration of individuals. A sufficient amount of deck or dock area must be provided to allow the patrons and the lifeguards to move safely from one area of the facility to another. The following are examples of formulas that have been used to establish capacity limits for bathers and nonbathers:

X number of persons per X square feet of surface area of the total facility

X number of persons per X square feet of surface area for a specific water depth (In this formula, "shallow" and "deep" water will have to be defined by the facility management or by the regulating agency.)

X number of persons in the water within X feet of distance to a diving board or tower

X number of persons on the deck within X feet of distance to a diving board or tower

X number of persons on the total deck area

- Lifeguard-to-patron ratios

When swimming capacity limits are determined for an aquatic facility, the next step is to determine the number of lifeguards required to properly supervise that number of patrons. Some facilities are too large for one lifeguard to supervise properly, no matter how many patrons there may be. Other facilities, because of their size and shape, will require that more than one guard be on duty at all times.

If a regulatory agency, such as a department of health, sets the lifeguard-to-patron ratios, a facility may still have to adjust them according to its peak hours, lifeguard schedules, breaks, environmental conditions, and emergencies that may occur. The following examples may be used to establish lifeguard-to-patron ratios:

X number of lifeguards per X number of patrons in the facility

X number of lifeguards per X number of patrons in the water

X number of lifeguards and a manager or assistant manager at all times, regardless of adding lifeguards as the number of swimmers increases

Provisions should be made to adjust the number of lifeguards accordingly as the number of patrons increases or decreases. Specific activities, such as instructional programs or swim meets, should have a direct supervisor, instructor, or coach for the participants. **The facility should provide separate lifeguard supervision for additional safety during these activities.** One individual cannot safely perform the duties of a lifeguard and a coach or instructor simultaneously.

SUPERVISION OF BATHERS

The management of an aquatic facility has a legal and moral obligation to its patrons to provide the safest conditions possible. The mangement of the facility delegates this responsibility to the lifeguards, who are expected to recognize facility conditions or situations that may be hazardous. Uninterrupted and proper supervision of the facility and the patrons is required at all times. Each facility should establish a system of supervision that will allow for the safety of the patrons and, at the same time, will not put undue responsibilities on the lifeguard.

FACILITY SECTIONS

One preventive step that can be taken by the facility management to manage various activities is to divide the swimming area into sections or zones. The total area can be zoned according to various activities, such as —

- Recreational swimming.
- Swimming laps for physical conditioning.
- Diving.
- Instruction — swimming, lifesaving, and so on.

All zones or sections should have a lifeguard on duty, including sections for instructional activities. In open-water facilities, sections may also be designated for boating or fishing. Where there are zones that have hazards such as tree stumps, rocks, large areas of weeds, or shallow water (less than five feet in depth), they should be posted "Danger — No Swimming," "Danger — No Boating," or "Danger — No Diving."

AREAS OF RESPONSIBILITY

Proper supervision will, in most instances, prevent accidents. The placement and positions of the lifeguards and the lifeguard stands will vary from one facility to another. Some of the factors that should be considered in determining these positions are as follows:

- Size and shape of facility

  Certain sections of the swimming area will have larger concentrations of patrons than other sections. For example, at any given time, there are usually more swimmers in shallow water than in the deep-water area.

- Number of patrons in the facility

  Warmer days, weekends, and holidays are times when there is an increase in the number of patrons in the facility.

- Number of lifeguards

  When large numbers of patrons are expected in the facility, arrangements should be made to ensure that there will be enough lifeguards on duty to provide proper supervision.

- Environmental conditions

  In facilities where lifeguard stands are stationary, proper supervision can be maintained by roving lifeguards who cover areas of the water that are blind to lifeguards in certain stands because of sun reflection, waves, wind, or debris. "Blind spots" are also discussed later in this chapter.

VISUAL SURVEILLANCE

The practice of good visual scanning techniques is very important to lifeguards. It greatly improves the chances of seeing someone who needs assistance, since the lifeguard's primary responsibility is to the swimmers in the guard's assigned area of responsibility. However, communication and cooperation with lifeguards in adjacent areas ensures safety throughout the facility.

The lifeguard should continually scan back and forth over the water. This should be done slowly enough to be able to see what each swimmer is doing. Each sweep must cover the total area of responsibility. If a swimmer goes underwater, the lifeguard watches to see that the swimmer surfaces before continuing the sweep of the area. The water area directly in front of and below the lifeguard stand should be of particular concern. This area is a potential "blind spot" to the lifeguard in the stand.

ZONE COVERAGE

The procedure of dividing the total swimming area into separate areas of responsibility is frequently used. A section of the water area is designated for each lifeguard station, with an overlapping of zones.

The following examples of zone coverage (Figs. 4-4 to 4-7) are suggested for stationary lifeguard stands. They may need to be adapted for different facilities.

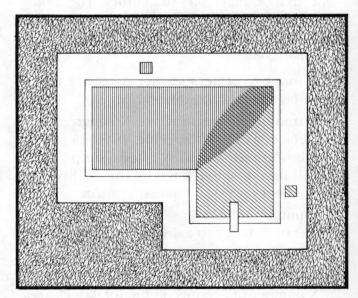

FIG. 4-4

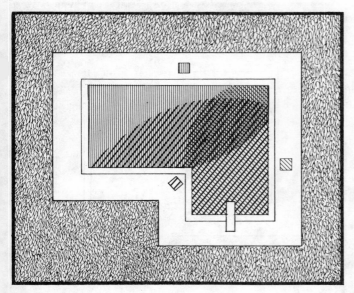

FIG. 4-5

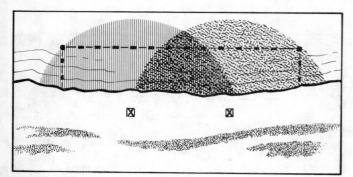

FIG. 4-6

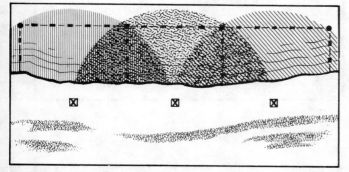

FIG. 4-7

Some advantages of zone coverage are as follows:

- Guards can concentrate on a limited area.
- Overlapping allows for double coverage.

Some disadvantages of zone coverage are these:

- Large facilities require more zones, thereby requiring more staff.
- Lifeguards may be confused as to their area of responsibility where zones overlap.
- Lifeguards may not scan their entire area of

responsibility if boundaries are not clearly marked (lifelines, ladders, diving boards).

Some suggested methods for dealing with these disadvantages are the following:

- Large swimming areas can be controlled by consolidating swimmers into a smaller number of sections for easier supervision.
- Lifeguards must be made aware of their area of responsibility.
- An effective system of communications should be established between lifeguards.

TOTAL COVERAGE

Another procedure for supervising bathers is for one lifeguard to have responsibility for the entire swimming area. This procedure should be used only if a small number of swimmers are in the water and there are only one or two lifeguards on duty. An advantage to this system is that it requires a smaller number of staff members. There are also several disadvantages to this system:

- Lifeguards are required to observe a larger area and may not see a problem as quickly as with zone coverage.
- Lifeguards may concentrate too much of their attention on the extreme boundaries of the area. They must be fully aware of all activity in their area of responsibility. They must continuously scan the entire area with their eyes.

Some suggested methods for dealing with these disadvantages are the following:

- Concentrate the swimmers into a smaller area.
- Close some sections of the water area.

BACK-UP COVERAGE

In emergency situations, when there are two or more lifeguards on duty and one lifeguard must enter the water, each lifeguard who remains out of the water will have a larger area of responsibility to supervise. It may be necessary for the lifeguards remaining out of the water to move to better vantage points. This will be determined by the design of the facility and the number of patrons in the facility at the time. The following suggested back-up systems may be adapted to different facilities (Figs. 4-8A, 4-8B, 4-9A, 4-9B, 4-10A, and 4-10B). In each of the following situations, the primary lifeguard will enter the water. The back-up lifeguard will move to a position that allows better surveillance of both areas of responsibility.

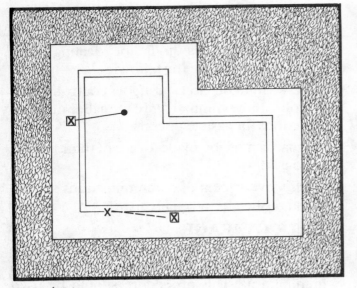

FIG. 4-8A

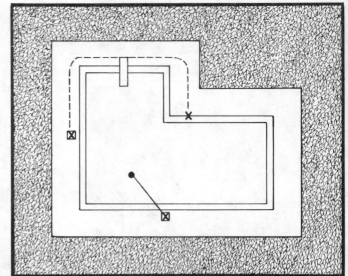

FIG. 4-8B

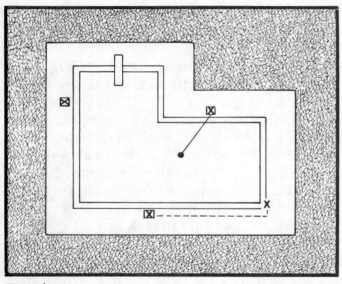

FIG. 4-9A

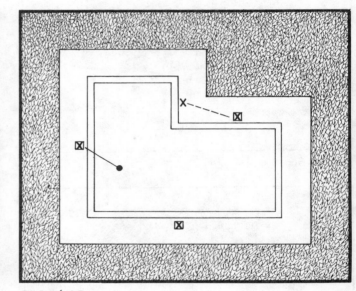

FIG. 4-9B

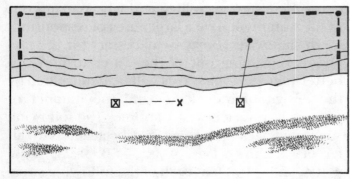

FIG. 4-10A

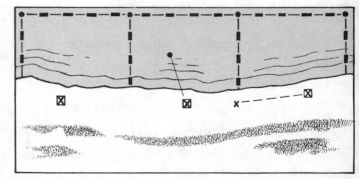

FIG. 4-10B

In facilities where there is only one lifeguard on duty, it may be necessary to clear all swimmers from the water. This procedure is discussed in detail in Chapter 5, "Emergencies."

There may also be times when it may be advisable to allow the patrons to remain in the water during an emergency — for example, at a pool with a small deck area. In this instance, the patrons remaining must be moved to shallow water and must have continued supervision. When there is only one lifeguard on duty, it may be necessary to recruit a volunteer or to notify another staff member that an emergency situation exists and that assistance is needed for the supervision of the facility. Examples of communications and signal systems are discussed in Chapter 5, "Emergencies."

SAFETY CHECKS

Lifeguards should check the facility periodically each day, especially before the facility is opened to the public. This includes walking around the area to ensure that no one has gotten into the facility while it was closed and to ensure that all equipment is operational.

Safety checks may be used to allow for rotations or breaks at facilities where there is only one lifeguard on duty. The lifeguard signals the patrons to clear the water and to sit or stand on the deck or the pool edge. Some facilities require that the patrons move away from the edge of the pool or deck. This eliminates the possibility of someone's falling into or being pushed into the water. The lifeguard may then rotate to another position to supervise the area or to take a short break, once all of the patrons are out of the water. The patrons should not be allowed to reenter the water until the lifeguard returns or is in the proper position and the proper signal is given to reenter the water.

Safety checks can also be used at facilities when there are large numbers of patrons in the water and when there is more than one lifeguard on duty. Lifeguards should check the bottom of the swimming pool for anyone who may have gone underwater unnoticed. During these safety checks, the patrons have an opportunity to rest. This may help to prevent swimmers from becoming overly fatigued.

A complete inspection of the facility must be made when the facility closes at the end of each day. This inspection should include the water area, locker and shower rooms, and any adjacent areas where patrons may go while in the facility — for example, the small craft area, playground area, and snack bar and eating areas. At waterfront facilities, it may be necessary to walk through the shallow water area to ensure that there is no one lying on the bottom.

After the closing inspection, a brief statement that the water area is clear and that all other safety precautions have been taken should be entered in the daily log. The name and signature of the person making the inspection, the time of day, and the signature of a witness should be included.

BUDDY SYSTEMS

The buddy system for supervising swimmers is frequently used at camp waterfronts. Swimmers of the same skill ability are paired when they enter the swimming area. The buddies may be restricted to a specific area according to their swimming abilities. If two swimmers of unequal swimming level are paired up, they must stay in the area restricted to the level of the less-skilled swimmer.

On a given signal, such as a whistle blast, the buddies grasp one of each other's hands, raise their arms over their heads, and remain in place until the lifeguard can get an accurate count of the number of swimmers in each section of the facility. Swimmers in deep water should be required to swim to the side of the dock or raft while the count is being taken.

"Buddy boards" that are located at the entrance to the swimming area can be used to check swimmers in and out of the facility (Fig. 4-11). After taking a swimming test to determine

FIG. 4-11

their respective skill levels, individuals are issued name tags showing which group they are in — beginners, nonswimmers, and so on. The name tags are kept in the "out" section (Fig. 4-12A) when the swimmers are not in the facility. As they enter the facility, they move their respective tag to the "in" section (Fig. 4-12B) and are then paired up with a buddy. A lifeguard, or another responsible person, should be stationed beside the buddy board to help ensure that the tags are put in their proper positions. These types of boards may also be used to indicate buddies in small craft activities (Fig. 4-13).

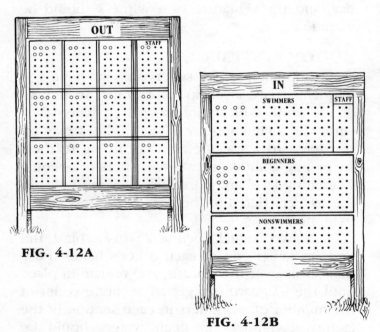

FIG. 4-12A

FIG. 4-12B

FIG. 4-13

All tags must be put back into the "out" section when the waterfront area is cleared of swimmers. Tags that remain in the "in" section indicate that (1) swimmers have forgotten to move their tags to the "out" section or (2) a swimmer may be missing in the waterfront area. Each facility must develop procedures to handle these situations quickly and efficiently. At waterfront facilities where the small craft area is located some distance from the swimming area, separate "in" and "out" boards may be required for both areas.

Another type of buddy board is one that has every tag numbered. All tags are painted red on one side and white on the other. Each swimmer or boater is assigned a number and is issued the corresponding tag. The master roster of these numbers and names is kept at the facility or camp director's office. When the swimmer is out of the waterfront area, the tag is left in the "out" section with the white side showing. As the swimmer enters the waterfront area, the tag is turned to the red side and moved to the "in" section of the board.

Another application of the buddy system is to assign each pair of swimmers a number as they enter the facility. The safety check is made by having them count off in numerical sequence. A method of supervising bathers at waterfront areas is to require bathers to wear bathing caps of different colors. Each color designates the wearer's swimming ability, such as red for nonswimmers, white for beginners, and blue for swimmers. Campers may also be required to wear caps for easy recognition when they are in the small craft area.

LIFEGUARD STATIONS

Supervision of the patrons in an aquatic facility may be maintained either from the deck or beach or from the water. This supervision may be either mobile or stationary. The object is to provide optimum coverage for the total facility.

The lifeguard stand should be located where lifeguards can easily observe and can react quickly to any situation in their assigned area of responsbility. These stands or chairs are for the use of lifeguards only. They are not intended to be used as gymnastic or diving equipment or storage areas for the personal items of patrons or lifeguards. Food, drinks, and radios should be kept off the lifeguard stands. Patrons should be politely asked to keep the area around the stand clear at all times, especially the area in front of the stand.

LOCATION

Some of the factors used for determining the location of lifeguard stations are as follows:

- Size and shape of facility
- Depth of water
- Number of patrons in facility
- Movement of sun and wind
- Condition (clarity) of water
- Deck or dock area surrounding water
- Type of activity: recreational swimming, swimming lessons, diving

These factors may not apply to all facilities. Some facilities may have different conditions that will indicate the location of the lifeguard stations. Each facility should establish a system of coverage that allows the lifeguards to be in positions that will be most advantageous to the safety of the patrons.

ELEVATED STATIONS

Lifeguards usually have a better vantage point to visually scan their area of responsibility when they are in elevated stations such as towers, stands, or chairs. They may need to use binoculars in facilities that have large open-water areas. In camp facilities, the person in the elevated station acts as a lookout or observer and directs lifeguards on the ground to patrons who may need assistance.

Care must be taken to ensure that the areas directly in front of the elevated stations are kept clear at all times. An injury to a lifeguard or to a patron who is sitting or standing nearby can result from a guard's jumping down from a platform. Some facilities suggest that their lifeguards climb down rather than jump. The height of a lifeguard stand may vary from one facility to another, and the safety of the lifeguards in getting up and down from the stand in an emergency must be considered when establishing the height of these stands.

Rescue equipment that is kept on or near an elevated stand should be placed in a location where it is ready for use and where it will not interfere with the lifeguard's getting up or down from the stand, especially in an emergency situation.

Further information on lifeguard stands and chairs is in Chapter 7, "Equipment."

GROUND-LEVEL STATIONS

Lifeguards may have to be in positions where there are no elevated stations, especially in small facilities. Roving lifeguards may be needed where there is a large concentration of swimmers or when a sudden change in water depth occurs.

Lifeguards who are stationed at ground or deck level may be assigned to specific locations in the facility (stationary), or they may be required to move around the area (roving). In both instances, and where appropriate, a piece of rescue equipment, such as a rescue buoy or reaching pole, should be carried by the guards or be placed at the guard station.

An advantage to lifeguards who are at ground level is that they are in closer proximity to the patrons. This allows disciplinary actions to be more quiet and effective, since the lifeguards may not have to shout or blow a whistle to attract the attention of a patron. However, this advantage is usually outweighed by the advantages of having the lifeguards in elevated stations. Having all or most of the lifeguards at ground level is the least desirable method of supervision.

BOAT STATIONS

In open-water areas, such as camps or parks, it may be necessary to station one or two lifeguards in a boat at the outer edges of the swimming area. The boat should not enter the swimming area except in an emergency. The lifeguards can easily patrol the deep water in a boat and can be in a good position to give assistance to swimmers more quickly than lifeguards who are stationed on the shore. Additional equipment, such as a first aid kit or resuscitator, may be carried in a boat. This equipment, in addition to the rescue equipment, allows the lifeguard to initiate first aid procedures immediately, if necessary. Procedures for boat rescues are discussed in Chapter 12, "Waterfront Areas."

ROTATING AND RELIEVING LIFEGUARDS

Lifeguards who sit or stand at the same station for an extended period of time can easily become physically and mentally fatigued. Periodic rotations from one station to another, plus relief breaks, should be scheduled to keep lifeguards alert. Rotating the lifeguards also allows them to become familiar with the conditions and hazards of the total facility, rather than in just one location. For example, at some facilities the sun glare from the water may prohibit the use of a specific stand during certain times of the day.

ROTATING SYSTEMS

Rotations for lifeguards should occur at set times according to a schedule made up by the head lifeguard or the manager. The schedule should be flexible enough to allow for any changes that may become necessary because of the number of swimmers suddenly increasing or decreasing.

The amount of time a lifeguard spends on duty and on a break can vary. One system is to have a guard spend 20 or 30 minutes at one station, rotate to another station for 20 to 30 minutes, and then have a 20- or 30-minute break. Another system is to spend 45 minutes at one stand, have a break for 15 minutes, and then go to another stand. Methods of rotating the guards may vary with the number of guards who are on duty. One method of rotation is to have a lifeguard who is on a break (Guard A) relieve one who is on duty (Guard B). Lifeguard B then rotates to the next station and relieves the lifeguard there (Guard C). This process continues around the facility to the last station. The lifeguard who is relieved at the last station then goes on a break or to whatever other duties are required at that time. Another method is to rotate all of the guards simultaneously if there are enough guards to cover all of the stations.

PROCEDURES FOR RELIEVING LIFEGUARDS

There must be no break or delay in the supervision of the areas of responsibility during the rotation of the lifeguards. Changes in orders or special instructions may be exchanged during the rotation. At a ground-level station, the new lifeguard need only walk to the side of the lifeguard who is being relieved. The following is a suggested procedure for relieving a lifeguard who is in an elevated station:

- The incoming lifeguard takes a position next to the stand and observes the area of responsibility for that stand (Fig. 4-14). When the incoming lifeguard has scanned the area and is aware of the ongoing activity, the new lifeguard signals the lifeguard in the stand, who can then climb down.

FIG. 4-14

- Once on the deck, the outgoing lifeguard takes a position next to the stand and scans the area (Fig. 4-15), then signals the incoming lifeguard to get up in the stand. The incoming lifeguard is in charge of the area after climbing up in the stand and scanning the area. The new lifeguard then signals that the outgoing lifeguard can leave (Fig. 4-16). The outgoing lifeguard should continue to observe the activity in the water and on the deck while going to the next station or to the guard room. Some facilities require lifeguards to circle the facility before going on a break. This allows for periodic

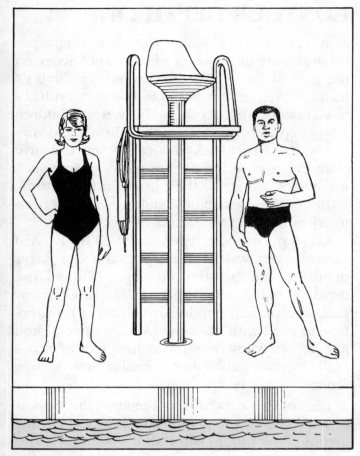

FIG. 4-15

FIG. 4-16

checks of areas that are at the extreme boundaries of an area of responsibility.

The procedure for relieving boat stations is for one rescue boat to remain on station until the second boat has arrived and has taken over the observation of the area. If only one lifeboat is being used, the relief must be coordinated with other lifeguards. The relief can be made during a safety check when all swimmers are out of the water; or the lifeguard at the closest station can scan the water area until the new lifeboat crew arrives on station.

BREAKS

Relief breaks should be worked into the rotation schedule and should allow for the continued supervision of the facility. The schedule should allow each lifeguard a relief break every hour. All lifeguards must be aware of the schedule and should not be allowed to make changes or substitutions without the consent of the head lifeguard or the manager. Lifeguards should not leave the facility during a break without notifying the head lifeguard or the manager about where they are going and when they will return.

At facilities where there is only one lifeguard on duty, it will be necessary to clear the water while the lifeguard takes a short break. Patrons should not be left in charge of the facility while the lifeguard goes on a break.

ACCIDENT CHARTS

A key to effective preventive lifeguarding is knowing where and how accidents may happen and then eliminating or minimizing any conditions that may jeopardize the safety of the patrons. All lifeguards should have a thorough knowledge of the facility and its hazardous areas. A method of gathering this information is by maintaining an accident chart or a diagram of the facility on which the locations and types of all accidents can be recorded.

All pieces of equipment, such as lifeguard stands, lifelines, ladders, and diving boards, should be indicated on the diagram. Fences and deck and grass areas should also be shown. Whenever there is an accident or injury, it should be coded and posted on the chart (Fig. 4-17). By recording all incidents and their frequency and locations, it is possible to determine the causes and effects of the different types of accidents. Corrective actions can then be taken to perform necessary maintenance, to install safety equipment, or to place extra lifeguards on duty or reassign lifeguards for better supervision.

SUGGESTED ACCIDENT CHART

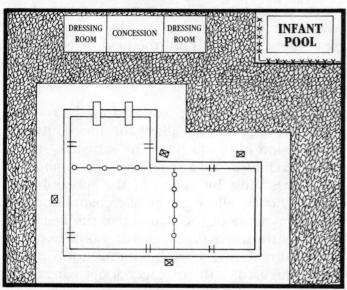

FIG. 4-17

```
+++  LADDER          ┌─┐ DIVING BOARD
o─o─o LIFELINE       └─┘
x─x─x FENCE          ⊠ LIFEGUARD STAND
```

All staff members must be familiar with the codes that are used at their facility to indicate accidents. Any combination of codes can be used to describe an accident. Each accident should be marked on the chart. The following are examples of codes that may be adapted to different facilities:

Cause	Injury
1. Fall	a. No injury
2. Running	b. Bruise
3. Slipped	c. Abrasions
4. Tripped	d. Cut
5. Pushed	e. Dislocation
6. Stepped on	f. Fracture
7. Hit	g. Burn
8. Tired swimmer	h. Drowning
9. Diving board	i. Head
10. Ladder	j. Arm
11. Slide	k. Leg
12. Steps	l. Body
13. Diving from deck	
14. Diving from starting blocks	

CONTOUR DEPTH LINE

Many accidents and injuries that occur at an aquatic facility are the result of a lack of knowledge on the part of the victim concerning the facility's features. A common example is the individual's not knowing the depth of the water. Children may jump into water over their heads and may not be able to get back to safety. Others may dive from the edge of the pool or the dock into shallow water and strike their head on the bottom. Either of these examples could result in serious injury or death to the victim.

Accidents of these types can often be avoided when proper warnings are posted about water depths. Some facilities use signs. Others use depth markings on the deck. However, many people, especially children, pay little or no attention to the depth markings. Also, some children just do not know how deep four feet of water really is. Many adults do not realize how shallow four feet really is.

The contour depth line is a method that is used in some facilities to graphically show the various depths of the water (Fig. 4-18). It is simply a line

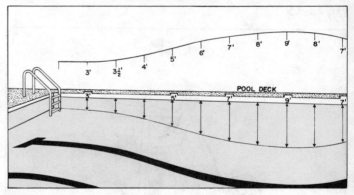

FIG. 4-18

that is drawn or painted on a wall or fence that is parallel to, and relatively close to, the side of a pool. The line is marked to show the depth of the water that is directly in front of the wall. People can stand in front of the wall at any given place on the line and know immediately how deep the water is in relation to their own height.

A contour depth line can be made easily. Starting at the shallow end of the pool, a pole or some other measuring device is placed in the water. The depth of the water is marked on the pole. The pole is then placed next to the wall directly in line with the point where the water depth was measured, and a mark is made on the wall. This process is repeated every two feet along the entire length of the pool. All of the depth marks on the wall are then joined with one continuous line of paint or waterproof tape. Depth numbers can be placed on the wall that correspond to depth number markings that may be on a pool deck, for example, three feet, five feet, seven feet. Another method of making a contour depth line at outdoor facilities is to weave a colored rope through a wire fence in a manner that will show the proper heights (depths). Depth markings may be painted on a small wall if there is no wall or fence that runs the entire length of a pool. Patrons can then stand against the wall to compare their height to the depth of the water. Depths of less than five feet should be marked "No Diving."

POTENTIALLY HAZARDOUS AREAS, EQUIPMENT, AND ACTIVITIES

There are hazardous areas that are common to all aquatic facilities as well as those that are peculiar to individual facilities. Preventive lifeguarding requires identifying these areas, minimizing or eliminating the hazards if possible, helping patrons to avoid the areas, or constantly providing supervision of the hazardous areas. Hazardous areas that are common to many facilities are discussed below.

ENTRANCE AREAS
Patrons rushing to the water may be pushed and fall or may slip on wet surfaces and fall. If an entrance is near the deep end of the facility, nonswimmers or weak swimmers may jump or dive into water that is over their heads. If the entrance is near the shallow water, patrons may jump or dive into water that is too shallow.

Warning signs should be posted at these entrance areas. The signs should indicate slippery areas and different water depths and should caution about running and diving.

DECK AND BEACH AREAS
Running is a common cause of accidents in deck and beach areas. Patrons who run, usually small children, can be injured by falling or by running into someone else. The "walk only" rule must be strictly enforced.

Docks at outdoor facilities may be slippery when wet. They should be coated with a nonslip material. Patrons should be cautioned about running. Out-of-line boards that will allow a person to catch a foot or toe should be replaced. Splinters and exposed nails or bolts can also cause injury to patrons. These should be removed or covered. Beach areas should be cleared of any glass, shells, or rocks to protect the patrons from possible injuries.

LADDERS AND STEPS
Ladders and steps may become gathering places for patrons. Weak swimmers or nonswimmers may be ducked or pushed into water that is over their heads. Depending on the type of construction of ladders, swimmers may become caught in the rungs or between the ladder and the pool. Wooden ladders that are used at waterfronts may be rotten, and nails could become exposed. Swimmers may attempt to use the ladders as pieces of gymnastic equipment. Steps can become slippery and may be chipped. Patrons should not be allowed to play or gather around ladders or steps. All necessary repairs to ladders and steps should be made as quickly as possible.

SHALLOW-WATER AREAS
The major dangers in shallow-water areas are in diving from the deck or dock and the ducking of weak swimmers or nonswimmers. Patrons, especially children, should be cautioned about horseplay in the water or on the deck. Inexperienced divers may dive into water that is too shallow, resulting in cuts, injured fingers or hands, and possible severe neck and back injuries. Diving should not be permitted in water that is less than five feet in depth. Water depths should be clearly marked. Patrons should be made aware of these depths and of changes in depths.

SEMI-DEEP-WATER AREAS
Weak swimmers and nonswimmers can misjudge the water depths or the distance back to standing-depth water and find themselves in trouble. Lifeguards should watch for swimmers who will not release their hold on the side of the pool or dock or who venture too far from some form of safety. These people should be sent back to shallow water. Patrons should be warned of any "step-offs" where the bottom dips sharply from shallow to deep water. Lifeguards working

at freshwater areas must be alert to fluctuation in the water depth due to storms, evaporation, or release of water from dams.

OVERFLOW TROUGHS

Overflow troughs (or gutters) are hazardous to patrons who may use them to work their way around the edge of the facility to get from shallow water to deeper water. Weak swimmers and non-swimmers who use the troughs to move to deeper water should be sent back to shallow water. The design of some overflow troughs will allow young swimmers to catch an arm or leg in the trough when they attempt to climb out of the pool. All patrons should be advised to use only a ladder or steps to climb out of the water.

DEEP-WATER AREAS

A constant danger in deep water is that poor swimmers may misjudge the water depth or their own skill level. If there is doubt about a patron's swimming ability, the person should be cautioned and, if possible, should be given a swim test before being allowed into deep water. An example of a swim test is having the individual swim a specific distance, such as 10 or 15 yards. This may not be possible in facilities where there are large numbers of patrons. In these situations, lifeguards will have to use their own judgment.

UNDERWATER SWIMMING

Underwater swimmers in all areas of the facility may be injured by being jumped on or dived on by another person, especially in lakes where the water is not clear or in pools that are congested. Another danger to underwater swimmers is "shallow-water blackout," which is the result of hyperventilation. This condition can occur in any depth of water when swimmers inhale and exhale deeply, fairly rapidly, and repeatedly before submerging in order to hold their breath longer. Underwater swimming should be discouraged except in designated areas where it can be properly supervised and controlled.

DIVING BOARDS AND TOWERS

Serious accidents can occur from the improper use of diving boards and towers. Some accidents may occur through no fault of the diver.

Lifeguards must be aware of the kinds and causes of these accidents that can occur and of the ways to prevent them. Guards should be especially alert to poor swimmers or very young swimmers who obviously intend to use or continue to use diving boards or towers. Poor swimmers should be able to prove their ability to swim safely in deep water before they are allowed to use diving equipment.

Many divers, especially children, will jump rather than dive from a board. They must be instructed to swim out of the way of the next diver as soon as possible. Divers should be cautioned about the possibility of being hit by the next diver if they persist in swimming underwater in the diving area for a period of time before surfacing. Diving from the side of a board or tower is extremely hazardous and must not be permitted. The diver may strike another diving board, the side of the pool, or a person in the water.

Rules about the use of diving boards and diving towers should be placed near the boards and towers and must be strictly enforced. Examples of these rules are as follows:

- Divers must use the ladder to mount the diving board or tower. Mounting in any other way is prohibited.
- Only one bounce on the end of the board is allowed.
- Only one person is allowed on the board at a time.
- Diving or jumping must be done straight off from the end of the board or tower.
- Diving or jumping from the side of the board or tower is prohibited.
- Horseplay will not be tolerated.
- Individuals must look before diving or jumping and must make sure that no swimmer or previous diver is in the diving area.
- Patrons must swim to the nearest ladder as soon as possible after diving or jumping.
- The diver's hands must enter the water first during head-entry dives.
- Handstands on the board or tower are prohibited.
- Twisting or somersaulting dives should not be attempted by untrained divers.

Lifeguards must be aware of and eliminate potential hazards that can result in diving accidents. Patrons must not be allowed to dive or to jump from the side of a pool into the diving area. Such a diver may be struck by a person leaving the diving board or vice versa. Swimmers must not be allowed in the diving area. Divers should not run on the diving board or be allowed to attempt long distances through the air if there is the slightest chance that they will (1) strike the slope of the pool that rises from the deep section to the shallow section, (2) strike the floating line marking the boundary of the diving area, or (3) strike a swimmer who is supposedly outside the diving area. This problem is inherent in some older pools that have competitive-type diving boards. Striking the slope can cause, and has caused, serious neck and back injuries to divers. These slopes are also found under the board and along the side (Figs. 4-19, 4-20A, and 4-20B).

BLIND SPOTS
Blind spots are areas that cannot be seen or that are difficult to see from a lifeguard station. Such areas can result from the layout of the facility, the improper location of lifeguard stands, or the position of the sun or indoor lighting in relation to the position of the guards. Relocating guard stations or providing roving guards should be done to provide proper supervision of blind spots. Of particular concern is the water area directly in front of and below the lifeguard stand.

SLIDES
The hazards of slides in the swimming areas are similar to those of diving boards. Rules about the use of slides should be developed and posted next to the slides or on the ladder of the slides. These rules should consider the height, location, and configuration of the slides, the depths of the water where the slides are located, and the turbidity of the water.

Slides should be located where the exit area into the water has a minimum depth of eight feet. Only children should be allowed to use slides that exit into water having a depth of five feet or less (shallow water). Sliding in the **sitting position only** should be permitted. Headfirst entries into shallow water from the kneeling or prone position may cause the sliders to strike the bottom with their head.

Weak swimmers and nonswimmers are more likely to use slides than diving boards. Lifeguards must be particularly alert to these individuals.

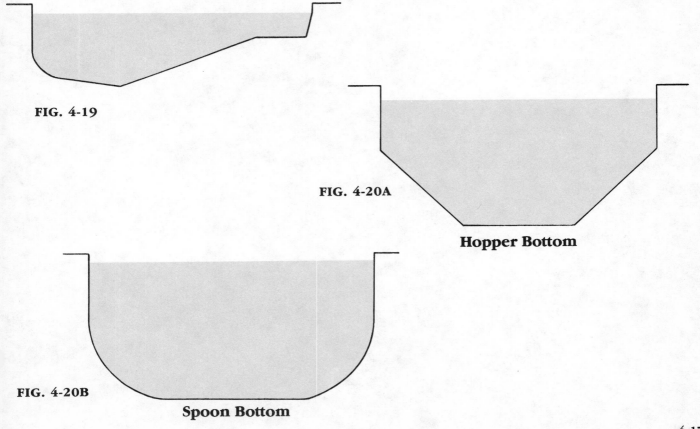

FIG. 4-19

FIG. 4-20A

Hopper Bottom

FIG. 4-20B

Spoon Bottom

STARTING BLOCKS

Only competitive swimmers should be allowed to dive from starting blocks. Starting blocks should be used only during swim team practices or swim meets. Starting blocks should be removed when not in use, if possible.

FLOATS AND DOCKS

Floats and docks can present several danger areas and hazards. One lifeguard may be unable to guard all sides of a float or dock properly. Swimming to a float can present a challenge to weak swimmers. Floats and floating docks may tip when overloaded, causing those on them to fall into the water. Swimmers may be trapped while swimming under floats and docks.

Floats and floating docks should be anchored securely to the bottom. In order to be stable in the water, they may need additional anchoring if they have diving boards or diving towers on them. Floats must be inspected periodically. Deterioration of the float material can cause instability of the platform. All floats should be stable enough to prevent adverse tipping when occupied by their maximum safe load of patrons. Floats of this type that can tip or shift direction can cause serious injuries to divers.

Swimmers should show evidence of good swimming ability before being allowed to swim out to floats (rafts). The maximum number of swimmers that are allowed at any one time on floats and docks should be established and enforced. No one should be allowed to swim under floats and docks.

OTHER HAZARDOUS AREAS

Areas of a facility that contain filtration and chlorination systems or that are used to store chemicals or maintenance equipment should be clearly posted, and access should be restricted to authorized personnel only.

Covers (plates) for drain holes in deep- and shallow-water sections of swimming and wading pools must be firmly secured in place over the holes. This will prevent a patron's extremities from becoming trapped in the hole owing to the force of the suction of the water flowing out of the pool. At impounded open-water areas all swimming areas should be located a safe distance from the intake points or the spillways of dams.

Chapter 5

EMERGENCIES

Handling emergencies is the responsibility of the lifeguard and the management of an aquatic facility. Consequently, every facility should have written, rehearsed procedures that are specific to every potential accident or emergency. Any delay during an emergency situation may cause additional problems that could lead to further injury or death. The patrons using the facility should also be made aware that their actions could add to delay. Their cooperation during an emergency will expedite procedures.

Various types of accidents can occur at an aquatic facility, even in one that is well guarded. Any situation that may endanger a patron and take the attention of the lifeguard away from supervising the bathers, and that requires immediate action, should be considered an emergency. Lifeguards trained in first aid and cardiopulmonary resuscitation (CPR) procedures are qualified to handle a wider range of emergencies.

CLASSIFICATIONS

Emergencies may be classified according to their degree of danger to the patrons.

LIFE-THREATENING EMERGENCIES

This classification of emergency would include such situations as stoppage of breathing, severe bleeding, or poisoning. Examples of these would be a drowning victim, a person who has a severely cut foot or hand, or a person who has been exposed to chlorine gas. Each of these situations calls for immediate positive action by the lifeguard to prevent the loss of human life or some level of permanent damage to the victim.

Additional examples of life-threatening emergencies are as follows:

- Spinal injury
- Heart attack
- Fire
- Natural disaster, such as a flood, hurricane, or tornado

NON-LIFE-THREATENING EMERGENCIES

This classification of emergency may require the action of one or more lifeguards, but the danger to the patron is considered minimal. There are two levels of non-life-threatening emergencies:

- Major — Includes situations such as broken bones, an out-of-the-water epileptic seizure, or a tired swimmer.
- Minor — Includes situations such as sunburn or abrasions.

A non-life-threatening emergency may become life-threatening if not handled properly. Although the immediate danger to the victim is minimal, the lifeguard still has the responsibility of providing the best care possible.

Some emergencies, whether they are life-threatening or non-life-threatening, may require the immediate action of only one lifeguard. Others may require the actions of the total staff of the aquatic facility. Some will also require the cooperation of other patrons. Because of the various types of accidents, it is necessary for all staff members of the facility to be educated in how to deal with these problems.

Lifeguard training emphasizes the development of certain aquatic and first aid skills. However, in an emergency the lifeguard will need additional skills to recognize the emergency, to assist the victim, and to reduce any chance of further injury. While this is happening, the other patrons in the facility must still be protected. It is for these reasons that educational programs in emergency procedures should be developed for staff members and the public.

EMERGENCY PLANS

A large number of people will usually gather at the scene of an emergency. Those directly involved may include the victim, the rescuer, any additional rescuers, personnel from law enforcement and fire departments, and rescue squad members. Those indirectly involved may include the victim's family and curious onlookers. In a small area, the people indirectly involved can cause a great deal of confusion and can contribute to a delay in rescue and first aid procedures. An emergency plan should contain procedures to control the crowd in an orderly fashion, to allow for the proper care of the victim, and to provide supervision of the facility.

In the initial development of an emergency plan, thought should be given to every type of emergency that may occur at the facility, both life-threatening and non-life-threatening. A detailed plan for emergencies should be put in writing in the manual of operation for the staff and the facility. The plan should be thoroughly reviewed and practiced regularly by all staff members, and the public should be involved at every opportunity. This promotes good public relations and educates the public to situations when they may be required to give assistance, such as lost-person drills, evacuation of the facility, crowd control, or the use of a backboard. The plan should also be posted for the public to re-

view so that patrons can become familiar with it. Visual aids such as large, colorful charts and printed handouts help to promote awareness of emergency plans. It is better to have a plan and have everyone aware of their responsibilities than to have an emergency situation take place and be unable to properly handle it. It would be impossible to develop a specific plan for every potential emergency; therefore, one or two general categories of emergencies should be selected, and plans can then be adapted for specific situations.

Additional personnel that should be involved in the development and practice of emergency plans include local law enforcement and fire departments, rescue squads, gas and power companies, water authority agencies, and chemical supply companies. Each of these groups will have helpful information on emergency procedures, and information, methods, and procedures can be updated by working in conjunction with these groups.

The following points should be considered when developing an emergency plan:

- The chain of command or table of organization should be referred to so that all persons clearly know and understand their limits of authority and responsibility for their own position and those of others in the structure. This must be clearly understood by all staff. (Refer to Appendix A.)
- State or local ordinances should be checked. Facility standards, policies, and procedures should be updated to coincide with all ordinances. This information can be obtained from health departments, police and fire departments, or local utility companies.
- Past records of accidents and emergencies should be reviewed and analyzed. These records will give insight to the staff as to the causes of previous accidents and the action steps that were taken by the staff during these situations. Every potential emergency situation should be defined and analyzed as to cause, prevention, and actions to be taken by each staff member. Conditions such as weather, number of patrons, number of lifeguards on duty, and any other influencing factors should all be considered. A comprehensive action plan should then be established for each of these situations.

- Support personnel should be consulted and involved in the development of emergency plans. Police, fire, and rescue personnel can provide valuable information about response times, limits of authority, and the amount and types of assistance that are available and may be needed. Emergency personnel who are expected to respond to a call from a facility should be given clear directions on how to approach the facility. The participation of these support personnel will help to establish a smooth transition process for the victim and all of the staff who are involved in an emergency.
- An area should be designated for first aid care for all victims of accident or illness. When there is no danger of causing further injury to the victim, the person should be moved to the first aid area as soon as possible. The area should be as private as possible, with easy access for rescue personnel. The location of the keys to unlock the access doors and gates leading to the first aid area should be known to all staff. All personnel and equipment that will be used in this area should be specified so that there will be no confusion during an emergency. This area should have clear identification, such as "First Aid Station" or "Emergency Room."
- All rescue and first aid equipment should be inspected and should be situated for easy access. Any piece of equipment that is not in good condition should be removed and repaired or replaced. The inspection should be conducted every day before the facility is opened for use.
- Each facility staff member should have primary and also secondary responsibilities to follow in the event of an emergency. These procedures should be rehearsed at least monthly. Repetition develops confidence and the likelihood of smoother procedure conducted by competent lifeguards. Lifeguards must remember that in all cases their main responsibility is the safety of the patrons. They must remain calm in all situations and do what they are trained to do.
- The potential for multiple-victim rescues must be analyzed. Lifeguard reactions to these situations and back-up coverage must be rehearsed.

- Arrangements should be made to replace all equipment and materials used during an emergency as soon as possible. For example, if a victim has a suspected spinal injury and is transported to medical care on the aquatic facility's backboard, a second board should be available.
- All rescue and accident cases should be reported in writing. A system of records and reports should be developed, and every lifeguard should be thoroughly trained in the proper procedures for filling out and filing accident reports. Further information on records and reports can be found in Chapter 6, "Records and Reports," and Appendix B.
- In case of an emergency, the owner or operator of an aquatic facility should designate one person to be responsible for informing the victim's relatives and for providing information and news releases. This eliminates the possibility of misinformation being released concerning the injury to the victim or the cause of the accident.
- Crowd control is an important part of any emergency plan. Patrons cleared from the water during an emergency must continue to have supervision if they remain in the area. Curious onlookers, who gather whenever an emergency vehicle arrives, must be kept at a distance. A coordinated program for crowd control during an emergency must be established with local law enforcement personnel. Limits of authority for lifeguards and other facility staff should be thoroughly understood.

The points above apply to all aquatic facilities and to all staff members. The patrons of the facility should have the benefits of safe conditions and a well-trained staff.

The following charts and procedures are suggested emergency plans that can be adapted to different facilities. The steps in these plans may not necessarily be performed in the exact sequence in which they appear. Some may be performed simultaneously by the lifeguard or by other personnel. Some steps may not be necessary. Action steps and sequences will depend on the type of emergency, the number of staff on duty, available equipment, and the type of facility.

RECOMMENDED PROCEDURES FOR AN EMERGENCY ACTION PLAN IN A MULTISTAFF FACILITY

The following are explanations of the procedures listed in the flowchart in Fig. 5-1:

- *Accident or situation.* Any unexpected situation that would demand immediate action on the part of a lifeguard or other trained facility personnel.
- *Lifeguard awareness.* The lifeguard becomes aware of the situation. It should be noted that in some instances another person may call the attention of the lifeguard to a victim who needs assistance.
- *Victim recognition.* The trained lifeguard will be able to recognize a person who is actually in trouble and needs immediate assistance.
- *Lifeguard reaction.* Whenever a lifeguard leaves an assigned station, a prearranged signal, such as a whistle, flag, or alarm bell, should be given to notify other lifeguards or staff members of a potential emergency. The lifeguard's area of responsibility must be covered by another lifeguard.
- *Lifeguard enters water?*
- *No.* If it is unnecessary for the lifeguard to enter the water.
- *Lifeguard contacts victim.* If the victim is close enough to the side of the pool or dock, the lifeguard may perform an extension rescue or a reaching assist.
- *Yes.* If it is necessary for the lifeguard to enter the water, supervision for that area of responsibility must continue.
- *Lifeguard alerts second lifeguard.* If it is necessary for the lifeguard to enter the water, a prearranged signal, such as a whistle, flag, or alarm bell, should be given to alert a second lifeguard.
- *Second lifeguard supervises bathers.* Once the first lifeguard has entered the water, the second lifeguard must supervise the area of the facility that is left unattended. If there are more than two lifeguards on duty, each of them would assume a larger area of responsibility to ensure that there is total supervision of the facility.
- *Lifeguard contacts victim.* The lifeguard uses the proper rescue techniques to prevent further injury to the victim. If the victim is conscious, attempts should be made to calm the person by talking. If the victim is unconscious, the lifeguard must establish whether the person is breathing. If it is necessary to give artificial respiration in the water, the lifeguard should begin mouth-to-mouth resuscitation as quickly as possible in shallow water or while holding on to a boat, the side of a pool or dock, or a suitable buoyant aid, such as a rescue tube or rescue buoy.
- *Victim to safety.* Once contact is made with the victim, from the deck or in the water, the victim is brought to safety — to shallow water, to the deck or dock, or to shore. The victim should be moved only as far as necessary and only as much as any injuries will allow. For example, a victim with a suspected back or neck injury should not be moved until a backboard has been properly applied.
- *Victim OK?* The victim's condition should be evaluated by the lifeguard.
- *Yes — lifeguard returns to duty.* If the victim was not injured and is capable of caring for himself or herself, the lifeguard should return to duty after cautioning the victim, e.g., restricting activity to shallow water or pointing out changes in water depth. If the victim received only minor injuries, such as when a child scrapes a knee, another staff person should care for the victim. The lifeguard should return to duty as soon as possible.
- *No — lifeguard calls for assistance.* If the lifeguard needs help to properly care for the victim, e.g., needs to administer cardiopulmonary resuscitation (CPR), a prearranged signal should be given to summon other lifeguards or staff members. (Refer to the section on communications that appears at the end of this chapter.)
- *Second lifeguard alerts third guard.* The second lifeguard should alert the third lifeguard by a prearranged signal that two lifeguard stands will be empty owing to an emergency. The second lifeguard should then take whatever additional equipment (e.g., backboard or resuscitator) that may be necessary to

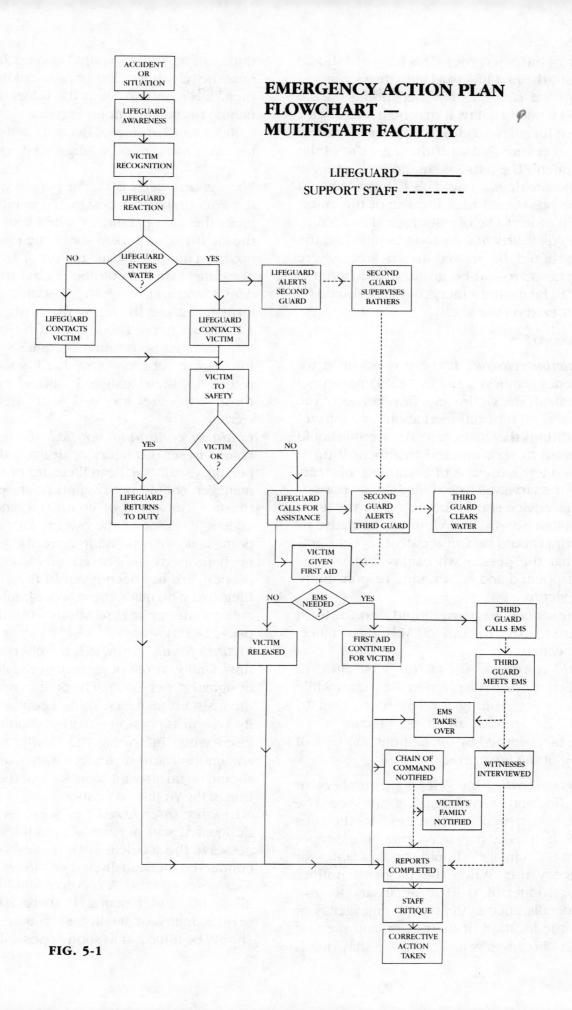

**EMERGENCY ACTION PLAN
FLOWCHART —
MULTISTAFF FACILITY**

LIFEGUARD ————————
SUPPORT STAFF ---------

ACCIDENT OR SITUATION

LIFEGUARD AWARENESS

VICTIM RECOGNITION

LIFEGUARD REACTION

LIFEGUARD ENTERS WATER ?

NO — LIFEGUARD CONTACTS VICTIM

YES — LIFEGUARD ALERTS SECOND GUARD --- SECOND GUARD SUPERVISES BATHERS

LIFEGUARD CONTACTS VICTIM

VICTIM TO SAFETY

VICTIM OK ?

YES — LIFEGUARD RETURNS TO DUTY

NO — LIFEGUARD CALLS FOR ASSISTANCE

SECOND GUARD ALERTS THIRD GUARD --- THIRD GUARD CLEARS WATER

VICTIM GIVEN FIRST AID

EMS NEEDED ?

NO — VICTIM RELEASED

YES — FIRST AID CONTINUED FOR VICTIM

THIRD GUARD CALLS EMS

THIRD GUARD MEETS EMS

EMS TAKES OVER

CHAIN OF COMMAND NOTIFIED

VICTIM'S FAMILY NOTIFIED

WITNESSES INTERVIEWED

REPORTS COMPLETED

STAFF CRITIQUE

CORRECTIVE ACTION TAKEN

FIG. 5-1

the site of the emergency. This lifeguard should also assist the first lifeguard with the victim.

- *Third guard clears water.* Depending on the size and type of facility, it may be necessary for the third lifeguard to clear the water of bathers — and to ensure that all bathers get out of the water safely. The patrons should be kept away from the accident scene. This lifeguard should then be positioned near the site of the emergency in order to be of assistance, if needed.
- *Victim given first aid.* As soon as possible, the victim should be moved to an area where emergency care can be given. If the victim is unable to be moved, emergency care should be administered on the site.

- *EMS needed?*

- *No — victim released.* If there is no need for emergency medical services (EMS) personnel to be called, the victim and/or relatives of the victim should be cautioned about any injuries or conditions that may exist. The victim should be advised to seek medical treatment if there has been any stoppage of breathing, obstruction of the airway, severe bleeding, or poisoning. This advice should be noted on the accident/rescue report. The victim or a relative of the victim should sign an accident report signifying that the person who signs understands what happened and is assuming responsibility for the victim.
- *Yes.* The second lifeguard should alert the third lifeguard to make the call to EMS for assistance, if it is needed.
- *First aid continued for victim.* First aid care should continue to be given to the victim while lifeguards are waiting for EMS personnel to arrive. The amount and type of care given should be governed by the amount and type of training of the lifeguards.
- *Third guard calls EMS.* Telephone numbers for police, fire, and rescue organizations should be posted in a visible location next to the telephone. If it is a pay telephone, the proper amount of change should be available for emergency use. When the lifeguard notifies EMS personnel, it will be necessary to give exact details, such as the type of emergency or injury, the location of the victim, and the first aid care already given. To ensure that this is

done, a suggested "script" should be posted near the telephone. The person making the call then needs only to fill in the information pertaining to the current emergency.

Refer to Chapter 6, "Records and Reports," for an example of a suggested emergency script.

- *Third guard meets EMS.* The person who called the EMS or another designated person should meet the EMS personnel when they arrive at the facility. This person should be easily recognizable (in appropriate uniform) by the EMS personnel. They should be guided to the accident scene and be given assistance or any information about the victim that is needed.
- *EMS takes over.* There should be an orderly transfer of responsibility to the EMS personnel for the care of the victim. Facility staff should return to their assigned duties, except for those who are involved with helping the victim.
- *Chain of command notified.* If the accident results in serious injury or death, a designated person, usually the head lifeguard or the facility manager, should notify appropriate persons in the facility's chain of command, such as the aquatic director or the owner. This should be done as soon as possible once the facility has been properly supervised or closed and the proper care has been given to the victim. The lifeguard who made the rescue should be available to answer any questions from the appropriate facility staff.
- *Victim's family notified.* If members of the victim's family were not present at the accident, a designated person, such as the manager or the assistant manager, should contact the family as soon as possible. Caution should be exercised when informing the family, to prevent any undue alarm or unnecessary worry. There should be no attempt to make a medical evaluation of the victim's condition.
- *Witnesses interviewed.* As soon as possible, designated staff persons should interview witnesses to the accident. All interviews should be conducted individually and privately.
- *Reports completed.* A record should be kept of all assists and rescues. If there has been a serious injury or fatality, all required reports should be filled out as soon as possible. Actions

taken by all staff members with possible time frames and sequences should be recorded while they are fresh in everyone's memory. These reports will be used during the critique of the accident and for insurance information. Equipment and material used during the emergency should be reported and replaced as soon as possible.

- *Staff critique.* All staff members involved in the emergency should meet to critique the incident as soon as it is practical to do so. The accident, its probable cause, the rescue procedures, and the actions of all personnel should be discussed and evaluated. If this meeting does not occur on the same day as the accident, it should be held as soon as possible, with the entire staff in attendance.
- *Corrective action taken.* In order to minimize or eliminate the conditions contributing to the accident, corrective action should be taken as soon as possible.

RECOMMENDED PROCEDURES FOR AN EMERGENCY ACTION PLAN IN A SINGLE-LIFEGUARD FACILITY

Many aquatic facilities may have only one lifeguard on duty at a time. Examples are swimming pools at apartment complexes, swim and racquet clubs, hotels and motels, and some smaller, private summer camps. This practice may be necessary because of limited finances or the size of the facility. One-lifeguard facilities present their own unique problems for supervision and emergency action plans. For example, how is the facility supervised when the guard goes on a break? Who supervises the area, who sends for help, who gets the first aid equipment? These and other matters of proper supervision should be discussed and clearly understood by the lifeguard and the management of the facility.

The development and implementation of an emergency action plan at a single-lifeguard facility will depend greatly on an effective communications system and the education of the patrons. Once the plan has been developed, the proce-dures and actions of support personnel should be clearly posted and rehearsed periodically with patrons. A communications system involving police, fire, and rescue personnel is very important for these facilities. The following chart outlines the recommended procedures that may be followed.

The following procedures correspond to the flowchart in Fig. 5-2:

- *Accident or situation.* Any unexpected situation that would demand the immediate action of the lifeguard.
- *Lifeguard awareness.* The lifeguard becomes aware of the potentially dangerous situation. Another person may call the situation to the attention of the lifeguard.
- *Victim recognition.* The trained lifeguard will be able to distinguish if the victim is actually in trouble and needs assistance.
- *Lifeguard reaction.* Whenever the trained lifeguard leaves an assigned station in an emergency, a prearranged signal should be given to patrons and other facility staff, such as locker room attendants or snack bar personnel. An established communications system and an educated public are very important in this step of the procedure. The lifeguard should take the necessary rescue equipment (e.g., reaching pole or rescue tube) when leaving the station.

- *Lifeguard enters water?*
- *No.* If it is unnecessary for the lifeguard to enter the water.
- *Lifeguard contacts victim.* If the victim is close enough, the lifeguard may use a reaching assist or extension to make contact.
- *Yes.* If it is necessary for the lifeguard to enter the water.
- *Lifeguard alerts second person.* After a quick evaluation of the situation, the lifeguard alerts a second person. This person should be ready to get any equipment, such as a backboard or re-suscitator, or supply any assistance that may be necessary. There should be some prearranged signal that will let patrons and other staff members know that an emergency exists and that the lifeguard needs assistance.
- *Lifeguard contacts victim.* The lifeguard uses the proper rescue technique to ensure against any further injury to the victim.

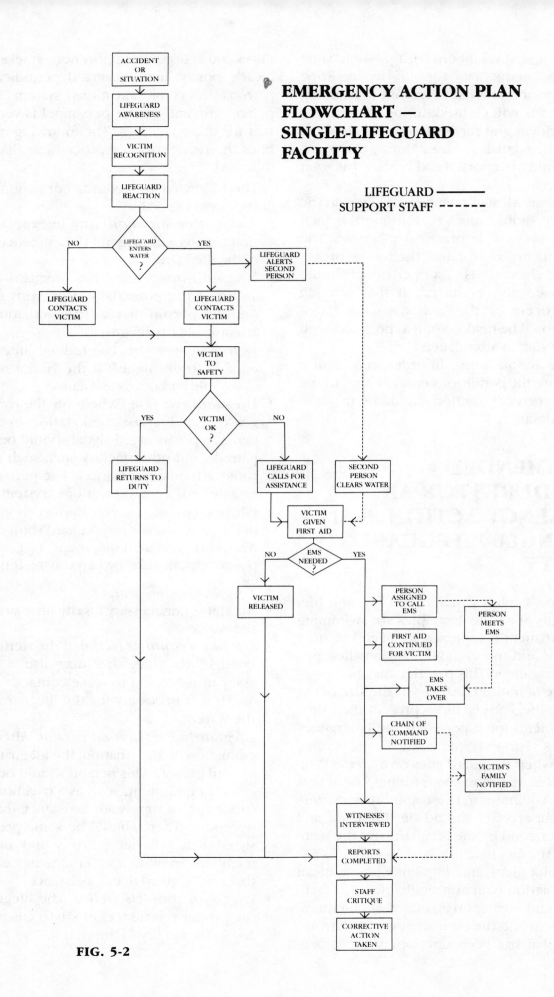

EMERGENCY ACTION PLAN FLOWCHART — SINGLE-LIFEGUARD FACILITY

LIFEGUARD ————
SUPPORT STAFF - - - - - -

ACCIDENT OR SITUATION

LIFEGUARD AWARENESS

VICTIM RECOGNITION

LIFEGUARD REACTION

LIFEGUARD ENTERS WATER?
NO → LIFEGUARD CONTACTS VICTIM
YES → LIFEGUARD ALERTS SECOND PERSON
YES → LIFEGUARD CONTACTS VICTIM

VICTIM TO SAFETY

VICTIM OK?
YES → LIFEGUARD RETURNS TO DUTY
NO → LIFEGUARD CALLS FOR ASSISTANCE

SECOND PERSON CLEARS WATER

VICTIM GIVEN FIRST AID

EMS NEEDED?
NO → VICTIM RELEASED
YES → PERSON ASSIGNED TO CALL EMS

PERSON MEETS EMS

FIRST AID CONTINUED FOR VICTIM

EMS TAKES OVER

CHAIN OF COMMAND NOTIFIED

VICTIM'S FAMILY NOTIFIED

WITNESSES INTERVIEWED

REPORTS COMPLETED

STAFF CRITIQUE

CORRECTIVE ACTION TAKEN

FIG. 5-2

- *Victim to safety.* Once contact is made with the victim, from the deck or in the water, the victim should be brought to shallow water or to the deck or dock area. The victim should be moved no farther than necessary at this time.

- *Victim OK?* Once the victim is brought to safety, the person's condition should be evaluated by the lifeguard. This is only possible in cases where the lifeguard is trained in first aid and CPR.

- *Yes—lifeguard returns to duty.* If the victim, e.g., a nonswimmer or a tired swimmer, has no injuries and is capable to taking care of himself or herself, the lifeguard should return to duty after cautioning the victim, such as pointing out changes in water depth.

- *No—lifeguard calls for assistance.* If the victim has an injury or requires additional care, the lifeguard should call for assistance. This should be done by some prearranged signal, such as a hand signal.

- *Second person clears water.* If the lifeguard is unable to return to duty immediately, the second person should clear the water of all patrons. There should be a prearranged signal for clearing the water, such as a whistle or a blast on an air horn. Only qualified lifeguards should supervise bathers in the water. Once the patrons are out of the water, the second person should assist the lifeguard by getting any necessary equipment or helping with the victim.

- *Victim given first aid.* As soon as possible, the victim should be moved to an area where emergency care can be given. If the victim is unable to be moved, emergency care should be administered on the site.

- *EMS needed?* The lifeguard must be able to evaluate the condition of the victim and decide whether or not EMS personnel will be needed.

- *No—victim released.* If the victim's condition does not require EMS attention (if there is minor bleeding or a sprain, for example), the lifeguard should caution the victim and/or the victim's family, if they are available, concerning the victim's injury and condition. The lifeguard should always advise that they seek medical assistance. This advice should be included in the accident/rescue report. The victim or a relative of the victim should sign an accident report signifying that the person who signs understands what happened and is assuming responsibility for the victim.

- *Yes—person assigned to call EMS.* If the victim's condition requires EMS attention, such as a suspected back injury or a cardiac arrest, the lifeguard should designate a specific person to notify emergency medical personnel. The telephone numbers of police, fire, and rescue units should be posted near the telephone. If there is no telephone in the immediate area, directions to the nearest telephone should be clearly posted in the facility. The person making the call to EMS should give as specific directions as possible concerning the route to the facility and the location where they will be met upon arrival. Refer to Chapter 6, "Records and Reports," for an example of a suggested emergency script.

- *Person meets EMS.* Emergency medical personnel should be met upon their arrival and should be guided to the victim. The person meeting the EMS personnel should be easily identifiable in order to expedite their getting to the victim as quickly as possible.

- *First aid continued for victim.* While waiting for EMS personnel to arrive, the lifeguard should continue to administer first aid care to the victim. The type and amount of care given to the victim should not exceed the level of training of the lifeguard.

- *EMS takes over.* There should be an orderly transfer of responsibility for the care of the victim to the EMS personnel. The lifeguard should supply the EMS personnel with any information about the victim that may be required.

- *Chain of command notified.* If the accident results in serious injury or death, the lifeguard should notify the appropriate person in the facility's chain of command, such as the manager or the owner. This should be done as soon as possible once the facility has been properly supervised or closed and the proper care has been given to the victim.

- *Victim's family notified.* If members of the victim's family were not present at the accident, they should be contacted as soon as possible. Caution should be exercised when informing the family of the victim's condition, to prevent any undue alarm or unnecessary worry. There should be no attempt to make a medical evaluation of the victim's condition.

- *Witnesses interviewed.* The lifeguard and other facility staff members should interview any witnesses to the accident as soon as possible. The interviews should be conducted individually and privately.

- *Reports completed.* The lifeguard should complete an accident report as soon as possible for all rescues and serious injuries. Possible time frames and actions taken should be recorded while they are still fresh in the lifeguard's mind. All witnesses' statements and accident and equipment reports should be collected by the designated person in the chain of command, such as the manager or the owner. All equipment and material used during the accident should be reported and replaced as soon as possible.

- *Staff critique.* A meeting of all staff members should be held as soon as it is practical. The accident, its probable cause, the rescue procedures, and actions of all personnel involved should be discussed and evaluated.

- *Corrective action taken.* In order to prevent similar accidents or minimize their chances of happening again, corrective action resulting from the staff critique should be taken as soon as possible.

COMMUNICATIONS SYSTEMS

Each facility should have its own communications system, which must be learned by all lifeguards and other staff. The type of signals used will depend on the type of facility and the budget of that facility. The signals must be simple, clear, and easily understood, when using any of the following methods of communication.

- Whistle
  It is important that the whistle be used sparingly and only when needed. For example:

  One short blast — to get the attention of a swimmer

  Two short blasts — to get the attention of another staff member

  Three short blasts — to signal that there is an emergency, and help is needed

  One long blast — to clear the water. (Use for

rest periods or buddy checks also.) The same signal is used to indicate when patrons can reenter the water.)

These signals should be repeated at least twice, especially in indoor pools, where the noise level may be so high that the patrons may not hear a single signal.

- Hand signals
  Once the lifeguard uses the whistle to contact another person, the following hand signals can be used to communicate a further message:

  To gain attention. Lifeguard points directly to individual (Fig. 5-3).

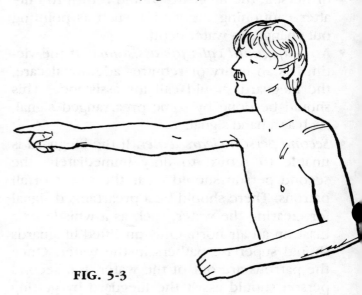

FIG. 5-3

Directing movement. Swimmer is in area of potential danger and needs to move to safer area. Arm and hand move in desired direction. Palm of hand should face desired direction (Fig. 5-4).

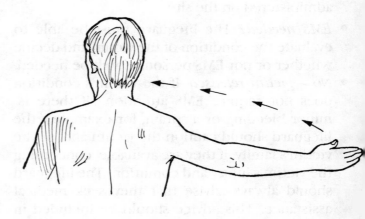

FIG. 5-4

Stop or stay where you are. Individual is told to stay in one place. Arm is straight out and palm of hand is facing individual. Arm is kept stationary (Fig. 5-5).

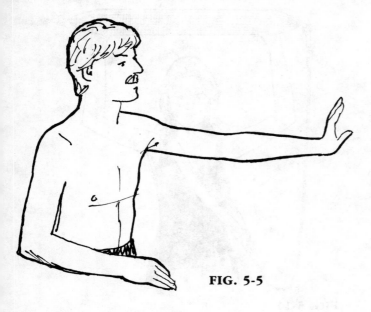

FIG. 5-5

Situation is under control. Hand is placed on top of head from side (Fig. 5-7).

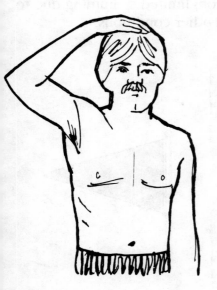

FIG. 5-7

Assistance is needed. Arm is raised up and down over head with fist clenched (Fig. 5-6).

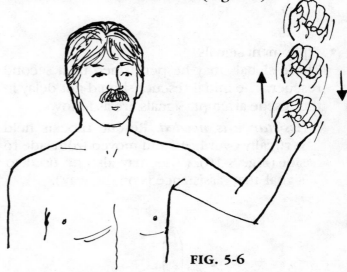

FIG. 5-6

Danger or potential rescue. Lifeguard repeats pointing or jabbing of arm with a closed fist (Fig. 5-8). (Used in conjunction with a whistle.)

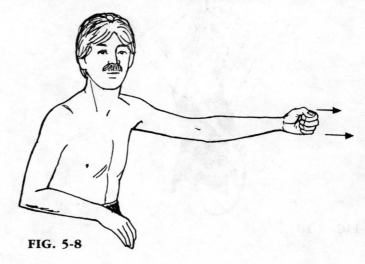

FIG. 5-8

Pull on line. Situation is under control. Arm is extended, waving from side to side, palm of hand facing shore (Fig. 5-9).

FIG. 5-9

- Equipment signals
  These signals may be performed by a second rescuer. The initial rescuer should not delay in the rescue attempt. Signals are as follows:

  Assistance is needed. Rescue tube is held vertically over head and moved from side to side (Fig. 5-10). (This may also be used to signal that assistance is on the way).

FIG. 5-10

Situation is under control. Rescue tube is held horizontally over the head (Fig. 5-11). Rescue buoy or oar may be used instead of rescue tube.

FIG. 5-11

- Flags.
  Flags of different colors that are displayed on permanently installed flagpoles may be used to indicate swimming and boating conditions (see Chapter 12, "Waterfront Areas.") Examples are as follows:

  Green — Safe; facility open for swimming.
  Red — Unsafe; facility closed for swimming.
  Yellow — Caution; limited swimming due to currents and other conditions.

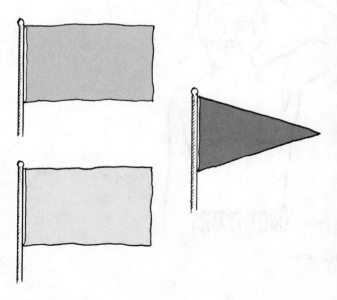

FIG. 5-12

A flag, made of plastic or strong nonfading material, on a staff about four feet long, should be attached to the lifeguard stand. The lifeguard should raise or lower it to indicate a normal or emergency situation. Examples are shown below (Figs. 5-13 to 5-15).

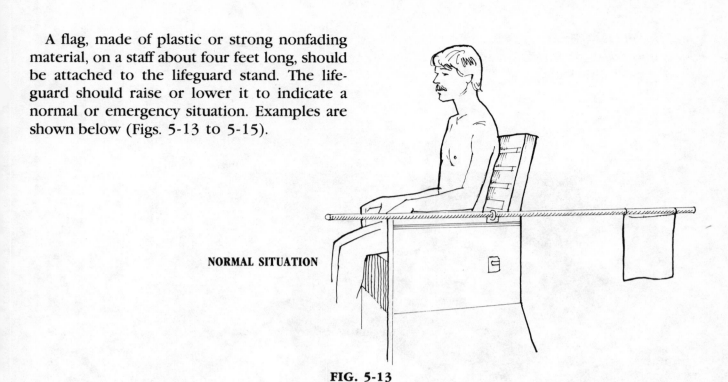

NORMAL SITUATION

FIG. 5-13

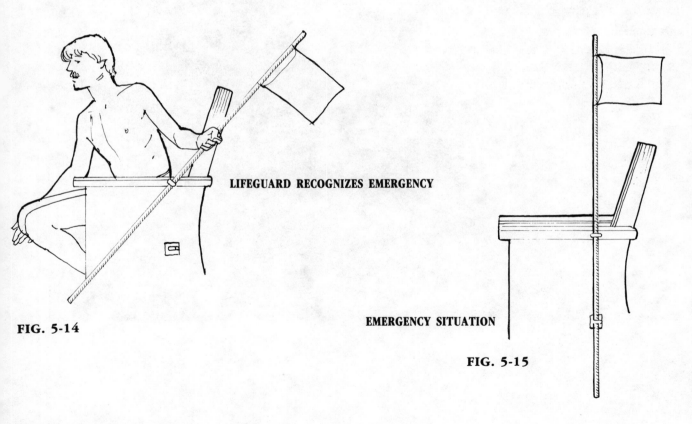

LIFEGUARD RECOGNIZES EMERGENCY

FIG. 5-14

EMERGENCY SITUATION

FIG. 5-15

- Additional methods
  Other methods of communication that can be used at aquatic facilities are as follows:

  Two-way radios   Public address systems
  Telephones   Air horns
  Bullhorns

Chapter 6

RECORDS AND REPORTS

The records and reports discussed in this chapter are required at many aquatic facilities. Some, such as financial records or payroll sheets, may be used only on a management level. Some, such as the accident report forms, are used specifically by lifeguards. Others will be used by personnel who are in supervisory positions for in-service training and personnel evaluations. The purpose of presenting all of the records and reports in this chapter is two-fold: (1) to educate all personnel involved with the operation of an aquatic facility to the proper records and reports that may be required and (2) to inform the personnel of the purpose of these records and reports. This information should help to develop a smoother operation in an aquatic facility. It may also help personnel to move higher in the chain of command at a facility by increasing their knowledge of the total operation of the facility.

Accurate records and reports are essential components of sound management practice in aquatic facility operations. It is usually true that the larger the facility and its management structure, the more records and reports there are to be completed. Each facility or department will have its own forms, with a certain number of copies of each that are usually required. Although the reporting system will differ from one facility to another, the basic information forms are usually similar in content. Every lifeguard should be

thoroughly familiar with each record or report form and its purpose. Records and reports should be kept for the following reasons:

- To provide data that will be helpful in making decisions regarding equipment, schedules, personnel, procedural changes, and improvements
- To provide data that can be used for research into the causes and prevention of injuries and fatalities
- To provide the basis for budget recommendations and future expenditures and the justification for them to management
- To comply with state and local ordinances that require specific information regarding sanitation and maintenance of aquatic facilities
- To provide documentation of accidents and incidents for use in possible legal action

Whenever possible, record and report forms should be standardized for all aquatic facilities that are under the same management supervision. They should be filled out, dated, and signed by the person responsible for making the report. Copies should be filed and forwarded through the proper channels as soon as possible. The manager's copies can be combined to form an annual manager's log.

Copies of all records and reports should be kept on file at the facility. These files should not be accessible to the general public. All records and reports, once completed, should be turned in to the manager, to the assistant manager, to the head lifeguard, or to a person designated by the manager, so that they may be checked for accuracy before being filed.

Report forms may be classified by category in relation to the time period during which the aquatic facility is in operation. Some forms may be used in all of the time categories discussed in the following sections. Some aquatic facilities are open year-round and have no definite season. The records and reports discussed in this chapter may be used continually or might not be used at all at these facilities. The following sections discuss some common types of records and reports. The format of each record or report contains a general list of common information that can be easily adapted for use by a specific facility.

PRESEASON RECORDS

The preseason time period is the period before the facility opens for use by the patrons. The forms and information listed below, in whatever format used, should be available at the facility.

APPLICATION FOR EMPLOYMENT

If departmental or agency forms are used, there should be an attachment about information that is pertinent to the lifeguard position. Some information listed on an application may be confidential. This information should be kept at the proper-level office, such as personnel, department headquarters, or the camp office. Applications submitted to a personnel department should include copies that can be kept at the facility. These copies may be helpful if there is a need to replace or to substitute lifeguards later in the season. The attachment could include the following information:

- Name
- Address
- Age
- Date of birth
- Social security number
- Telephone numbers—home, other work number
- If the agency has different facilities and types:

   Name of facility you are applying for:
   Pool _____ Lake _____ Surf _____

- Certifications:

   Lifesaving, first aid, CPR; any others that may be needed

   Organization(s) and type of certificate(s), date certificate(s) expires; name(s) of instructor (Photocopies of all certifications should be kept on file at the facility.)
- Physical examination: date of last examination. (Attach form, if needed.)
- Experience, if any, in lifeguarding
- Preemployment test scores
- Recommendations—for maturity, judgment, reliability

PREEMPLOYMENT TESTS

- A written test covering lifeguarding and/or lifesaving, first aid, cardiopulmonary resuscitation (CPR), and any other areas pertinent to the job responsibilities, for example, maintenance and filtration.
- Skills tests covering lifeguarding, first aid, and CPR. (Scores and times should be attached to the application and shared with the candidate during interviews.)

CHAIN OF COMMAND

A copy of the chain of command structure for the facility should be shared with each candidate. The lifeguard's position in the chain of command must be clearly explained to and understood by each candidate before employment (reference, Appendix A).

JOB DESCRIPTION SHEET

Job requirements, limits of authority, and information pertaining to a lifeguard's position and accountability, both for on and off duty, should be shared with each candidate.

EMPLOYMENT FORMS

- State and federal tax forms
- Physical examination form
- Employment benefits brochure or information
- Policies of employer

INVENTORY

All equipment and material used at the facility, its condition, and the quantity of each item should be included in the inventory.

EMERGENCY TELEPHONE NUMBERS

A complete list of emergency telephone numbers should be given to each employee, and one list should be posted near the telephone at the aquatic facility. This list should also contain the names of one or two persons who are on the management level in the chain of command. The following emergency organizations are not listed in any order of priority:

- Poison control center
- Rescue unit (ambulance)
- Police department
- Fire department

At isolated facilities, emergency telephone numbers may also include:

- Physicians — at least two. This is not for seeking advice. In a camp setting, the medical person may be the medical adviser or a staff member for the camp, such as the camp nurse.
- U.S. Coast Guard (Search and Rescue).
- County police or sheriff's department.
- Helicopter — for emergency evacuation of an accident victim.
- Hyperbaric chamber — for pressure-related diving accidents.

Additional telephone numbers that may be needed at an aquatic facility are as follows:

- Manager
- Head lifeguard or assistant manager
- Health department
- Water department
- Gas department
- Chemical supply company
- Weather service office
- Electric department
- Animal shelter
- Local American Red Cross chapter or office
- Diving Accident Network (DAN) — relates only to pressure-related accidents.

If there is a need to contact emergency personnel, such as police, fire, or rescue departments, specific information will be required. To ensure that this information is communicated properly, a suggested script for the caller to follow should be prominently posted near the telephone. This script should include the following information:

- Name of caller
- Location and telephone number of caller (and location of emergency, if different)
- Nature of emergency (drowning, cardiac arrest, severe bleeding)
- Required assistance (ambulance, fire, police)

- Suggested approach route (including entrance to facility, e.g., front, rear, or side)
- Location where emergency personnel will be met and method or description by which emergency personnel will recognize individual who will meet them when they arrive

The caller should ask if any further information is required and should **not hang up** until the other party (police, fire, or rescue unit) does so first.

IN-SEASON RECORDS

The in-season period is the time period starting from the first day the aquatic facility is open to the patrons until the day that it closes for the season. The following list includes some forms that are commonly used. Additional forms may be needed and used in different locations. Some of these forms will be used daily, weekly, monthly, once a season, or at other specific times. The number of copies of each will vary with the facility and its management structure. At least two copies of each report should be made, with one copy maintained at the facility in a permanent file.

WORKING REPORTS

- Daily schedule — should include:
  Hours of operation of the facility.
  Lifeguards on duty and times.
  Rotation system.
  Special activities — swim classes, swim team practices, and so on.
- Financial records — should include:
  Admission receipts.
  Snack bar or canteen receipts.
  Instructional class receipts.
  Sales receipts for equipment or clothing, such as kickboards, swim goggles, T-shirts, or jackets.
- Instructional course reports — should include:
  American Red Cross course worksheets and course record forms.
  Enrollment and registration forms.
  Attendance.
  Health clearance, if required.

One person should be designated to keep the instructional course records. However, each instructor is responsible for the accuracy of these forms. Red Cross instructors should be sure that the forms are turned in to the local Red Cross chapter as soon as possible after courses are completed. Copies of worksheets and progress reports should be kept by each instructor and by the facility.

- Payroll
Time sheets, daily and weekly, are required by many departments and agencies. The time sheets should allow places for —

  Names of staff members.
  Time checking in.
  Time checking out.
  Responsibility (lifeguard, maintenance, locker room attendant).
  Wage and salary schedule.
  Substitution: name of person this employee is working for. This should be done only after it has been cleared with the manager or the head lifeguard.

- Health and sanitation
Some of the following records and reports are required by state and local health departments. Some may also be required by the regulating agency, such as the park authority or the recreation department. These records should include —

  Water conditions. (The name of the person making the tests should be listed as well as the time of day the tests were made.) Conditions should include —
      Temperature.
      Turbidity.
      Chlorine: free, combined, total — or other halogen that may be used.
      pH level.
      Back-wash schedule.
      Vacuum schedule.
      Alkalinity.
      Microbiological tests.
  Daily attendance. (This can be counted by the total number of entrance fees, by turnstile counters, by periodic buddy checks or troop counts, or, in small facilities, by head counts taken several times each day.)
  Weather.
  Locker room and rest room cleaning report.
  Electrical equipment.

Facility data sheets, including —
  Name of facility.
  Depth of water — from…to….
  Length and width.
  Capacity — gallons.
  Filters — type and number.
  Turnover rate of circulation system.
  Types of pumps and their respective capacities.
  Capacity limit — per day; at one time.
  At waterfronts, the following additional information may be needed:
      Currents, if any
      Type of bottom
      Wind direction and velocity
      Cross-section drawing of area showing drop-offs, ledges, and other hazards
      Pollution
  Trash pick-up schedule

- Daily log
A narrative of the daily operation should be kept by the manager or the head lifeguard. General comments about opening and closing times, along with comments about the conditions of the physical plant, personnel, and equipment, should be entered in the log. Any changes in scheduling due to illness or emergency, discipline problems, and routine maintenance should be included. All accidents and injuries should be noted, with reference to the specific record for that accident or injury. The log may be used by the management of an aquatic facility to evaluate the total facility, personnel performances, and day-to-day operations.

ACCIDENT, INCIDENT, AND INJURY REPORTS

Reports for accidents, incidents, assists, rescues, or submersion cases can be separated into major and minor classifications. These classifications can be separated further into categories, such as water rescues, first aid, and cardiopulmonary resuscitation (CPR). Forms required by the facility with regard to state or local ordinances must be completed as soon as possible after an incident.

Many agencies and organizations have adopted the use of a checklist format for injuries. For example:

Location of injury:

☐ Head ☐ Trunk
☐ Neck ☐ Back
☐ Arm ☐ Leg
☐ Shoulder ☐ Foot

Another method is to use a diagram of the body, showing a front and rear view.

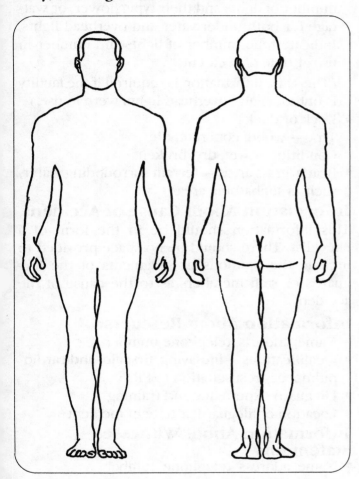

FIG. 6-1

The person filling out the report needs only to circle or check the area of the injury (Fig. 6-1). These formats are being used more often, since they can be filled out quickly and can be evaluated rapidly. Some agencies add a column for comments. Other agencies and departments prefer to have the lifeguard give a narrative description of an accident (refer to Appendix B).

Lifeguards should exercise care not to imply any fault when accident, injury, or fatality forms are filled out. Information on these forms should be as specific as possible, without attempting to suggest fault. Reports should contain only facts. There should be no personal assumptions or observations by the lifeguard.

The following lists include some of the more commonly required categories of information that are found on accident and rescue report forms. Some of the information may not be required or needed at some facilities. It is advisable to check with the facility's legal and insurance advisers for suggestions for priority information.

Information About Victim and Accident

- Name of injured person. (If the person was unconscious and had to be identified by another person, that person's name, address, and telephone number should also be included.)
- Address of injured person
- Age, telephone number, and sex of victim. (At a camp or school, the injured person's home address and telephone number should be included.)
- Date and time of report
- Date and time of accident
- Location of accident — name and location of facility
- Area of facility in which the accident occurred (shallow water, deck, locker room, deep water)
- Witnesses — names, addresses, and telephone numbers. (Witnesses' statements should be on separate forms.)
- Type of injury — drowning, fracture, burn
- Location of injury — head, neck, arm, shoulder
- Type of activity — diving, running, swimming
- Description of accident. (Briefly include any equipment that may have been involved, such as a diving board or a deck chair.)
- Violation of rules — statements as to whether or not the victim was violating any facility rules at the time of the accident. (Also indicate if the victim had been previously cautioned or corrected by the lifeguard.)
- Status of victim. (Explain final status of victim.)
- First aid care given
- Taken by family. (A signature should be required from the individual accepting responsibility for the victim, particularly in cases where the victim is a minor.)

- Transported by EMS. (Refer to section on first aid, medical treatment.)
- Left facility on his or her own. (Signature of victim or guardian is required. In case of a minor, a witness should also sign the report.)

Information About Rescue, Assistance, or Aid Given

- Type of rescue — reaching, wading, swimming
- Distance to victim — distance lifeguard had to travel to get to victim
- Assistance. (List any other staff that may have been involved.)
- Equipment used — ring buoy, rescue tube, rescue buoy, backboard
- First aid — was it administered? If no, why? If yes, what type?

  Artificial respiration — for how long and by whom? If resuscitator was used, by whom and for how long?

  Cardiopulmonary resuscitation (CPR) — for how long and by whom?

  Bleeding controlled, care for shock, bandage applied

  Back or neck injury — description of complete care, including approach to victim, turning victim over in water, and application of backboard

- Medical treatment — if emergency medical personnel were called:

  By whom and at what time?

  Time of arrival

  EMS personnel actions — what did EMS personnel do?

  Victim transported by EMS — names of EMS personnel and location where victim was taken

  If injury was minor (scrape, bruise) and victim was released, a record of care given should be kept on file. This should include victim's name, address, and telephone number. Victim, or relatives of victim in case of minor, should sign this record.

Information About Conditions at Time of Accident

- Weather — clear, cloudy, rain, temperature, electrical storm, fog, wind direction, and wind velocity, if possible

- Water — temperature, clarity, and depth of water at site of accident

  Additional information needed at waterfront facilities:

  Current, surface calm or choppy

  Beach area — sandy, rocky, level, steep
- Capacity — number of people in water and on deck or beach at time of accident
- Lights

  If facility is indoors, information should include number of lights and their type, power, or wattage for both underwater and overhead lights. Indicate total number of lights and number in use at time of accident.

  (The same information is required if the facility is outdoors and overhead lights were in use.)
- Deck or dock

  Type — wood, concrete, tile

  Condition — wet, dry, broken
- Beach/grass areas — terrain surrounding water, such as sunbathing areas

Information About Cause of Accident

This information should be in the form of a checklist. There should be no space provided to include the opinions or judgments of the lifeguards or staff members as to the cause of the accident.

Information About Rescuers

- Name, address, telephone number
- Qualifications — lifesaving, first aid, and cardiopulmonary resuscitation (CPR)
- Lifeguard experience and training
- Location of lifeguard at time of incident

Information About Witnesses' Statements

- Name, address, telephone number
- Date of statement
- Description of incident. (This should be a narrative statement by witnesses as to what was seen. Witnesses should be allowed to make statements in their own words without influence from facility staff members.)

MAINTENANCE REPORTS
Inspection Reports

Routine inspections (daily, weekly, monthly) of the total facility should be in a checklist format, using categories for conditions, such as satisfactory, unsatisfactory, and damaged. Action suggested and taken should be indicated.

Supply Records

The current supply stock should be known at all times. Any items that are low in stock should be reordered before anything runs out. These items may include soap, toilet paper, paper towels, first aid supplies, and pool chemicals. Daily checks on supplies should be made, especially first aid supplies. Perhaps the most important time to check and reorder supplies is immediately after an emergency. Always replenish anything that was used as soon as possible.

Maintenance Requests

All requests for maintenance should be submitted as soon as possible and should be followed up, at least weekly, until the maintenance is completed. They should include the date, the name of the person submitting the request, and an indication of how soon the jobs should be completed. Copies of all requests should be kept at the facility.

IN-SERVICE TRAINING REPORTS

Reports should be kept on all in-service training sessions. This information should include —

Names of all persons who were in attendance and of those who were absent.

Subjects that were covered.

Names of instructors.

Schedule.

Times and scores of participants.

A statement as to whether or not the practical training session was open to viewing by the public. This is a good public relations procedure for all aquatic facilities.

A copy of this report should be posted on the lifeguards' bulletin board with a statement relating to make-up training for those who were absent.

PERSONNEL EVALUATION

Lifeguards should be evaluated on a regular basis. Each evaluation should be reviewed with the lifeguard concerned. Once completed, copies of the evaluation forms should be forwarded to the proper offices (aquatic director, personnel). A copy should be kept at the facility, and the lifeguards should retain their copies. Some of the criteria that the lifeguards are evaluated on are as follows:

- Skills and knowledge — swimming, first aid, lifesaving, time tests
- Uniforms — cleanliness and proper uniform
- Attitude—accepting responsibility and authority
- Cooperation with management and with other staff members
- Conforming with standards, rules, and regulations
- Participation during in-service training sessions
- Relationships with other staff and patrons (public relations)
- Performance during emergencies
- Promptness and dependability
- Any other strengths or weaknesses that may affect performance

Comments should be included about any equipment that may have been issued to the lifeguard at the start of the session. Examples: swimsuit, shirt, jacket, whistle, and identification.

There are a number of methods used for evaluating lifeguards. Some facilities use a number scale, such as 1 being low on the scale and 5 being high. Another method is a rating scale for poor, average, superior, and excellent. A third method could be a combination of the first two. Each performance factor is given a point grade, such as 1 — does not perform, 2 — performs to minimum standards, and 3 — performs above minimum standards. Since lifeguards are evaluated on a number of factors, a total is reached by adding the points given. Then each category is given a range of points.

Written criteria for all of these categories should be included in the lifeguard manual. Any of these methods can be adapted by an aquatic facility. Whatever method is used, it must be standardized for all lifeguards. The same individual or team of individuals should evaluate all of the lifeguards at one facility, if possible.

ADDITIONAL RECORDS AND REPORTS

- Missing person
- Lost and found articles
- Disturbance
- Insurance — explanation of coverage and worker's compensation forms
- Swim meet material:
    Names, addresses, and telephone numbers of coaches, officials, judges, and timers

Miscellaneous forms — list of events, entry forms, rules and regulations, giving the most up-to-date information
- Schedules of events — daily and weekly

POSTSEASON RECORDS

The postseason time period is the period after the facility has been closed to the patrons. All postseason records should be maintained by the facility manager or the owner in order to have them ready for the start of the following season. In facilities that are operated year-round, records can be maintained on an ongoing basis. Examples of postseason records are as follows:

INVENTORY

A complete list of all supplies and equipment, identifying their condition and the quantities on hand, should be filed at the facility, and a copy should be kept by the manager or the owner. This list must be accurate, since it will be used as a projection for budget items for the next season.

MANAGER'S REPORT

This report is usually done in a narrative format, although it could be simplified by using a checklist format. The report could include information such as the total attendance for all activities, evaluations for the facility operations, first aid records, rosters, schedules, and any recommendations for the future.

SUMMARY

This chapter (Chapter 6) discusses the more common types of records and reports that are, or may be, used at aquatic facilities. Other forms or information may be useful or necessary. Lifeguards and managers should be sure that an adequate supply of all record forms is available at the facility.

Chapter 7

EQUIPMENT

A responsibility at each aquatic facility is to provide necessary safety and rescue equipment, which may include personal uniform equipment for lifeguards. The types and amounts of equipment will be governed by the number of lifeguards who are employed, by the size and type of facility, and by budgetary considerations. Since the primary concern of the lifeguard is to provide for the safety of the patrons, it is the responsibility of the lifeguards to ensure that the equipment is in good condition and that it is readily available at all times. A daily check of the equipment for necessary repairs or replacement should be made before the facility opens. Any item that is questionable should be reported to the facility management and should be replaced, repaired, or removed. A facility should not be operated without a minimum amount of safety equipment. Minimum standards for equipment may be established by local and state ordinances. Such items should include a reaching pole and a ring buoy. Arrangements should be made to substitute or replace pieces of equipment and materials that could be used during emergencies, such as a backboard or first aid materials.

Safety and rescue equipment have become standardized over the years. Not all of the equipment described in this chapter will be necessary for all facilities. Further information on the use of certain pieces of this equipment can be found in

Chapter 9, "Water Rescues and Special Situations," and also Chapter 10, "Search and Recovery Operations."

PERSONAL EQUIPMENT

UNIFORM

Many facilities require a specific type of uniform to be worn by the lifeguards. Some employers may provide all or part of the uniform. The uniform should be kept neat and clean at all times and should be worn in the prescribed manner and only while on duty. A uniform may consist of the following items:

- Swimsuit
  A nylon swimsuit is ideal, since it dries quickly. It should be of a color that is easily recognized.
- Shirt
  A shirt may be either a special T-shirt or a blouse that provides protection from the weather and easy identification of the lifeguard.
- Jacket
  A jacket provides identification and protection from the weather at an outdoor facility. A light windbreaker may also be worn at an indoor facility. A jacket should be designed so that it can be removed easily in an emergency.
- Hat
  A hat provides protection from the sun for the head and face.

- Foul-weather gear
  This type of gear should be available where weather dictates its use.
- Whistle
  A small, shrill whistle should be available for instant use.
- Sunglasses
  Sunglasses should be of good quality, designed to filter sunlight, and should not reduce vision.
- Shoes
  Tennis shoes, sandals, or thongs should be worn to protect the lifeguard's feet.

ADDITIONAL EQUIPMENT

Personal equipment may include the following items:

- Binoculars
  Binoculars are very useful on large beaches where there are large areas of responsibility.
- Blanket
  A blanket can be used to cover the lifeguard's legs for warmth and can be used to cover or shade a victim after rescue.
- Suntan lotion
  As a precaution against overexposure to the sun, lifeguards should use suntan lotion or a sunscreen.

Jewelry such as earrings, bracelets, watches, necklaces, chains, and pins should not be worn when the lifeguard is on duty, because it can cause injury to the lifeguard or the victim during a rescue.

SAFETY EQUIPMENT

- Lifelines
  Lifelines are buoyed lines that mark and separate swimming and diving areas (Fig. 7-1). They help to prevent accidents from happening by restricting bather activity to designated areas. They also can provide temporary support to a victim who is in a distress situation. They should be stretched tightly, enough to support an adult with his or her head above water.

FIG. 7-1

- Lifeguard stands
  Lifeguard stands provide vantage points for lifeguards while supervising bathers. The lifeguard stand can be stationary or mobile. Chairs must be located so that the lifeguard can see over the edge of the pool immediately in front of the chair. Types and sizes of stands will vary with facilities. Some standard features are as follows:
- The seat should be from five to six feet above the level of the ground or deck.
- On larger beaches, the seat may be from 10 to 16 feet above the level of the beach.
- Footrests and backrests are important. Straight-backed chairs will help to prevent the lifeguard from slouching.
- There should be some provision for shade and shelter for the lifeguard, such as an umbrella or a canopy.
- A hook, stand, or supports for rescue equipment should be available to allow the lifeguard to store and reach the equipment with little effort.
- The stand should have a place for first aid equipment.

Many lifeguard stands at swimming pools are constructed of galvanized pipe or stainless steel and are anchored to the deck (Fig. 7-2A).

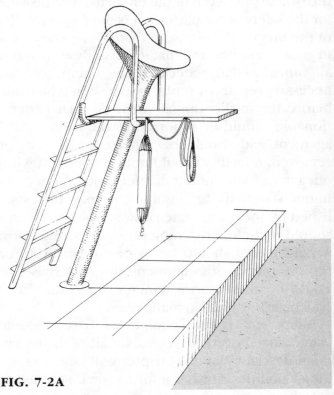

FIG. 7-2A

At lakes and nonsurf beaches, the stand may be wooden and can be attached to the dock or sometimes can be anchored in the water (Fig. 7-2B). A mobile stand or chair at pools or beaches provides flexibility for the lifeguard. It may be moved to a location where the lifeguard can observe a special class or to an area that has a larger concentration of swimmers (Fig. 7-2C).

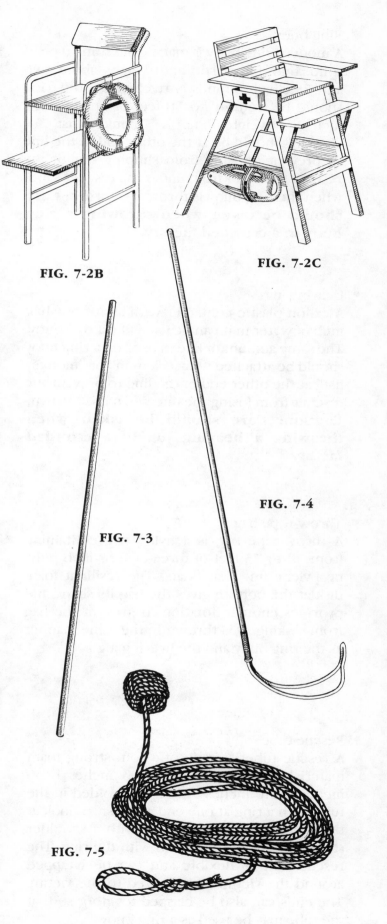

FIG. 7-2B

FIG. 7-2C

FIG. 7-3

FIG. 7-4

FIG. 7-5

RESCUE EQUIPMENT

This section deals with equipment that can be used by a lifeguard to assist a person in either a distress or drowning situation. Pieces of equipment that are extended or thrown to a victim can be used only in distress situations where the victim will be aware of their presence and will have enough self-control to grab hold of the equipment.

- Reaching pole
  The reaching pole (Fig. 7-3) is used mostly at pools and camp waterfronts. A pole should be approximately 10 to 15 feet long. Poles are usually made of bamboo, aluminum, or fiberglass.
- Shepherd's crook
  A shepherd's crook (Fig. 7-4) is a long, lightweight pole with a blunted hook at one end. The hook should be long enough to encircle a victim. It may be used with either a conscious or unconscious victim. It can also be used as a reaching pole.

- Heaving line
  A heaving line (Fig. 7-5) is any strong, lightweight line, from 40 to 50 feet in length. There should be an eye splice in one end to go around rescuer's wrist. A "monkey fist" or a similar weighted object attached at one end of the line adds weight to help direct the line out to the victim when it is thrown by the rescuer.

- Ring buoy

  A modern ring buoy is made from some type of solid, buoyant plastic and weighs about two and one-half pounds. Attached to the ring should be from 40 to 50 feet of one-quarter-inch lightweight line. A "monkey fist" or "lemon" should be at the other end of the line to prevent the line from slipping out of the rescuer's hand or from under the rescuer's foot when the ring buoy is thrown. **Caution: Care should be taken when throwing a ring buoy in a crowded facility.**

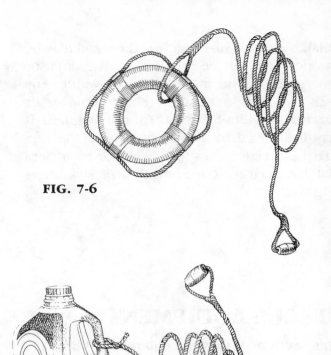

FIG. 7-6

- Heaving jug

  A gallon plastic container with about one-half inch of water in it can be used like a ring buoy. The same amount of line as used on a ring buoy should be attached with a "lemon" or "monkey fist" at the other end of the line to prevent the rescuer from losing the line when it is thrown. **Caution: Care should be taken when throwing a heaving jug in a crowded facility.**

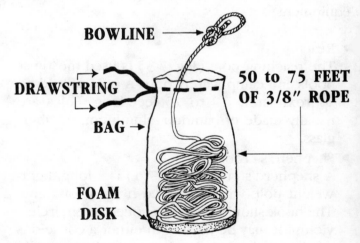

FIG. 7-7

- Throw-rope bag

  A throw-rope bag is a nylon bag containing from 50 to 75 feet of three-eighths-inch polypropylene line that floats. The resilient foam disk at the bottom gives the bag its shape and provides enough flotation to prevent the bag from sinking. It is thrown in the same manner as the ring buoy and the heaving jug.

BOWLINE

DRAWSTRING

50 to 75 FEET OF 3/8" ROPE

BAG

FOAM DISK

FIG. 7-8

- Rescue tube

  A rescue tube is made of a soft, strong foam material. It is approximately 3 inches by 6 inches by 40 inches. A strap is molded in the tube with a ring at one end and a snap hook at the other. A six-foot towline with a shoulder strap is attached to the end with the ring. The rescue tube is flexible and can be wrapped around the victim and secured to the victim. The ends can also be clasped together so that the tube may be used as a ring buoy.

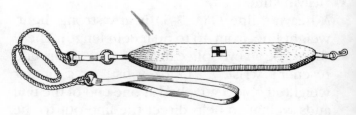

FIG. 7-9

- **Rescue buoy**

  A rescue buoy is made of a lightweight, hard, buoyant plastic. Molded handgrips along each side enable a victim to maintain a firm hold on the buoy and may also be used by the rescuer to hold the victim to the buoy. Plastic buoys are tough, almost indestructible, and virtually maintenance-free. A towrope, about four to six feet in length with a shoulder strap, is attached to one end of the buoy.

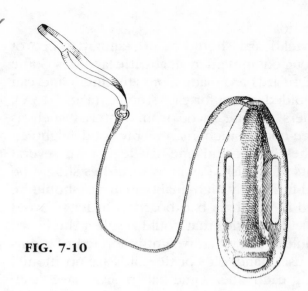

FIG. 7-10

- **Torpedo buoy**

  Older models of this type of buoy were made of metal; however, newer ones are made of plastic. There are handholds or grip ropes along each side. Smaller versions have a towrope and shoulder strap that allow the rescuer to tow the buoy while the victim holds on to it. Larger versions are usually attached to a line that is fed out from shore. The victim and the rescuer can be towed to safety by other lifeguards on shore.

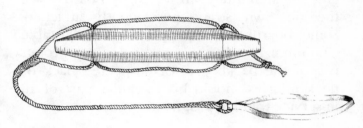

FIG. 7-11

- **Lines and reels**

  Lines and reels are sometimes called surf lines or beach lines. They are valuable for surf, multi-victim, or ice rescues. The line should be a polypropylene line that floats, one-quarter inch in diameter and approximately 500 to 600 feet in length. One end of the line has an eye splice or a snap hook that allows the rescuer to make a shoulder loop or to attach the line to a rescue tube or rescue buoy. The rest of the line is coiled on a reel or is kept in a small box or basket. Reels can be fastened to a lifeguard stand or mounted on portable stands. Larger beaches may have reels mounted on vehicles. A second lifeguard attends the reel to keep it from snagging or fouling. Once contact with the victim has been made, both the victim and the rescuer can be towed to safety.

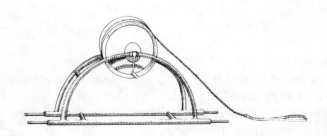

FIG. 7-12

- Backboard

  A backboard should be a standard piece of rescue equipment at all aquatic facilities. Some backboards are made from aluminum and can be folded in half for easy storage. (Fig. 7-13A). Others can be made from material such as three-quarter-inch marine plywood, eighteen inches by six and one-half feet, with several coats of varnish. Paints or varnishes should be lead-free. Only high-quality material should be used in making a backboard in order to avoid possible injuries that could result if the board should break when weight is applied to it during use. Handholds or tie holds are positioned along each side. Some backboards have "runners" on the bottom side to allow for easier lifting (Fig. 7-13B). Runners should be affixed to the board with wooden dowels, waterproof glue, or aluminum screws. Many boards have the tie-down straps permanently attached. Some boards are equipped with adjustable aluminum foot plates. Practice in the proper use of the backboard for suspected back or neck injuries should be a regular part of all in-service training programs.

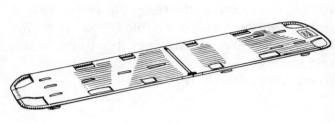

FIG. 7-13A

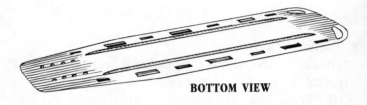

BOTTOM VIEW

FIG. 7-13B

- Litters and stretchers

  These pieces of equipment can be used for emergency transportation. A common litter is the folding type, with aluminum handles and a canvas or vinyl bed.

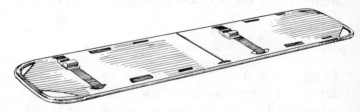

FIG. 7-14

- Rescue board

  A rescue board is a piece of rescue equipment used at open-water facilities. The rescue board or paddle board is larger and provides more flotation than the modern surfboard. It can readily support both the victim and the rescuer. (Refer to Chapter 9, "Water Rescues and Special Situations.") Approximately ten feet by twenty-two inches, the board can be made of foam, fiberglass, balsa wood, or marine plywood (Fig. 7-15). Lifeguards should be skillful enough to maneuver the board through crowded swimming areas. In an emergency, a board used for surfing can be used for a rescue.

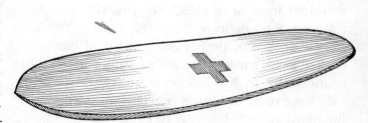

FIG. 7-15

- Rescue boat

  The rowboat is a common type of craft used for lifeguard operations. A canoe may be used, although it is not very practical. In recent years, there has been an increase in the use of power-boats. The rescue boat should be stationed for easy access and speed in launching. It can also be used to patrol along the edge of the swimming area. The biggest advantage that a boat provides is its use for long-distance rescues. The lifeguard has the option of using the boat to make contact with the victim, extending something to the victim, or, when there are two lifeguards in the rescue boat, entering the water to assist the victim. Generally, and depending on the type of craft, the following equipment may be found in a rescue boat:

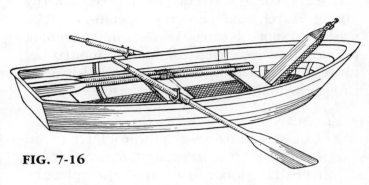

FIG. 7-16

Extra set of oars	Bailer
Rescue buoy/tube	Towline
Reaching pole	First aid kit
Anchor and line	

Personal flotation devices (PFDs)
Marker buoys (minimum of 3)

  Powerboats are recommended for use as patrol rescue boats in small-craft areas. Further information on the use of rescue boats is in Chapter 12, "Waterfront Areas."

- Swim fins

  Lifeguards at open-water areas may use swim fins for assistance during rescues when a great distance must be covered to get to the victim and back to safety. They can be helpful if a lifeguard has to dive to the bottom of a deep diving well to recover a victim. They are also helpful when the lifeguard must stabilize both himself or herself and a victim in open water while attempting to administer mouth-to-mouth resuscitation. They are also very useful during search and recovery operations in open-water areas.

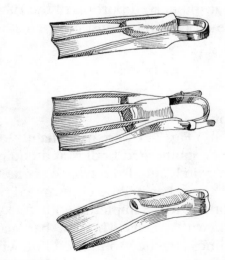

FIG. 7-17

SEARCH AND RECOVERY EQUIPMENT

This section deals with equipment used primarily during search and recovery operations. Face masks and snorkels can be used during swimming rescues. However, their use may be limited because of the possibility of the lifeguard's having to struggle with the victim during a rescue.

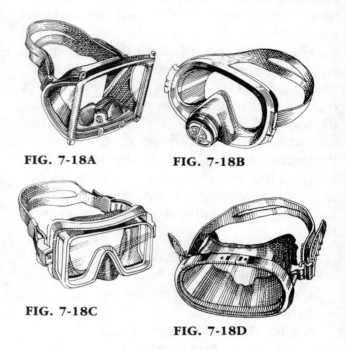

FIG. 7-18A   FIG. 7-18B

FIG. 7-18C

FIG. 7-18D

- Face mask
  A mask should have a shatterproof, tempered glass faceplate. The faceplate should be set in a soft, flexible rubber skirt that is held in place by a corrosion-proof metal or plastic reinforcement band (Figs. 7-18A and 7-18D). An individual can choose a mask with any of the extras that are available. A mask may have a purge valve (Fig. 7-18B) or molded indentations in the skirt (Fig. 7-18C) that allows the wearer to pinch the nose when attempting to equalize pressure in the ear or ears.

- Snorkel
  A snorkel is a hollow rubber tube from 12 to 15 inches in length, with a soft-rubber flanged mouthpiece (Fig. 7-19). It can be of one-piece molded construction or can have a ribbed, flexible section at the curved portion of the tube. The longer end of the tube must be open at all times.

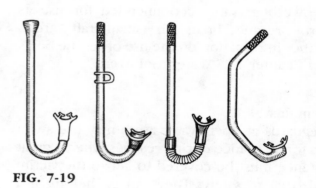

FIG. 7-19

- Grappling irons
  Grappling irons (Fig. 7-20) are used mainly for the recovery of submerged bodies and equipment. They vary in length from two to six feet. The size of the tow bar will be determined by the type of bottom, for example, smooth, rocky, or overgrown with weeds. The tow bar may have several lines attached to it. Each line will have a series of one-inch barbless hooks. Light chain hooks should be used, so that the rig can be freed more easily if it should become snagged. A cable, chain, or rope is attached to each end of the tow bar for dragging operations.

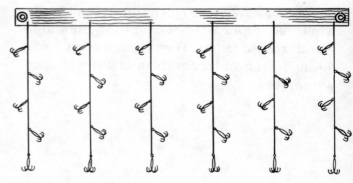

FIG. 7-20

- Grappling pole

  In areas where the bottom is grassy or is littered with debris or tree stumps, a grappling pole (Fig. 7-21) from 12 to 16 feet in length, with a large, barbless hook at one end, can be used to probe for a body or a lost piece of equipment. Only a trained person will be able to distinguish between a rock, a piece of wood, or a human body.

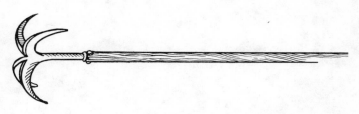

FIG. 7-21

- Grappling lines

  A large, pointed hook attached to the end of a line can be used for dragging operations in narrow, deep channels or in small areas between rocks (Fig. 7-22). Procedures for the use of grappling equipment and search patterns are discussed in Chapter 10, "Search and Recovery Operations."

  Additional items such as scuba equipment, vehicles, and aircraft are being used in some areas of the United States to aid in rescues. The use of this equipment will be based on the type, location, and size of the facility. The use of oxygen therapy equipment such as a self-inflation bag and mask or a mechanical resuscitator will require specialized training. Lifeguards should be thoroughly trained with the type of equipment used at their facility.

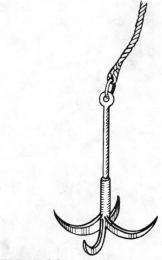

FIG. 7-22

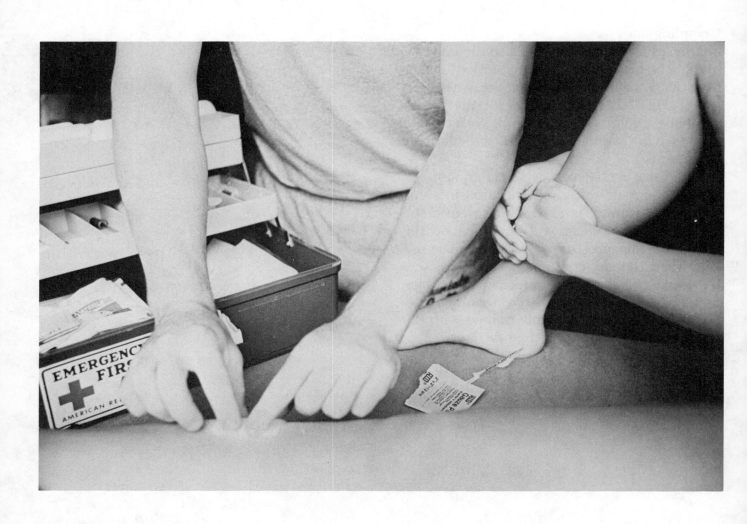

Chapter 8

HEALTH AND
SANITATION

GENERAL INFORMATION

The health and safety of the patrons is the responsibility of the total staff of an aquatic facility. The management of the facility has an obligation to provide as safe a facility and as well trained a staff as possible. The lifeguards are obliged to ensure the safety of the patrons by supervising activities in the facility and, when possible, preventing hazardous situations from occurring. Other staff members, such as locker room attendants and maintenance personnel, are obliged to provide a clean and sanitary facility. However, not all aquatic facilities have a large enough staff to separate these duties. Frequently, it is the lifeguards who perform most of the health and sanitation duties. Each facility will vary in the amount and type of duties that are required of the lifeguards.

This chapter deals with the most common health and sanitation duties performed by the lifeguards. It points out some of the differences between the duties of lifeguards at swimming pools and those at waterfronts. It is not intended to take the place of a pool operator's course or to teach an in-depth environmental control program. There are organizations such as the National Swimming Pool Foundation, pool chemical companies, and departments of health that conduct training courses in these subjects. Many colleges and universities also offer this type of training.

The degree of healthfulness and sanitation of an aquatic facility is determined primarily by three factors: (1) the patrons' personal hygiene practices, (2) the amount of attention given to the safety and cleanliness of the facility by the staff, and (3) the quality of the water in the swimming area. These factors can be influenced by the lifeguards in the following ways:

- Patrons should be required to take a shower before being allowed to enter the pool. Patrons who have open sores or skin diseases should be prohibited from using the facility.
- Daily inspections and maintenance should be conducted for the entire facility. Equipment should be kept clean and free of hazards. Hazardous items should be removed or controlled to protect the patrons.
- The clarity and sanitary characteristics of the water in swimming pools are controlled by having filtration and disinfection systems that are in good working order and that are operated by personnel who are trained in the proper use of this equipment. The water in waterfront facilities is monitored by using systems that are established by boards of health or by other regulatory agencies.
- All lifeguards should constantly be checking for patrons who show signs of overexposure to heat or to cold temperature. It is important that lifeguards be able to recognize the symptoms that may signal this overexposure.

The principles of health and sanitation are similar for most aquatic facilities. Each facility should have a detailed manual of operation for its staff members. The manual should include, as a minimum, the following information about the health and sanitation of the facility:

- A list of items that should be inspected on a daily or weekly basis, the reasons for inspecting each item, and the procedures to be followed regarding any necessary maintenance or repairs
- The areas of the facility that need to be cleaned on a daily or weekly basis and the cleaning procedures that are to be followed
- The procedures to be followed for testing and maintaining the quality of the water in the swimming area
- Samples of all records and reports used by the lifeguards during the operation of the facility.

DAILY INSPECTIONS AND MAINTENANCE

There should be daily inspections of all of the equipment in the facility, including recreational as well as safety equipment. Any piece of equipment that is found to be unsatisfactory should be removed or restricted for use until it can be repaired or replaced. The management should be notified in writing as to equipment condition. There should also be an inspection of all areas that are used by the patrons, including locker rooms, showers, toilets, and beach and deck areas. These areas should be inspected before any patrons are allowed into the facility.

The following list includes some of the most common areas that need to be inspected. It includes hazards that may be found in swimming pools and waterfront areas. In each of these areas, the hazards or problems can be handled by the lifeguards or other staff members, such as locker room attendants or maintenance personnel. Areas and some hazards are as follows:

- Locker rooms and showers —
  Standing pools of water and slippery surfaces
  Leaky faucets, shower heads, and toilets
  Broken chairs and benches
  Stopped-up floor drains
  Broken pipes and spigots
  Temperature of water too hot in showers

- Decks, docks, and entrance areas —
  Slippery surfaces
  Broken or loose concrete
  Broken or loose boards
  Exposed nails
- Ladders —
  Loose or broken steps
  Splinters
  Sharp edges or exposed nails or bolts
- Diving boards or towers —
  Loose or broken steps
  Loose or broken frame and railings
  Splinters
  Sharp edges or exposed nails
  Diving boards in poor condition
- Lifeguard stands —
  Loose or broken steps
  Loose or broken frames
  Sharp edges or exposed nails or bolts

- Beach area —
  Glass or sharp objects
  Holes
  Excessive amount of rocks
- Floats (docks and rafts) —
  Exposed nails
  Broken or splintered boards
  Stability
- First aid rooms —
  Unclean, messy
  Insufficient supplies
  Damaged supplies

The first aid station should be checked daily to ensure its cleanliness and to make sure that there is a sufficient supply of necessary first aid items such as the following:
- Desk and chairs
- Locking cabinets for storing supplies
- Bulletin board
- Pens, pencils, and paper
- Accident and incident report forms
- Clock
- Counter-top work area
- Hot and cold running water
- Sink
- Additional sink or basin at lower level for treating knee and foot injuries
- Liquid soap
- Refrigerator (for ice)
- Cot, blankets, and pillow
- Flashlight (extra batteries kept in refrigerator)

- Plastic bags of various sizes
- Paper towels and paper cups
- Trash receptacle
- Telephone, CB radio, or other communications system
- Emergency telephone numbers and procedures
- Portable first aid kit containing —
  - Adhesive compresses of various sizes
  - Adhesive tape
  - Eye dressing pads (4" x 4" and 3" x 3")
  - Gauze pads (4" x 4" and 3" x 3")
  - Roller gauze (2", 3", and 4" widths)
  - Scissors and tweezers
  - Triangular bandages
- Red Cross Standard First Aid textbook
- Resuscitator and oxygen*
- Cervical collars of various sizes*
- A litter
- Splints (14 inches and 36 inches) with ties
- Long backboards with ties and material for immobilizing the head and neck

All emergency equipment, such as respirators, must be kept in good working order. Units that contain electrical connections should be kept locked. Disinfection equipment, such as chlorine gas, should be checked periodically each day to ensure its safe operation. Maintenance equipment, like power mowers, should be checked to make sure that it is in good working condition before being used.

Another area of concern for lifeguards is the bottom and sides of the swimming facility. In swimming pools, because of the clarity of the water, inspections can usually be made by just walking around the pool and looking for any hazards such as grates over the drains being removed or loosened and underwater lights that may have worked loose or that may have broken glass. "Bathtub ring" is still another maintenance problem. This condition is caused by a buildup of grease and suntan oil on the walls at the surface of the pool. It can be removed by scrubbing with a brush and using an appropriate cleaning solution.

At waterfront facilities, the lifeguards will have to check the bottom by carefully walking through the shallow water and by swimming through the deeper areas while using masks, fins, and snorkels. In facilities that are part of a river system or that are influenced by currents, it is possible for debris to be brought into the swimming area. Therefore, these areas should be checked daily, especially after a storm or a sudden change in the weather.

Rescue boats should be inspected daily to see that they are in good working condition, that they are ready for immediate use, and that all necessary equipment is on board and in good condition.

The following is a suggested routine of daily maintenance that may be adapted to different aquatic facilities:

1. Before opening
   a. Check bottom of swimming areas for objects.
   b. Sweep out and hose down locker rooms, bathhouses, showers, toilets, and entranceways. These areas should be scrubbed daily if facility is used heavily.
   c. Skim surface of water and clean out overflow troughs in swimming pools.
   d. Vacuum pool.
   e. Rake beach at waterfronts. Inspect area for other debris.
   f. Empty all trash containers. These containers should be washed out on a weekly basis.
   g. Clean out office, guard room, and first aid room. Treatment surfaces in first aid room should be washed with a disinfectant.
   h. Hose down deck or dock area. At waterfronts, this can be done with buckets of water. Wash in a direction away from swimming area, if possible, to avoid splashing or washing any debris from deck into swimming area.
2. During hours of operation
   The following areas should be inspected on a periodic basis throughout the day. All trash should be removed, and any supplies that are needed should be replaced.
   a. Pool deck or beach area
   b. Area designated for sunbathing
   c. Locker rooms
   d. Showers and toilets
3. Closing
   a. Check bottom of swimming area for objects or bodies.

*These items require specialized training.

b. Put trash in cans and station it where it can be picked up.
c. Hose down locker rooms and shut off showers and faucets.
d. Hose down decks.
e. Put all found articles in lost-and-found lockers.
f. Return all equipment to proper areas.
g. Turn off all unnecessary lights. Turn on any security lights.
h. Double-check all windows, doors, and gates to be sure that they are locked.
i. Be sure that all small craft have been returned.

SWIMMING POOL MAINTENANCE

Persons who are responsible for the proper operation of the filtration and disinfection equipment at swimming pools must have a technical knowledge of water chemistry. This knowledge should include the various types of disinfectants that can be used; the methods of testing and controlling the chemical balance of the water, including the pH level and the turbidity; the physical and biological properties of water; and the bacteriological standards that are established for the water in the facility.

The information about water chemistry that follows is not intended to thoroughly educate lifeguards. It is presented only as a foundation and as a stimulus to individuals to further their education on this subject. Lifeguards are encouraged to purchase and read one of the texts that are available on pool maintenance chemistry. Owners and managers of swimming pools should allow lifeguards who are given responsibility for pool sanitation to attend pool maintenance clinics. Local ordinances may require the lifeguards to pass an examination on this subject. Periodic recertification may also be required. A file containing textbooks or manufacturer's directions relating to the pool operation and water sanitation should be kept at the facility. It should also include a list of possible problems relating to operation and sanitation and some solutions to these problems.

WATER CIRCULATION

Each swimming pool will usually have a different arrangement of the components that make up the circulation system. It is the lifeguard's responsibility to identify and locate each component at the facility where the lifeguard will be working. The following list of components may be found in most modern facilities. Not all of those listed will be found at every facility.

- Drains, on pool bottom — Take water into system.
- Overflow troughs — Take water into system.
- Skimmers — Remove oils and waste floating on water surface.
- Balance tank (surge tank) — Maintains water level in pool when water is displaced by swimmers.
- Strainers for hair and lint — Remove hair, lint, and other materials from system.
- Pump — Forces water through system.
- Tanks for chemicals — Hold chemicals to be put into system.
- Valve — Controls flow of water and chemicals.
- Gauges — Indicate pressures in system.
- Flow meter — Indicates rate of water flow.
- Filters, sand and gravel or diatomaceous earth — Remove material from water.
- Soda ash or caustic soda feeders — Allow soda ash or caustic soda to be put into system.
- Water heater — Heats water before its return to pool.
- Sight glass — Allows visual inspection of water clarity while back-washing a sand filter.
- Return inlets at pool — Return water to pool.
- Slurry tanks — Feed diatomaceous earth into filters.

Depending on the type of filter, additional components that may be found are a slurry tank to mix the diatomaceous earth or an alum feeder to put alum into the system of a sand-gravel filter.

BALANCED WATER

Balanced water is one of the most important factors contributing to the life expectancy of a swimming pool. The results of the various chemical tests performed on the pool water during daily operations will reflect the need for the addition of necessary chemicals or for other courses of action to be taken by the pool operator. Failure to maintain proper chemical levels can be very costly.

The single most significant aspect of balanced water is the pH factor. The pH indicates how

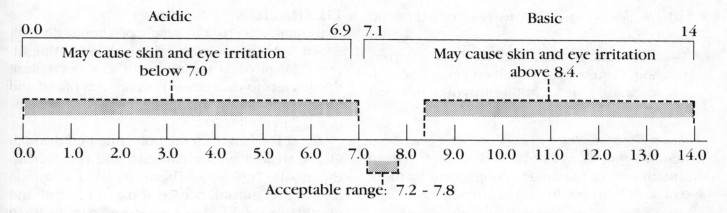

FIG. 8-1

basic or acidic the pool water is on a scale of 0 to 14. The number 7.0 represents neutral (neither basic nor acidic). Water ranging from 0 to 6.9 is acidic, and water ranging from 7.1 to 14 is basic (Fig. 8-1).

A pH level below 7.0 prohibits flocculation, which removes suspended materials from the water, and the proper functioning of sand filters. It can cause corrosion of plumbing, filter tanks, and the heater as well as cause discomfort to the eyes, skin, and mucous membranes. A pH of 7.8 or above reduces the effectiveness of halogen disinfectants (chlorine, bromine, iodine), allows for calcification in sand filters and pool heaters, promotes the growth of algae, and also causes irritation to the eyes. Attention to the proper pH and other chemical levels will provide for safer operation, more comfortable swimming, and longer pool life, and all at much lower operating and maintenance costs.

Different types of filtration equipment, unique water conditions, and chemical combinations will determine chemical levels in a swimming pool. Swimming pool operators should check with the health department or other regulatory agencies for local required standards. The following levels are not specific and therefore may vary for different states and localities:

Chlorine — Minimum free chlorine residual of 1.0 ppm (parts per million) maintains good clarity of water and causes less eye irritation.

pH — A range of from 7.2 to 7.8 will maintain water that is in an acceptable pH range.

Alkalinity — A range of from 80 to 100 ppm will prevent the pH level from rising and falling with various bather loads.

Hardness — A range of from 100 to 200 ppm is favorable. A water hardness that is too low may cause the water to become corrosive, and this condition can damage pipes, concrete, plaster, and heater coils. Too high a water hardness also may cause damage to pipes and heater coils.

DISINFECTION

Some means of disinfecting pool water is required by all states for the purpose of killing bacteria, since water serves as a transportation medium for many diseases, such as cholera, typhoid fever, hepatitis, and dysentery. Disinfection is usually accomplished by using one of the three halogens: chlorine, bromine, and iodine. Other methods have been attempted (e.g., ozone, ultraviolet light, sulfamic acid, silver salts), but they have not proved to be cost-effective or successful. The halogens remain the most popular, with chlorine the most commonly used. Each of the following disinfectants has its own unique characteristics, advantages, and disadvantages:

Chlorine

Chlorine disinfects the water by killing algae and bacteria and oxidizing solid matter in the water.

Gas Chlorine

Gas chlorine requires use of soda ash or caustic soda, and bicarbonate of soda for balancing water.

Advantages — Least expensive method; good algaecide.

Disadvantages — Most potentially dangerous method; requires use of self-contained breathing apparatus when working around it or when changing gas cylinders.

Calcium Hypochlorite

Calcium hypochlorite requires use of an acid to maintain proper pH range, along with bicarbonate of soda to maintain proper balance.

Advantages — Inexpensive; good algaecide.

Disadvantages — Some types are flammable and explosive when contacted with organic material such as paper, oil, and gasoline; raises pH of water.

Sodium Hypochlorite

Sodium hypochlorite requires use of an acid to maintain proper pH range, along with bicarbonate of soda to maintain proper balance.

Advantages — Easy to use; relatively inexpensive; good algaecide.

Disadvantages — Shelf life of only 60 to 90 days under ideal storage conditions; raises pH of water.

Lithium Hypochlorite

Lithium hypochlorite is a newer chlorine compound. It is not widely used at this time. It is also higher priced than other hypochlorites.

Bromine (Organic)

Bromine requires soda ash and bicarbonate of soda to maintain balance.

Advantages — Good algaecide, oxidizer, and disinfectant.

Disadvantages — Stains pool walls; pool water can develop suds, dark green color, and strong odor; more expensive than gas chlorine.

Iodine

Iodine requires an algaecide along with soda ash and bicarbonate of soda to maintain balance.

Advantages — Less eye irritation; good oxidizer and bacteriacide.

Disadvantages — Requires simultaneous use of chlorine to enable iodine to work. Discolors jewelry. Ineffective against algae.

FILTRATION

Sparkling water is the result of chemically balanced water along with effectively operating filters. The physical cleaning of the water (filtration) refers to the removal of particles of dirt and the organic and inorganic materials that are suspended in pool water.

Water is taken from the pool, pumped through filters, treated with chemicals, and returned to the pool (Fig. 8-2). There are two common methods of filtration used today: (1) sand and gravel and (2) diatomaceous earth. Both methods refer to the filter media used to remove the dirt and other impurities.

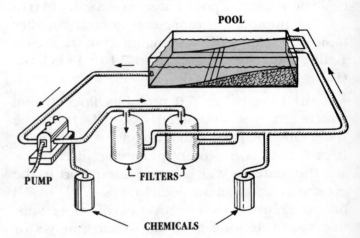

FIG. 8-2

Sand and Gravel Filters

Sand and gravel is a perpetual-type medium in that it does not usually have to be replaced. Rapid-sand pressure, high-rate pressure, and vacuum gravity are the three types of sand filters that are used commercially. Both pressure types operate on the same principle: utilizing a pump motor to force the water through the filter. Water enters the top of the filter through a baffle plate and then passes through two or three layers of sand and several layers of gravel to a manifold or collection pipe at the bottom of the filter tank. The water exits at that point and is returned to the pool (Fig. 8-3). Pressure filters sometimes include a layer of powdered anthracite coal over the top layer of sand. Almost all pressure filters employ a coagulant, such as alum, to aid in filtering out tiny particles of suspended material. However, high-rate pressure filters are smaller than rapid-sand pressure filters, and fewer in number are required for use, since water is forced through them at much faster rates than through rapid-sand pressure filters.

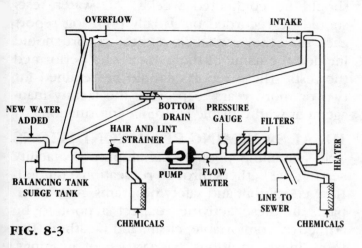

FIG. 8-3

Diatomaceous Earth Filters

Although sand and gravel filters use the same means of removing physical impurities as nature does, the diatomaceous earth (DE) system (Fig. 8-4) is unique. The use of diatomaceous earth was developed during World War II because of the necessity to provide better drinking water for U.S. military personnel.

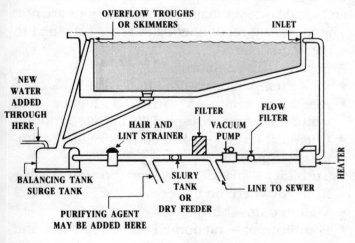

FIG. 8-4

Diatomaceous earth is at present the most efficient filtration system yet developed for pools. The filter medium is a temporary material that is subsequently discarded after use, which makes it more expensive to use than sand. However, newer DE systems are now using the same medium for as long as one year (regenerative cycle DE filters). Diatomaceous earth is the fossilized remains of marine plants called diatoms.

Vacuum and pressure systems are the two basic types of DE filter systems now being used.

Vacuum filter elements are composed of a plastic or metal framework covered with a synthetic fabric such as nylon. Pressure DE elements have been made from porous stone and more recently from fiberglass and stainless steel mesh. A coating of diatomaceous earth is applied to the filter elements and thus provides the means of filtration. Water passes through the DE, on through the element, into a manifold pipe, and returns to the pool. The filtered particles remain on the surface of the DE until the channels fill up. Then the filters must be cleaned. While DE filtration is expensive, owing to the continual replacement of the medium, very little water is wasted in the cleaning process. This conserves valuable chemicals and the heat that is normally lost in cleaning a sand filtration system.

Backwashing Sand Filters

Simply stated, the term "backwashing" means the reversing flow of water through the filter. This carries away to the sewer all of the material that has accumulated on the filter surface. Backwashing on a regular basis helps to extend the filter medium life. Manufacturer's instructions should be followed for the best results when backwashing. The backwashing procedure can be a delicate operation. It is highly recommended that a step-by-step procedure be posted in the filter room for easy reference. Never trust the procedure to memory.

Cleaning Diatomaceous Earth Filters

Depending on the type of filter, there are several ways of cleaning DE filters. Examples of techniques are compressed air, agitation, or spray washing. Manufacturer's instructions should be followed for the best results. Never trust the procedure to memory. The operator doing the cleaning should wear a mask that covers the nose and mouth during the cleaning procedure. This will help to prevent inhaling fumes or dust.

WATER TESTING

The chemical analysis of pool water is a daily requirement. All states require the daily monitoring of the disinfectant levels and the pH level along with written reports to be maintained by the operator. Some facilities are required to submit these reports to the state or county health office having jurisdiction for swimming pools. Maintaining proper levels of disinfectants will ensure that the bacteria count will be within acceptable levels. The procedures for determining the bacteria count must be performed by a certified laboratory technician rather than a member of the pool staff.

Testing for the various residual levels of chemicals in swimming pool water is accomplished through the use of some type of color slide comparator or titration. The proper test kits must be used, depending upon the type of disinfecting agent that is used. Test kits for water analysis are available through several leading manufacturers in a variety of price ranges. The higher priced kits are usually more sophisticated and provide more detailed results. However, readings as fine as 1 ppm or less may not be necessary for testing the hardness and alkalinity of the water. Therefore, a much less expensive kit will provide adequate results.

Test kit reagents are also a very important consideration. Only chemicals manufactured by the company making the test kit should be used. Reagents from one company will not produce the colors that correspond with the slide comparator of a different company. The pool operator should also be aware that most reagents have a shelf life of less than one year. Reagents should not be exposed to extremes of heat or cold or to direct sunlight for any length of time.

The testing process provides important information about water quality. It should be performed accurately to get the best results.

It is essential to conduct the test with clean hands and to maintain clean test components. The method of taking the water sample from the pool is also important. Samples should be taken between the water inlets, not in front of them. When the sample is taken, the container should be kept capped until it is approximately one foot below the surface, where it is then filled. The manufacturer's directions should be followed when the water is tested. Fresh reagents should be used in the proper amount in order to realize accurate measurements. Water samples should be flushed into a waste disposal system instead of being poured back into the pool.

Pool water should be tested for chlorine residual and for pH while the pool is in operation. Other tests, such as those for total alkalinity, total hardness, total dissolved solids, and bacteria, should be conducted weekly. All water tests should be recorded on a daily pool log report each time they are taken, and the report should include the name of the person who performed the tests. These reports should be retained for two or more years to provide the facility management with valuable reference information.

IDEAL SWIMMING POOL CONDITIONS

The swimming pool is a multipurpose facility serving the bathers through recreation, competition, education, and safety programs. All participants in these activities expect a pool to be attractive, comfortable, clean, and healthful. The term "ideal conditions" has a variety of meanings, depending on the nature of the program or activity and the age of the participants. Tiny tots, young children, disabled persons, and adults enrolled in Beginner Swimmer courses appreciate having a water temperature of about 82° to 85°F. Competitive swimmers and coaches prefer to have the water temperature somewhat cooler.

Some chemical, bacteriological, and maintenance conditions for pools are specified by state and local laws, yet many other conditions are not. The following recommendations are provided to serve as guidelines:

- Bacteria — no coliforms
- Water temperature — 78° to 83°F
- Air temperature — 5° to 10°F higher than water temperature, especially in indoor pools
- Chemical levels — balanced to provide healthful environment
- Turbidity — sparkling water; bottom visible from anywhere on deck
- Water color — blue
- Pool bottom — vacuumed and free of dirt and other materials, such as hair
- Total dissolved solids — less than 200 ppm
- Decks — clean; free of stagnant water and algae; not slippery
- Diving boards and starting blocks — surface clean; free of fungus; not slippery; in good condition

WATER PROBLEMS

Turbidity or colored water (other than blue) is usually the result of ignorance, neglect, or unusual chemical and mineral combinations. Two things are certain: (1) cloudy or colored water conditions do not usually occur within a few hours and (2) some water problems may take days or weeks to correct. The following water problems and their causes are common. They are presented with the hope that staff members will remember the causes and will be alert enough to prevent them.

Problem	Causes
• Turbid (cloudy) water	• Low disinfectant residual • Tear in a DE filter cover • Water level below gutters or skimmers when pool is not in use • Filters that need cleaning • Precipitate from a pH above 7.8
• Algae	• Low disinfectant residual • Using a disinfectant ineffective against algae • Having pH above 7.8 • Water too warm
• Colored water	• Water not balanced • Green — high copper or iron compound content • Red or reddish brown — high iron content (rust) • Brown or black — high manganese content
• Eye irritation	• Having pH too low — below 7.0 • Having pH too high — above 8.4 • High level of chloramines (chlorine and ammonia compound)
• Chlorine odor	• Low chlorine content in water • Chlorine and ammonia forming chloramines

CHEMICAL SAFETY

Safety in reference to bathers has been discussed in this book. Years of experience and training in water safety have alerted managers and staff to other dangers at a swimming pool. There are many unseen dangers involving the various chemicals used for disinfection, balancing, testing, and cleaning. The following list contains some of the more dangerous chemicals and the problems they present:

Chemical	Problems
• Chlorine gas	• Leakage could necessitate evacuation of pool and surrounding area. (Emergency plans should be developed for this situation.) • Inhaled fumes can easily cause death. • Chlorine gas is heavier than air, stays at or near ground level.
• Calcium hypochlorite and lithium hypochlorite	• Some types are explosive and flammable when contacted by organic substances, such as paper, oil, and gasoline. (No smoking around these chemicals.) • Used improperly, can cause water to become cloudy. • Can be fatal if swallowed. • Can cause severe burns if they get into eyes. • Chlorine gas created while burning.

Chemical	Problems
• Sodium hypochlorite	• Contact with skin may cause irritation. • Inhaled fumes can damage lung tissue. • Can cause severe burns if it gets into eyes.
• Chlorinated cyanurates (all types)	• Irritating to eyes, mucous membranes, and open cuts. • Flammable under certain conditions. (Do not allow contact with organic substances.) • Chlorine gas created while burning.
• Bromine (organic)	• Flammable and explosive. (Prevent contact with organic materials. No smoking around this chemical.)
• Iodine (KI crystals)	• Harmful if swallowed or comes in contact with eyes.
• Test kit reagents (general)	• Harmful or fatal if swallowed. • Harmful to eyes if contacted. • Ortho tolidine (reagent used for chlorine tests) is carcinogenic (cancer-causing). (Wash hands after using.) This chemical is prohibited in some states.

Extreme caution should be used when dealing with chemicals around a swimming pool. Storage areas should be kept locked and marked "off limits" to unauthorized personnel. All chemicals should be stored in a cool, dry place. The area should be kept clean and well ventilated. Heat, fire, lighted cigarettes, and matches should be kept away from the chemicals. The chemicals should be kept in the orginal containers, and the containers should be closed when not in use. Residue from the bottom of barrels should not be added to pools.

Personnel responsible for the operation of disinfection and filtration equipment must be properly trained in the operation of that equipment, in the procedures for performing necessary maintenance, and in the appropriate emergency procedures.

A self-contained breathing apparatus should be kept near the room containing the chemicals. All aquatic facility staff should be trained in the proper use of this equipment. This training should include —

• Method of checking air supply.
• Proper method for putting on the equipment.
• Testing to verify proper functioning of equipment.

• Emergency procedures if equipment does not function properly.
• Where to get air supply recharged.
• How to perform preventive maintenance on equipment.

ELECTRICAL SAFETY

Electrical shock is a very real hazard in the operation of swimming pools. The possibility of electrical fixtures and wires coming in contact with water exists with underwater lights, tape recorders, record players, automatic-timing devices, pace clocks, pool vacuum cleaners, and many other appliances having wires stretched across the pool decks. All underwater lights should be protected by a ground-fault interrupter. This eliminates the danger of electrocution in the event of a cracked or leaking lens. State electrical codes are very stringent about the positioning of electrical outlets and the use of electrical appliances around pools. Rooms or boxes containing electrical connections or equipment should be kept locked. Only authorized personnel should be allowed in these areas. Swimming pools should be empty of patrons whenever vacuum cleaners are being used.

WATERFRONT FACILITIES

At all waterfront facilities, the swimming and diving areas must be operated and maintained in accordance with state and local laws, ordinances, and regulations. It is the responsibility of the owners, operators, and managers of these facilities to check with the local regulating agencies, such as the public health department.

There should be specific regulations covering such subjects as water quality, safety and rescue equipment, electrical safety, insect and rodent control, and plumbing. Each waterfront facility will differ in the responsibilities that are given to lifeguards for these matters. However, lifeguards must be aware of the health hazards inherent to waterfront facilities. Some of the most common health and sanitation problems faced by lifeguards at waterfront facilities are as follows:

- Water quality

The biological, bacteriological, and radiological qualities of the water must be tested according to the times and standards of the regulating agency. Lifeguards must be properly trained to administer and evaluate these tests if they are responsible for this testing.

In waterfront areas that are part of a river system, the water quality will be influenced by anything that may enter the river upstream from the site, such as sewage, liquid wastes, or erosion materials from a construction site, power station, laboratory, or industrial plant. In addition, all waterfront areas should be constantly checked for debris, such as rocks, logs, seaweed, and swamp growth, that may be brought in by currents, tides, storms, or recreational boaters.

- Temperature

Lifeguards must check the temperature of the water and the air frequently. Since nothing can be done to control these temperatures, aquatics activities, particularly instructional classes, should be scheduled, if possible, for the times of the day when the air temperature is warmest. Lifeguards should be trained in the prevention, recognition, and first aid care for victims of hypothermia. Lifeguards must realize that they also are susceptible to overexposure to heat and cold. Proper precautions, such as wearing the correct type and amount of clothing, should be followed.

- Marine life

The area should be checked for leeches, snakes, open or broken shells, and any other marine life that could be hazardous to patrons.

- Animals

The management of the facility should be informed immediately of any animals that are in the area. Animals should not be permitted at swimming, diving, or snack bar areas. Any animal bites of patrons must be immediately reported to the management and to the local board of health or other appropriate regulating agencies.

- Electrical safety

Lifeguards should check electrical outlets at waterfront facilities daily for damage that would allow water to enter the outlets. Any piece of electrical equipment that is damaged and needs repair should be reported to the management. All damaged electrical equipment should be removed or disconnected from the electrical source until it is repaired. Rooms or areas containing electrical equipment, such as motors or breaker boxes, should be kept locked, and only authorized personnel should be allowed to enter these areas. Grounding requirements for electrical equipment and circuits should be checked and followed.

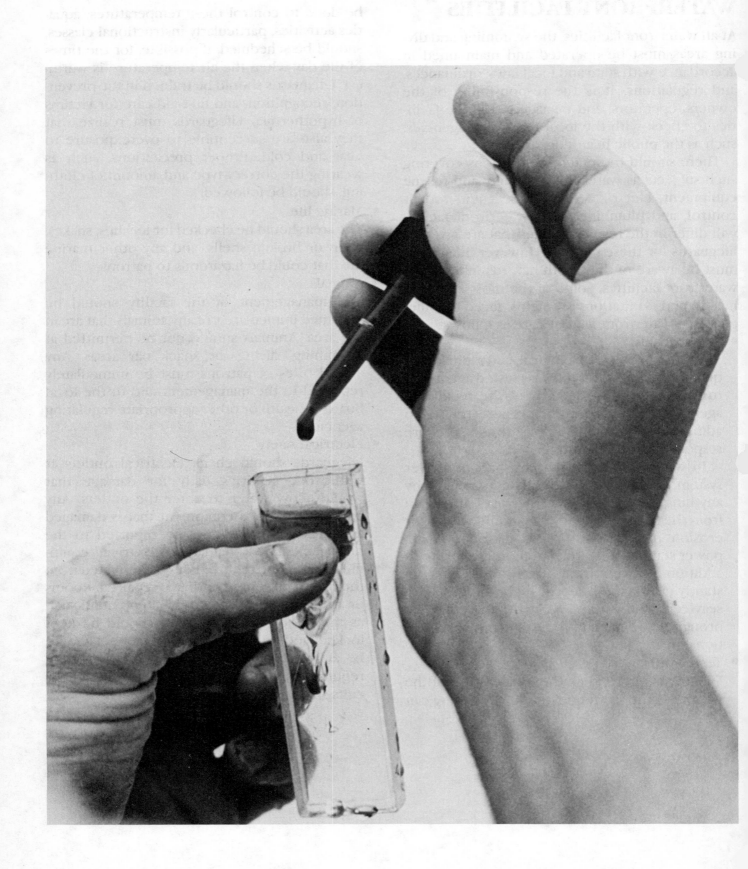

Chapter 9

WATER RESCUES AND SPECIAL SITUATIONS

Despite the best efforts of the lifeguard to provide proper supervision, accidents may happen, and the lifeguard may have to perform a rescue. The lifeguard must rely on proper training, knowledge, and experience to evaluate each situation and act accordingly. This chapter reviews some of the assists and rescue skills that are taught in a lifesaving course and also presents new material. It is not, however, intended to be a complete lifesaving review course. It also deals with special situations that lifeguards may face.

VICTIM RECOGNITION

An important skill that must be developed by lifeguards is the ability to recognize a person needing assistance. Initially, the lifeguard should not be concerned with whether the victim has suffered a cramp, is fatigued, or has swallowed water. The primary concern should be: Can the victim support himself or herself, and what type of behavior can be expected from the person? Usually, the movements of the victim will provide the lifeguard with the needed information.

DISTRESS SITUATION

This is a situation in which a person is unable to get to safety without assistance. The victim may be able to wave his or her arms and to call for help. Examples of a possible distress situation are —

- A person is attempting to swim but is making no progress.
- Two or more persons are holding on to a float, such as an inflatable raft or ring, that is designed for use by one person.

The distressed person's buoyancy may alternate between neutral and positive. This allows the victim to support himself or herself while waving for help. The victim's face will be out of the water, and thus the person will be able to get air for breathing and to call for help.

A distressed victim may quickly become a panicky or active drowning victim. The lifeguard must exercise caution in approaching this victim.

The distressed victim, once supported, can usually be calmed down by being talked to. The lifeguard can then tow the victim to safety.

DROWNING SITUATION

This is a situation in which a victim is unable to call for help or to wave his or her arms. A distress situation may become a drowning situation when the victim, for whatever reason, is no longer able to keep afloat. Drowning situations may be classified as passive or active.

Passive

In a passive drowning situation, the victim may suddenly slip underwater, making no attempt to call for help, or may float face down on or near the surface of the water.

A passive situation may result from any of the following causes:

- A heart attack or stroke
- Being hit by an object such as a boat or surfboard
- Hyperventilation and shallow-water blackout
- Cold water shock after sudden submersion in cold water. (The victim may feel a strong urge to gasp. This may cause the person to aspirate water, which, in turn, may cause panic and eventual suffocation.)
- Alcohol or drugs

Active

In contrast to a passive situation, the victim in an active situation is usually conscious. The person's actions may be violent or weak, depending on the amount of energy he or she possesses. A drowning victim's buoyancy will alternate between neutral and negative. The victim's arms will be extended outward from the sides, thrashing the water in a vertical movement, and the victim will be making no forward progress. Instead, the person will alternately raise and lower himself or herself in the water. Buoyancy may be lost each time the victim goes beneath the surface. As negative buoyancy increases, the victim becomes less able to take in air and has to work harder to stay on the surface. Panic will begin to set in during the process, and the victim will be unable to call for help because of concentrating all conscious efforts on breathing. The victim must be supported so that he or she can breathe freely after the initial contact and during the carry to safety.

WATER RESCUES

Lifeguards must be able to distinguish between a distress situation and a drowning situation. Factors that will then determine the lifeguard's actions will be the size and condition of the victim, the condition of the water, and the proximity to safety. However, the lifeguard should not take extra time to decide whether the situation calls for a swimming rescue or an elementary form of rescue. The rule is always to go get the victim, if there is any doubt as to which procedure should be used.

SIGHTINGS AND CROSS BEARINGS

In open-water areas, lifeguards may be unable to keep the victim in sight at all times because of

FIG. 9-1

wave actions or the victim's going underwater. To ensure that the lifeguard is swimming in a straight line toward the victim, the lifeguard can use sightings or cross bearings.

Sighting

As the lifeguard enters the water, the guard should sight a stationary object on the far shore, if possible. The lifeguard maintains this line of sight during the approach swim to the victim (Fig. 9-1).

An alternative to this procedure is for the lifeguard to pick out a stationary object behind himself or herself at the point of entry that is in line with the victim. By periodically looking back to shore and sighting on the stationary object the lifeguard can stay on a straight line while swimming to the victim.

Cross Bearing

When another lifeguard or a patron is available, a cross bearing can be taken by one or more persons spaced along the shore. Each person takes a sighting on the victim, as described previously. They all continue to point to the victim or to the spot where the victim was last seen. The life-guard, after taking his or her own sighting, enters the water and periodically checks these spotters on the shore for directions (Fig. 9-2).

FORMS OF RESCUE

Whenever possible, the lifeguard should use the most expedient form of rescue. This may include swimming, reaching, extending, wading, and throwing assists.

It should be noted, however, that a victim in a drowning situation may be unaware of a heaving line or ring buoy that has been thrown. When this happens, or in a situation where the victim is too far away for an elementary form of rescue to be used, a swimming rescue must be made. Some piece of rescue equipment, such as a rescue buoy or rescue tube, should be taken to help the victim whenever it is necessary to enter the water. Rescues using equipment should be made whenever possible, for the following reasons:

- Equipment rescues are safer types of rescues. Direct contact with the victim is kept to a minimum or is eliminated.
- There is more freedom for the lifeguard while swimming and towing the victim.

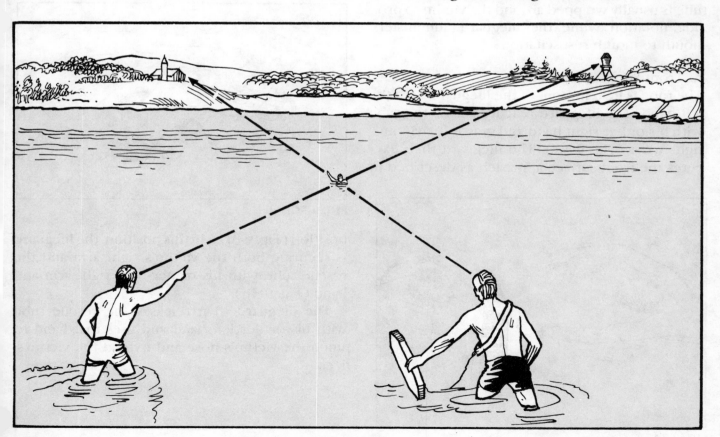

FIG. 9-2

- There is more flotation for the victim. This may allow the victim to calm down and regain enough self-control to follow instructions.
- Less energy is expended by the lifeguard.

RESCUE EQUIPMENT

The rescue tube and rescue buoy may be used in swimming rescues at both swimming pools and open-water areas. The rescue board, because of its size, is limited to use at open-water areas.

The following procedures may be done with either hand. The procedures are described here using the right hand.

Rescue Tube

The rescue tube is a very versatile piece of equipment. It can be extended to the victim from the deck, or its ends can be hooked together to form a circle and then thrown as a ring buoy. It can also be towed in its open position by the lifeguard to the victim. Once the lifeguard is close enough to the victim, the rescue tube is given for support. If the victim is unconscious or is too weak to hold on to the rescue tube, the lifeguard can place it around the victim and hook the ends together. For a nonbreathing victim, the rescue tube is usually wrapped around the victim to provide flotation while the lifeguard administers mouth-to-mouth resuscitation.

A. Front-Surface Approach
The tube is held in front of the lifeguard with the left hand. The lifeguard reaches across the tube with his or her right hand and grasps the victim's right wrist (Fig. 9-3A). The lifeguard then executes the front-surface approach as described in

FIG. 9-3A

the Advanced Lifesaving course (Fig. 9-3B). As the victim is being turned to a face-up position, the lifeguard submerges the tube with his or her left hand and extends both his or her left arm and the tube under the victim. The tube should come to rest across the victim's back, just below the vic-

FIG. 9-3B

tim's shoulders (Fig. 9-3C). The lifeguard releases the victim's right wrist, reaches over the victim's right shoulder, and secures the victim in a do-si-do

FIG. 9-3C

position (Fig. 9-3D). In this position, the lifeguard is securing both the victim's right arm and the rescue tube with his or her own right arm and hand (Fig. 9-3E).

The lifeguard then releases the rescue tube with his or her left hand and uses that hand to pinch the victim's nose and extend the victim's neck.

FIG. 9-3D

FIG. 9-3F

FIG. 9-3E

FIG. 9-3G

B. Front-Surface Approach — Alternate Method

The procedure for turning the victim and positioning the tube is the same as that described above.

Once the victim is turned and the tube is placed under the victim's back, the lifeguard releases the victim's right wrist. The lifeguard then secures the tube to the victim by wrapping the tube around the victim and snapping the hook in the center of the victim's chest (Figs. 9-3F and 9-3G). The lifeguard can now move to either side of the victim and assume the do-si-do position (Fig. 9-3H).

C. Block and Turn

The victim is passive and facing the lifeguard. The lifeguard is holding the rescue tube with his or her left hand in the center of the tube; the left forearm is parallel to the tube. The lifeguard then brings his or her right hand up under the victim's

FIG. 9-3H

FIG. 9-3I

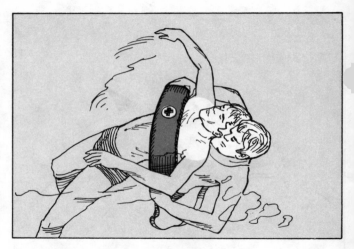

FIG. 9-3K

FIG. 9-3L

left arm and grasps that arm above the elbow with his or her thumb to the inside of the arm (Fig. 9-3I). A simultaneous movement of pushing the victim's left arm up and moving it across in front of the lifeguard will turn the victim. As the victim is turning, the lifeguard moves the rescue tube with his or her left hand and positions the center of the tube in the center of the victim's chest (Fig. 9-3J). Once the victim is completely turned, the lifeguard can release the victim's left arm.

FIG. 9-3J

The lifeguard then wraps the rescue tube around the victim, under the victim's arms (Fig. 9-3K). The tube is snapped, with the buckle behind the victim. The lifeguard moves to either side of the victim and assumes the do-si-do position (Fig. 9-3L). The lifeguard uses his or her free hand to pinch the victim's nose and extend the victim's neck.

D. Rear Approach
The lifeguard executes the single armpit level-off, using his or her right hand (this can also be done using a chin level-off). The rescue tube is held with the left hand, and the left forearm is parallel to the tube (Fig. 9-3M). As the victim is pulled

FIG. 9-3M

back, the lifeguard reaches around with his or her left arm and positions the tube in front of the victim (Fig. 9-3N). The tube is wrapped around

FIG. 9-3N

the victim and snapped, with the buckle in the center of the victim's back (Fig. 9-3O). The lifeguard can now move to either side of the victim and assume the do-si-do position. The lifeguard uses his or her free hand to pinch the victim's nose and extend the victim's neck (Fig. 9-3P).

FIG. 9-3O

E. Straddle the Tube

Before making contact with the victim, the lifeguard stops and snaps the ends of the rescue tube together. He or she then steps through the ring with one leg. The tube can be held in this position by squeezing the legs together. A variation of this method is to have the strap run between the legs instead of the tube.

If the tube is one of the thick models, it may be difficult for the lifeguard to submerge the tube after the ends are snapped together. An alternate

FIG. 9-3P

method for placing the tube between the legs is for the lifeguard to lie on the tube with the tube parallel to his or her body. As the lifeguard slides the tube down between his or her legs (Fig. 9-4A), the lifeguard sits up and straddles the tube. He or she can then snap the ends of the tube together (Fig. 9-4B).

FIG. 9-4A

Once the lifeguard has the tube properly positioned, he or she can move in to the victim and use any procedure to turn the victim to a face-up position. The lifeguard then assumes the do-si-do position on either side of the victim and uses his or her free hand to pinch the victim's nose and extend the victim's neck (Fig. 9-4C).

FIG. 9-4B

FIG. 9-4C

Rescue Buoy

Rescue buoys come in different sizes and provide support to a victim. The victim can hold on to the buoy while the lifeguard tows the victim back to safety. In an emergency situation with an unconscious victim, the lifeguard may tie the buoy to the victim, utilizing the towline. The buoy may also be used by the lifeguard to provide flotation while administering mouth-to-mouth resuscitation to a nonbreathing victim.

A. Front-Surface Approach — Buoy to Victim's Back

The lifeguard holds the buoy with his or her left hand holding one of the handholes on the far side of the buoy. The buoy is positioned between the lifeguard and the victim. The lifeguard reaches across the buoy with his or her right hand and grasps the victim's right wrist (Fig. 9-5A). The lifeguard then executes the front-surface approach

FIG. 9-5A

as described in the Advanced Livesaving course. As the victim is being turned to a face-up position, the lifeguard submerges the rescue buoy with his or her left hand and arm. The lifeguard should extend the left arm as he or she submerges the buoy. This movement will force the buoy under the victim. The buoy should be placed across the victim's back, just below the shoulder blades (Fig. 9-5B). This position will assist in extending the victim's neck for artificial respiration.

FIG. 9-5B

After the buoy is positioned, the lifeguard releases the victim's right wrist, reaches over the victim's right shoulder, and assumes the do-si-do position on the right side of the victim. The lifeguard grasps the rescue buoy with his or her right hand beneath the victim. The lifeguard then releases the buoy with his or her left hand and uses that hand to pinch the victim's nose and extend the victim's neck (Fig. 9-5C). During this procedure, the buoy may slip to the opposite side of the victim from the lifeguard. If this happens, the lifeguard should maintain a grasp on the buoy and continue to support the victim across his or her own arm.

FIG. 9-5C

B. Front-Surface Approach — Buoy to Victim's Side
The lifeguard executes the front-surface approach, using the right hand to turn the victim, as described in the Advanced Lifesaving course. The buoy is floating behind the lifeguard (Fig. 9-5D).

FIG. 9-5D

Once the victim is turned to a face-up position, the lifeguard assumes the do-si-do position using his or her left arm on the victim's left side (Fig. 9-5E).

FIG. 9-5E

The lifeguard then releases the victim's right wrist. Using the right hand, the lifeguard grasps the buoy and submerges it enough to allow him or her to grab it with the left hand, which is still under the victim (Fig. 9-5F). The buoy is allowed

FIG. 9-5F

to slide to the victim's right side. The lifeguard releases the buoy with his or her right hand; then uses his or her right hand to pinch the victim's nose and extend the victim's neck (Fig. 9-5G).

C. Rear Approach
The lifeguard executes the single armpit level-off, using his or her right hand to level the victim. The buoy is floating behind the lifeguard (Fig. 9-5H). As the victim is pulled back, the lifeguard assumes the do-si-do position, using his or her left arm on the left side of the victim. The lifeguard then

FIG. 9-5G

FIG. 9-5H

releases the victim with his or her right hand. Using the right hand, the lifeguard grasps the buoy (Fig. 9-5I) and submerges it beneath the victim to a point where he or she (the lifeguard) can grab it with the left hand. The buoy is allowed to slide to the victim's right side. The lifeguard releases the buoy

FIG. 9-5I

with his or her right hand. The lifeguard then uses his or her right hand to pinch the victim's nose and extend the victim's neck (Fig. 9-5J).

FIG. 9-5J

Lifeguards should practice, as often as possible, how to use the rescue buoy and adapt it to different situations.

Rescue Board

Properly trained lifeguards will find the rescue board a fast, stable, and easily maneuverable piece of equipment. The lifeguard must be able, in some instances, to safely move the board through a crowded swimming area to reach a victim. In-service training at waterfronts using rescue boards should stress the proper handling of the rescue board.

Lifeguards may use the rescue board to patrol the outer edges of a swimming area. Rescue boards should also be kept on the beach in a position for easy access in an emergency.

Two paddling positions are commonly used on a rescue board: kneeling and prone. The prone position is usually preferred because it offers a more comfortable position closer to the water, which facilitates paddling. The lifeguard may use a butterfly stroke arm pull or a crawl stroke arm pull to propel the rescue board.

Lifeguards should practice rescues of conscious and unconscious "victims" using the rescue board. Timed events and races help to develop the skill and confidence needed to properly and safely handle rescue boards in emergency situations.

Another skill that should be practiced while using a rescue board is the administration of mouth-to-mouth resuscitation to a nonbreathing victim. Two methods of administering mouth-to-mouth resuscitation from a rescue board are as follows:

- The lifeguard lies across the rescue board in a prone position, with the victim in the water (Fig. 9-6), supporting the victim in a "do-si-do" position. The do-si-do position may be taken from either side of the victim, but it is described here from the right side. The lifeguard slides his or her right arm between the victim's right arm and body. The lifeguard then grasps the victim's hair with the left hand and pulls the victim's head back into an extended position. The lifeguard's left hand is used to pinch the victim's nose if resuscitation is needed. The victim may be rolled slightly toward the lifeguard for easier positioning during mouth-to-mouth ventilation.

FIG. 9-6

- The victim is positioned on the rescue board perpendicular to the board in a supine position, with the victim's head and neck off the board and the shoulders remaining on the board. This position will extend the neck and open the airway. The lifeguard in the water alongside the board can pinch the victim's nose

with one hand and hold on to the rescue board or the victim with the other hand (Fig. 9-7).

FIG. 9-7

Other methods of using a rescue board while administering mouth-to-mouth resuscitation may be used, depending on the size and condition of the victim, the condition of the water, and the size, strength, and experience of the lifeguard. Practicing various positions and procedures will save time and will allow for easier administering of mouth-to-mouth resuscitation during an emergency.

MULTIPLE-VICTIM RESCUES
When two or more victims are in need of assistance, a lifeguard should provide flotation to support the victims until back-up lifeguards arrive. A rescue buoy, rescue tube, or rescue board can be used for flotation. After it is provided, the lifeguard should attempt to calm the victims.

LIFTS, ASSISTS, AND CARRIES
Lifeguards should practice removing a "victim" from both deep and shallow water. Lifts, assists, and carries that are taught in a lifesaving course must be practiced periodically so that valuable time will not be wasted during an emergency. Great care should be taken not to injure either the victim or the lifeguard when lifting or carrying the victim.

LIFT FROM WATER

Whenever it is necessary to lift a victim from the water onto a deck or dock, the lifeguard must always maintain contact with the victim while climbing out of the water (Fig. 9-8A). The life-

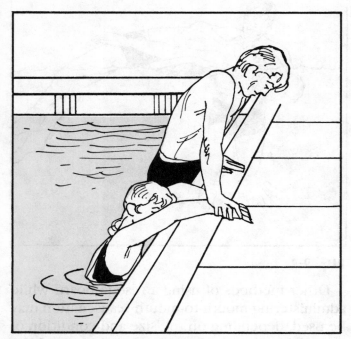

FIG. 9-8A

guard's primary source of power should be the legs instead of the back (Fig. 9-8B). The victim's head should be protected as the person is lowered to a prone position (Fig. 9-8C). While pulling the victim's legs out of the water, the lifeguard should take care not to twist the victim's back. The victim should be rotated as a unit (Fig. 9-8D). This procedure, as taught in the American Red Cross Lifesaving course, should be reviewed periodically by all lifeguards.

SHALLOW-WATER ASSIST

When assisting a conscious victim from shallow water, the lifeguard takes a firm grasp on the wrist of the victim's arm that goes across the lifeguard's shoulder. The lifeguard wraps his or her free arm around the victim's back and maintains a firm grasp at the victim's side (Fig. 9-9).

BEACH DRAG

The beach drag is the safest and easiest method of removing a victim from the water when the victim is unconscious, when there is a sloping beach, or when the victim is heavy. The lifeguard grasps the victim under the armpits and walks

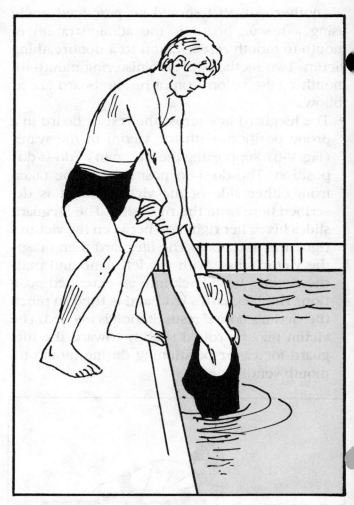

FIG. 9-8B

FIG. 9-8C

slowly backward (Fig. 9-10). If possible, the victim's head is supported by the lifeguard's forearms. The victim can be removed completely from the water or taken to a point where at least the person's head and shoulders are out of the water. The lifeguard's back should be as straight as possible during the drag.

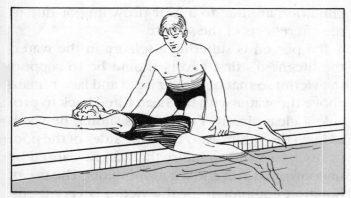

FIG. 9-8D

FIG. 9-9

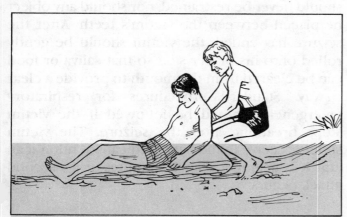

FIG. 9-10

PACK-STRAP CARRY

The pack-strap carry may be used for either conscious or unconscious victims. This carry must never be used when there is the slightest possibility that the victim has a neck or back injury. When the victim has been brought to chest-deep or waist-deep water, the lifeguard supports the victim while moving to the front of the person. With the lifeguard's back to the victim, the victim's arms are brought over the lifeguard's shoulders and the victim's wrists are crossed and held in front of the lifeguard's chest (Fig. 9-11A). The victim's arms should be straight, with the armpits directly over the lifeguard's shoulders. The victim should be well balanced on the lifeguard before the carry is started and all during the carry to the beach. The lifeguard should lean forward slightly to keep the victim well up on the lifeguard's back. The lifeguard lowers the victim carefully to the ground by kneeling slowly on one knee, then on both knees, while using one arm for support (Fig. 9-11B). The lifeguard gently rolls the victim to one side and onto the ground while maintaining a grasp on one of the victim's wrists (Fig. 9-11C). Care must be exercised during these movements to prevent the victim's head from hitting the ground.

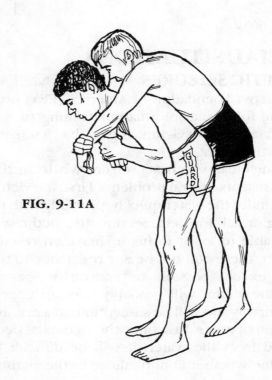

FIG. 9-11A

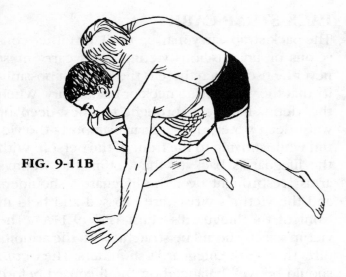

FIG. 9-11B

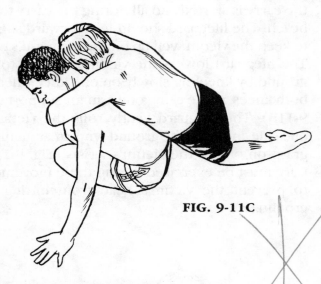

FIG. 9-11C

SPECIAL SITUATIONS
EPILEPTIC SEIZURES

The Epilepsy Foundation of America (EFA) provides the following information relating to the proper handling of a victim who has had a seizure while in the water:

An individual who has a seizure **while in the water** presents several problems. First, the victim will go under the water quickly, probably with no warning or call for help. Second, the victim will not be able to assist in his or her own rescue. However, there will not be any resistance to the rescue, except possibly by convulsive spasms. Third, the victim will probably have an unprotected airway and will be susceptible to a massive aspiration of water. Last, once the victim has been removed from the water, it will be difficult to determine whether abnormalities in the victim's

condition are due to a near drowning or due to the aftereffects of the seizure.

If a person is suffering a seizure in the water, the lifeguard's first efforts should be to support the victim so that his or her head and face remain above the water with the head tilted back to provide a clear airway. Precautions should be taken to keep the victim away from the sides of the pool or dock to avoid an injury that can be caused by uncontrolled arm and leg movements. The use of flotation equipment for the victim is very useful in these situations.

When possible, the victim should be removed from the water and placed on his or her side. Proceed with artificial respiration, if necessary. Watch the victim closely for an obstructed airway or loss of pulse. The standard procedures for relieving an obstruction of the airway and for giving CPR should be followed, if needed.

Victims who have seizures in the water are vulnerable to massive aspiration of water. Therefore, special precautions should be taken, and medical attention should be sought. Any victim who has aspirated large quantities of water, especially fresh water, may develop significant life-threatening medical complications within 30 to 60 minutes. The blood will become extremely diluted, causing hemolysis (breaking up of red blood cells).

A victim who suffers a seizure **while out of the water** should not be transported during the seizure. Any obstacle that might be struck by the victim, and that might cause injury, should be cleared from that area. Something soft, if readily available, should be placed under the victim's head. The lifeguard's hands may be used to cushion the victim's head. Convulsive movements should never be restrained, nor should any object be placed between the victim's teeth. After the seizure has ended, the victim should be gently rolled onto his or her side so that saliva or food can be cleared from the mouth to provide a clear airway. Standard procedures for respiratory emergencies should be followed if the victim stops breathing after the seizure. The victim should receive immediate medical attention if an attack lasts longer than 10 minutes or if a second attack occurs.

After a single seizure, the victim should be helped to a secluded area and should be observed until he or she is fully alert. A victim who provides no indication of having had any previous seizure, or a responsible adult, as appropriate, should be advised that the victim should seek immediate medical evaluation. An individual who has epilepsy and who has had a single seizure either in the water or out of the water should not enter the water again on that particular day. A family member or a responsible adult should be informed of the individual's seizure in the case of a minor, or when a person with a mental handicap is involved who cannot assume responsibility for himself or herself. An adult victim should be advised of the seizure episode as soon as he or she becomes fully conscious. In any event, the family member who is the responsible adult, or the individual adult himself, should be advised that the victim should notify his or her physician of the seizure. Information from bystanders about a description of the seizure, its duration, and the recovery time, or about other circumstances when the seizure occurred, could be very helpful if it is relayed to the victim's physician.

Medical assistance need not be summoned for a person who has an epileptic seizure out of the water unless that individual appears to be injured, does not regain full consciousness, or does not resume regular activities within 20 to 30 minutes. **All persons who have had a seizure in the water and who have submerged, regardless of their apparent recovery once out of the water, should be transported to a medical facility.**

Signs and Symptoms of a Seizure

1. The person may fall, and the body muscles may stiffen for a few seconds to perhaps half a minute, followed by convulsive movements for several minutes. The person may stop breathing and become bluish or pale, and the tongue may be bitten during the period of stiffening. The loss of bladder and bowel content may also occur.
2. Drooling or frothing at the mouth may occur as breathing resumes.
3. There will be gradual subsidence of the convulsive movements.
4. Confusion and sleepiness may occur afterwards.

First Aid

1. Prevent the victim from being injured. Place something soft under the victim's head, loosen tight clothing, and clear the area of any sharp or hard objects.
2. Do not force any objects into the victim's mouth.
3. Do not restrain the victim's movements.
4. Turn the victim on his or her side to allow saliva to drain from the mouth.
5. Stay with the victim until the seizure ends naturally.
6. Do not pour any liquids into the victim's mouth or offer any food, drink, or medication until the victim is fully awake.
7. Give artificial respiration if the victim does not resume breathing after the seizure.
8. Provide an area for the victim to rest in until fully awakened and where the victim can be observed by a responsible adult.
9. Be reassuring and supportive when consciousness returns.
10. Although a convulsive seizure is not a medical emergency, occasionally a seizure may last longer than 10 minutes, or a second seizure may occur. In such instances, prompt medical attention in a properly equipped medical facility is necessary, because this situation may be, or may lead to, a condition called status-epilepticus (nonstop seizure). Emergency preparations, after the 10-minute mark has passed, will ensure that prompt attention will be available if the seizure continues.

RESCUE OF A SCUBA DIVER

Scuba diving as a sport has increased in popularity, and many swimming pools have lifeguards or maintenance personnel who clean and vacuum the pool while using scuba equipment. Therefore, it is possible that a lifeguard may be called upon to rescue a scuba diver who is in distress. In areas where scuba diving is allowed, lifeguards should seek additional training in recognition of pressure-related illnesses or injuries and the functioning of the different types of scuba equipment such as quick-release buckles and buoyancy compensating devices (BCDs). The following procedure, known as the RABBI system, describes the necessary actions to be taken by a lifeguard when rescuing a scuba diver underwater, when the diver is wearing the following equipment: buoyancy compensating device (BCD), tank/regulator, mask/fins, and weight belt.

The word RABBI is an acronym for the steps to be followed during the following rescue procedure:

R — Release
A — Airway
B — Bring
B — Breathe
I — Inflate

The following steps describe the rescue of a scuba diver. The lifeguard takes a deep breath and surface dives to the side of the victim. The lifeguard should leave the victim's mouthpiece where it is found.

- R — *Release.* Release the victim's weight belt. This belt is identified by feeling for the belt that has the weights attached. Once the correct belt is identified, it is removed by opening the quick-release buckle and pulling the belt clear of the diver (Fig. 9-12).

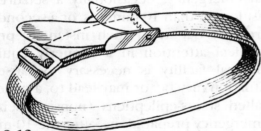

FIG. 9-12

The lifeguard must take care to ensure that the belt does not catch or get tangled on other gear or parts of the victim's body.

- A — *Airway.* Move the scuba diver into a standing position. Hold the diver's head so that the neck is not flexed or extended. The mouthpiece can be held gently in place if it is found in the diver's mouth. The lifeguard should not apply pressure to the purge button on the regulator mouthpiece if it remains in the diver's mouth.

- B — *Bring.* Bring the diver to the surface by using a modified armpit tow, or by holding on to the first stage of the regulator (Fig. 9-13) or the tank valve. The diver is kept in a vertical position with the head held erect during the slow ascent to the surface.

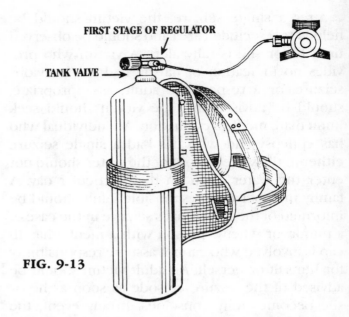

FIRST STAGE OF REGULATOR

TANK VALVE

FIG. 9-13

Special care must be exercised by the lifeguard to try to prevent the occurrence of an injury to the diver, which could result from bringing a downed diver too rapidly to the surface during the rescue. The rate of ascent should be approximately 1 foot per second, or 60 feet per minute. However, for a lifeguard without diving gear, the easiest way to maintain a safe ascent rate is to travel no faster than the smallest bubbles as they ascend.

- B — *Breathe.* Upon reaching the surface, the lifeguard immediately removes the diver's mask and mouthpiece. If the diver is not breathing, the lifeguard should give four quick, full breaths into the diver's mouth.

The lifeguard can maintain a firm hold on the diver and be in a position to administer the breaths if the diver is held in a "do-si-do" position, as described under the heading "Rescue Board" earlier in this chapter. A strong kick is needed by the lifeguard to maintain this position.

- I — *Inflate.* The diver's buoyancy compensating device (BCD) can be inflated to provide additional buoyancy. This may be done in three ways:
  1. Pull the lanyard that operates the CO_2 cartridge (Fig. 9-14A). The lanyard is usually located on the front of the BCD, toward the bottom on either or both sides.

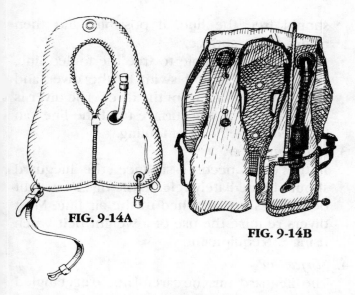

FIG. 9-14A

FIG. 9-14B

2. Some newer BCDs can be inflated by using an auto-inflator (Fig. 9-14B). There are various styles of auto-inflator connectors; therefore, lifeguards in areas where scuba diving is allowed should become familiar with the functioning of the different types of equipment used by scuba divers.

3. Use the oral inflation tube. This is usually located high on the chest of the BCD or on the collar (Fig. 9-14C). It is usually on the diver's left side. Most BCDs have a button at the end of the oral inflation tube that must be pressed to open the valve when blowing air into the BCD.

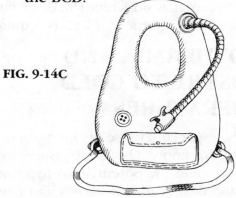

FIG. 9-14C

Continue artificial respiration, if necessary, while towing the diver to safety, where the required first aid, artificial resuscitation, or cardiopulmonary resuscitation (CPR) can be administered properly. Scuba gear should be removed before the diver is taken from the water.

If the local emergency medical system cannot adequately handle a diving emergency, it is important to have the contact information for the nearest operational recompression facility, or the number for the Diver Alert Network (DAN). The DAN number, which is (919) 684-8111, is especially important to divers because it provides immediate 24-hour access to the only nationally coordinated diving emergency information center in the U.S. (Collect calls are accepted in emergencies only.) This service is particularly useful when dealing with medical personnel unfamiliar with diving accidents, and who are in need of consultation with medical experts knowledgeable in diving medicine. In addition to consultation, DAN can coordinate all phases of treatment for the diving casualty through its network of personnel and facilities.

SURFACE-AIR-SUPPLIED (SAS) EQUIPMENT

Many modern aquatic facilities that have large swimming pools and deep diving wells have lifeguards or maintenance personnel who clean and vacuum the pools while using breathing equipment that is surface air supplied. This cleaning should be done when the facility is closed. However, there may be times when it is necessary to use the equipment while swimmers are in the pool. In either situation, there are certain steps that must be taken by personnel who use the equipment, and also by the lifeguards who may have to rescue someone who uses it. A thorough training program is required of anyone who will be using the SAS equipment. This program should include types, use, and maintenance of all equipment; physics of diving; and injuries related to diving. The following section relates to the actions of a lifeguard who is assigned to work with someone using SAS equipment.

Safety
Two-Person Operation
No one should be using SAS equipment unless there is another person on the deck who acts as a lookout or a "bubble watcher." There will be regularly spaced air bubbles breaking the surface.

Tether
The diver should wear a safety harness with a lifeline (tether) attached to it, separate from the

air hose. The lifeline should not be attached to the diver's face mask or breathing apparatus. The lifeline is used by the lookout to pull the diver to the surface when such help is necessary.

Communications

- Underwater communications systems, such as those used by competitive or synchronized swimming teams, may be used to communicate with the diver. However, since this is a one-way line of communication, its use is limited.

- Line signals can be a two-way communications system. Each signal that is sent is immediately answered by the receiver. For example, the diver signals, "Give me slack." The tender signals back, "Give me slack" and provides slack in the lifeline. The U.S. Navy Diver's Manual uses the following system of signals for divers who use SAS equipment. The signals are sent by a sequence of tugs to the line tender:

    1 tug on line — I am all right.

    2 tugs on line — Give me slack.

    3 tugs on line — Take up slack.

    4 tugs on line — Pull me up.

    2-2-2 tugs on line — Fouled, need assistance.

    3-3-3 tugs on line — Fouled, do not need assistance.

    4-4-4 tugs on line — Pull me up immediately.

    The personnel who will be involved with the use of SAS equipment must all be completely familiar with the communications system that is used at their aquatic facility.

Rescue Procedures

The most common problem facing a diver using SAS equipment is either getting tangled in or fouling the tether (lifeline). If either of these situations occurs, or if there is some other problem with the diver, the lifeguard who is on the deck should work with the line tender and follow these steps:

1. *Taking in slack*

    The line tender takes in the slack of the lifeline by pulling the line slowly. **The line tender should never pull on the air line.** Doing so could pull the face mask off the diver.

2. *Freeing fouled line*

    When it appears that the line is snagged or fouled after the slack is taken up, the lifeguard should enter the water and follow the line to the point where it is fouled. The lifeguard

should free the line, if possible, and then return to the surface.

    If it is not possible to free the fouled line, the lifeguard should swim to the diver and release the lifeline from the diver. The diver is then brought to the surface until the line can be freed at the point of fouling.

3. *Checking diver*

    If the diver needs assistance, the lifeguard should immediately release the diver's weight belt if it is not attached to the air line. Most divers require the use of a weight belt when using SAS equipment.

4. *Surfacing*

    The lifeguard must be careful not to get tangled in either the air line or the lifeline when bringing a diver to the surface. The lifeguard should not attempt to purge or to remove the diver's mask. The lifeguard should hold the diver with one hand under the diver's armpit or in a modified cross-chest carry. The lifeguard's other arm should stabilize the diver's head in an erect position. The rate of ascent should be approximately one foot per second. However, for a lifeguard without diving gear, the easiest way to maintain a safe ascent rate is to travel no faster than the smallest bubbles as they ascend. After reaching the surface, the lifeguard should remove the diver's mask. If there is a need, the lifeguard should administer four quick breaths to the diver. Artificial respiration should be started as soon as possible. The diver must be removed from the water if CPR is required.

HYPOTHERMIA AND EXPOSURE TO COLD TEMPERATURES

Lifeguards, especially those at open-water facilities, need to know about exposure to cold temperatures and the potential for hypothermia. This section deals with the causes and effects of exposure to cold temperatures, the signs and symptoms of hypothermia, and first aid care for hypothermia victims. Methods of preventing hypothermia and procedures for cold-water rescues are also presented.

    Hypothermia refers to a low body temperature, specifically a low body-core temperature. Lifeguards must be aware of the hazards relating to exposure to cold air and water. Hypothermia occurs when cold or cool temperatures cause the body to lose heat faster than it can be produced and the temperature of the vital organs (core temperature) falls below normal.

Factors that influence the onset and progression of hypothermia are air and water temperatures; wind velocity; length of exposure; amount and type of clothing worn; the individual's age, body size, and body build; and the mental and physical condition of the individual. The body loses heat through four processes:

1. Radiation — Heat lost to still air that surrounds the body, such as cold air with no wind.
2. Evaporation — Heat lost through water evaporating on the skin, such as perspiration.
3. Conduction — Heat lost through body contact with a cold object, such as water or the ground.
4. Convection — Heat lost through air or water movement around the body.

SIGNS AND SYMPTOMS

When the body temperature begins to drop, the body reacts to correct the heat loss. Shivering, usually a series of rapid, involuntary muscle contractions, is an example of the body's efforts to increase heat production. The body also reduces the flow of blood to the extremities in an attempt to prevent further heat loss. The following list identifies the body's reactions to decreases in body core temperature.

A person can become hypothermic from exposure to air that doesn't feel extremely cold, usually 30° to 50°F (-1° to 10°C). It can occur in some individuals in air temperatures ranging from 60° to 70°F (16° to 21°C) and from exposure to water that feels cool rather than cold. The initial stages of hypothermia have been observed in heated, indoor pools with water and air temperatures between 84° and 86°F (20° to 30°C). This combination of water and air temperatures with a mild breeze or air movement from ventilation fans can contribute to heat loss by convection and evaporation. Lifeguards should be aware of individuals showing the first signs of hypothermia, such as bluish lips or shivering. These persons should be moved to a warm area. If the persons are already indoors, they should be moved to an area where there is little air movement, such as an office or first aid room, or put under a warm shower. More advanced stages of hypothermia require first aid and subsequent medical treatment.

FIRST AID
Mild to Moderate Hypothermia

Lifeguards should be alert to individuals showing

Core Temperature	Body Reactions
98°-95°F (37°-35°C) Mild	The victim is conscious and alert but breathing deeply. Vigorous, uncontrolled shivering. The ability to perform simple tasks is impaired.
95°-90°F (35°-32.4°C) Moderate	The victim is conscious but with mental faculties and speech impaired. Voice is lowered. There is loss of coordination. Victim performs simple tasks with much difficulty.
90°-85°F (32.4°-29°C) Severe	The victim may be unconscious with mental faculties severely impaired. Shivering is replaced by muscle rigidity (stiffness). Skin may become cyanotic (bluish). Cardiac and respiratory arrhythmias (abnormal rhythms) may occur. The ability to perform simple tasks is nonexistent.
Below 85°F (29°C) Very severe	The victim is usually unconscious. This stage may be preceded by irrationality. There is continued slowing of respiration and pulse. Rigidity (stiffness) persists.
Below 80°F (26°C) Critical	The victim is unconscious and reflexes are nonfunctioning. Respiration is barely detectable. Severe cardiac arrhythmias, leading to ventricular fibrillation or cardiac arrest. Death (respiration and cardiac cessation).

the first signs of hypothermia, such as bluish lips or shivering. These persons should be moved to a warm area. If the persons are already indoors, they should be moved to, and kept in, an area where there is little air movement, such as an office or first aid room. They should be covered with a blanket or put under a warm shower until the hypothermic symptoms disappear. Warm, sweet, noncaffeinated liquids may be given. **Do not** give the victims coffee, tea, or alcoholic beverages or allow them to smoke.

Severe to Critical Hypothermia

Victims exhibiting the signs and symptoms for severe to critical hypothermia should be handled as carefully as victims of spinal injuries. **Do not** allow these victims to move around after being removed from the water. **Do not** rub or massage the victim's extremities. Any form of exercise will increase the flow of cold blood from the extremities back to the body core, which will increase the chances for "afterdrop." Afterdrop is the further decrease of an already-lowered core temperature of the body. It is caused by cold, metabolically imbalanced blood being sent from the extremities of the body back to the core. The effect of this blood on highly sensitive heart tissue could lead to cardiac arrhythmias, such as ventricular fibrillation, or cardiac arrest. Afterdrop can be fatal, especially to those victims whose core temperature is 90° F or below.

The following are the first aid procedures for handling victims of hypothermia:

1. Prevent additional heat loss. Remove wet or cold clothing as soon as possible. Remove the clothing gently and with no assistance from a severely hypothermic victim.

2. Allow the victim's body temperature to return to normal gradually. Provide warm, dry clothing. Wrap the victim in blankets, a sleeping bag, several layers of clothing, or all of these items. Add a mild heat source, such as warm, dry towels, or have one or two dry, warm rescuers lie on each side of the victim when he or she is under some form of cover, such as a sleeping bag. **Do not** use hot objects or high temperatures to warm the victim. Hot-water bottles, heating pads, or chemical heat packs should be wrapped in a towel or blanket to prevent burning the victim. These items are used to rewarm **only** the trunk, groin, neck,

and head, since these areas of the body have the highest rates of heat loss. Conversely, these areas have faster rates of transferring warmth to the body core. **Do not** apply warming items, such as heating pads, to the extremities. This warmth will dilate the blood vessels in the extremities, allowing cold blood to return more rapidly to the body core.

3. Maintain an open airway for the victim. Administer artificial respiration or CPR, if necessary.

4. If the victim is conscious and able to swallow, give a warm liquid such as soup. **Do not** give liquids to an unconscious victim.

5. The victim should not be allowed to smoke. Nicotine reduces circulation to the skin, which increases the risk of cold injury.

6. **Do not** give the victim any alcoholic beverages. Alcohol causes blood vessels to dilate, which increases heat loss.

7. Any victim of severe to critical hypothermia must receive medical care.

SUDDEN IMMERSION IN COLD WATER

A serious concern for lifeguards is the sudden immersion of an individual in cold water. Whether a person falls accidently into cold water or intentionally enters cold water without proper protection for the body, major changes in body functions can lead to unconsciousness and subsequent drowning.

Immersion in cold water, especially if it is sudden, causes the following reactions in the body:

- **A gasp reflex,** often a sudden uncontrollable attempt to "catch one's breath." If the face is underwater, this reaction could result in uncontrolled aspiration of the water. Every effort should be made to hold the breath if the person knows he or she will be entering cold water.

- **Hyperventilation,** the rapid taking in of oxygen and blowing off of carbon dioxide. This action could also result in the aspiration of water, if the person's face is submerged, or the mouth is at or near the surface of the water.

- **An increase in the heart rate and change in the blood pressure,** which may result in cardiac arrest or arrhythmias.

EDUCATION

Lifeguards at open-water facilities should try to educate patrons to the dangers of cold water and air, whenever possible. Instructional periods and demonstrations will help to develop a proper safety attitude. Signs and posters describing preventive measures and self-help techniques should be posted at all waterfront and small craft areas.

The following preventive measures can be taken by patrons:

- Dress properly for cold weather. Several layers of light clothing are better than one heavy layer.
- Always wear a PFD when taking any small craft out, especially on cold water or in cold weather.
- Never go boating alone. Have at least one other responsible person aboard. Always go boating in an area that is frequented by other boaters who can provide assistance, if necessary.

Following immersion, the victim's first objective is to get as much of the body out of the water as possible. The body loses heat many times faster in water than in air of the same temperature. When boating, the victim should get back aboard the boat or climb onto the hull if the boat is capsized. This should be done with as little expenditure of energy as possible.

The following rules apply when an individual cannot get out of the water immediately:

- Put on a lifejacket as soon as possible, if one is not already worn.
- Check to see that others involved in the mishap are all right.
- **Do not** attempt to swim to shore. Physical activity releases heat and permits cold water to flow through clothing, which will chill the body more rapidly. NOTE. In 50°F (10°C) water, even good swimmers find it difficult to cover a distance in excess of one-half mile.
- **Do not** remove any clothing, since clothing provides some insulation against heat loss.
- **Do not** perform survival floating (drownproofing) since this technique necessitates putting the head into the water. Wearing a PFD will help to maintain the head above water. If no PFD or other flotation device is available, the head can be kept above water by treading water as slowly as possible.

If a rescue is not imminent, additional protection against the cold can be obtained by adding flotation or clothing to the sides of the chest and to the groin area or by assuming the HELP or HUDDLE positions.

- Heat Escape Lessening Posture (HELP). This position is shown in Figure 9-15. Depending on the type of PFD and the flexibility of the individual, it may be necessary to lower the thighs to achieve a good balanced position in the water. Lowering of the thighs may also help to prevent cramping of the leg muscles.

FIG. 9-15

- HUDDLE position. The HUDDLE can be used with two or more people in the water (Fig. 9-16). The important part of the procedure is to have the sides of the chest touching, if possible. Small children and older adults should be placed in the middle of the HUDDLE for more warmth.

FIG. 9-16

Never try to use the HELP or HUDDLE positions in swift currents. The victims should get out of the water at the first opportunity.

If initial attempts to get out of calm water fail, the victim should remain as motionless as possible in order to minimize heat loss. Continued movements will lead to exhaustion and hasten the onset of hypothermia. A victim who is removed from the water should receive the same first aid care as a hypothermia victim.

MAMMALIAN DIVING REFLEX

Recent studies on cold water survival have found that some people, presumably dead after being underwater for an extended period of time, may retain enough air in their lungs and oxygen in their bloodstream to sustain life and prevent brain damage. This is attributed to a response known as the mammalian diving reflex. This reflex is a complex series of body functions that reduces blood circulation to most parts of the body except the heart, lungs, and brain. It allows oxygen-carrying blood to conserve heat and maintain normal functioning of the vital organs. The reflex was first observed in aquatic mammals, such as whales, porpoises, and seals, which are able to remain submerged for extended periods of time.

Victims who have been submerged in water colder than 70°F may appear to be clinically dead and may have the following signs:
- Decreased pulse rate. The pulse may be undetectable in many victims.
- No detectable breathing.
- Bluish skin that is cold to the touch.
- Muscle rigidity (stiffness).

RESCUES IN COLD WATER

Lifeguards must locate and remove victims who have been submerged in cold water as quickly as possible. There is a potential for survival for some of these victims, even if they have been submerged for an extended period. Some factors that increase the chance of survival are the following:
- Facial immersion — the mammalian diving reflex may occur when the human body, especially the face, is suddenly immersed in cold water.
- Victim's age — the mammalian diving reflex is believed to occur more often in younger victims.
- Water temperature — colder water may cause a

stronger reflex, which would mean more protection for the victim.
- Laryngospasm — water taken in by the victim may go to the stomach rather than the lungs because a spasm of the larynx could cause the airway to close.

The mammalian diving reflex alone will not guarantee anyone's survival. Survival depends on the several factors listed previously. It also depends on how well the lifeguards do their job. The quicker they can recover a submerged victim, the greater the victim's chances are. Once the victim has been removed from the water, appropriate resuscitation techniques should begin immediately. First aid procedures for hypothermia should be started as soon as possible. Victims must also receive medical care. As the core temperature of the victim approaches normal, the following vital signs may become more apparent:
- The return of normal skin color
- A contracting of the pupils of the eyes
- An increase in the rate and depth of breathing
- The return of a steady pulse
- An increase in the rate and strength of the pulse

An in-service training program should concentrate on the procedures for cold-water rescues. Lifeguards should not attempt swimming rescues in cold water without assistance. Since the lifeguard is subject to the same effects of cold as the victim, rescues and recoveries should be performed without the lifeguard entering the water, whenever possible. It must be remembered that the victim may not be able to hang on to an object such as a ring buoy or safety line. Therefore, if it is necessary for the lifeguard to enter the water, a piece of rescue equipment, such as a rescue tube, must be taken. It would be prudent for the lifeguard to wear a PFD. A towline should be attached to the rescue equipment used by the lifeguard. The victim and the lifeguard can then be towed to safety.

Training in the use of rescue boats should include how to handle the victim during the following procedures:
- Getting the victim into the boat
- Positioning the victim for artificial respiration and CPR
- Providing warmth during the trip back to shore
- Handling the boat in choppy water

- Removing the victim from the boat and transporting him or her to a facility for further treatment.

At open-water facilities, the presence of thermoclines in the water could pose a hazard to patrons and lifeguards. A thermocline exists when there is a sharp change in temperature from one layer of water to another. Surface water may be warm and comfortable, while water at a depth of several feet could be much colder. An unknowing bather could dive down to this depth and experience the same symptoms as described for sudden immersion. A thermocline could also present hazards to lifeguards attempting to rescue a submerged victim. Changes in temperature could severely reduce the lifeguard's swimming and breath-holding capacities. Water temperatures should be taken at varying depths and recorded at least three times daily. This information could help lifeguards in preparing for a swimming rescue or when setting up a search and recovery operation.

SPINAL INJURIES

A high percentage of spinal injuries at aquatic facilities are due to improper diving. Additional causes may be jumping, falling, or being pushed against a solid object. Improper use of the slide may also contribute to this type of injury. At many facilities, the slide is positioned into water less than five feet deep. Some swimmers slide down headfirst on their bellies. This, in effect, is a dive. The injury can occur when the victim's head hits the bottom of the pool or some other object, such as another bather.

This section provides information that will help lifeguards to recognize a victim with a suspected spinal injury and to handle the victim in such a way as to prevent any further injury. Although this section deals with spinal injuries in the water, lifeguards should also be trained to handle a victim on a deck or beach.

ANATOMY AND FUNCTION OF THE SPINE

A lifeguard must possess a basic understanding of the anatomy and function of the spine in order to make a proper rescue and evaluation of a victim with a suspected back or neck injury.

The spine is a strong, flexible column that supports the head and the trunk. It is the place where the ribs are attached. It also encloses and provides protection to the spinal cord of the nervous system. The spine consists of small bones (vertebrae) separated from each other by cushions of cartillage tissue called intervertebral disks (Fig. 9-17). This cartillage allows the back to twist and

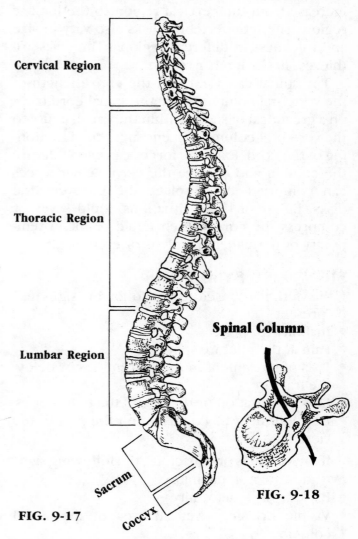

Cervical Region

Thoracic Region

Lumbar Region

Sacrum

Coccyx

Spinal Column

FIG. 9-17

FIG. 9-18

bend. It also acts as a shock absorber when a person is walking, running, or jumping. A vertebra is shaped like a circle of bone with a solid cylinder of bone forming the backside of the circle. The spinal cord runs through the hollow part of the circle (Fig. 9-18). Nerve branches extend to various parts of the body through openings on the sides of the vertebrae.

The spine is divided into five regions: the cervical or neck region, the thoracic or midback region, the lumbar or lower back region, the sacrum, and the coccyx (Fig. 9-17). There are 7 cervical vertebrae (C1-C7, starting at the top and going down the spinal column), 12 thoracic vertebrae (T1-T12), and 5 lumbar vertebrae (L1-L5). The vertebrae sit on a base provided by the sacrum. The coccyx is a small triangular bone at the lower end of the spinal column.

Most diving-related injuries occur in the cervical region. The size and mass of the vertebrae increase from the cervical region to the lumbar region. The intervertebral disks also vary in size and thickness in different regions. The disks are thickest in the lumbar region.

The spinal canal extends the entire length of the vertebral column. Since the spinal cord takes up a great deal of space within the canal, injury to the vertebral column can endanger the functioning of the cord. Extreme forces can even fracture the column and damage the cord. Lesser forces can compress and displace the intervertebral disks. Either of these situations could sever or compress the cord, which could result in temporary or permanent paralysis or even death.

SIGNS AND SYMPTOMS

If the victim is conscious, the following signs may be present:
- Inability to speak
- Pain at the fracture spot
- Loss of movement in the extremities or below the fracture
- Loss of sensation or tingling in the extremities
- Bewilderment or confusion on the part of the victim

If the victim is unconscious, the following signs may indicate a spinal injury:
- Back or neck deformity
- Visible bruising over an area of the spinal column
- Cessation of breathing
- Lacerations on the head or neck

If the lifeguard did not witness the accident, additional clues to a suspected spinal injury could be the location and position of the victim or information obtained from a bystander. A spinal injury is most likely to occur in water less than five feet deep. However, there have been injuries in diving areas where the bottom slopes are too close to the diving board. Further references to pool designs are in Chapter 4, "Preventive Lifeguarding." Areas where a spinal injury can most likely occur are near the side of the pool, in the corner of the pool, or where the bottom drops off to deeper water.

At open-water facilities, such as lakes or rivers, spinal injuries can occur in areas where water levels vary due to tides or currents and in areas where there are underwater hazards such as rocks or tree stumps.

PROCEDURES FOR HANDLING A SUSPECTED SPINAL INJURY

Lifeguards do not have the formal training or the equipment necessary to make an accurate diagnosis of a spinal injury. Therefore, all suspected spinal injuries should be considered as fractures and treated accordingly.

The following factors should influence the lifeguard's actions:
- The victim's condition — presence or absence of respiration or pulse
- The lifeguard's size — in comparison to the victim
- The location of the victim — shallow water, deep water, or on the bottom
- The availability of assistance — additional lifeguards, rescue squad or fire department personnel, untrained individuals
- The temperature of the water and/or air

As with any other emergency, an action plan for this type of injury must be established and then rehearsed continuously. Because of the great potential for further injury and risk to the victim, additional precautions must be taken during these procedures. Proper management of the airway must be maintained at all times. Depending on the degree of injury to the spinal column, the victim may not be breathing or may be experiencing breathing difficulty. If the injury is at vertebra C-5 or above, there may be paralysis of the chest muscles. This may cause shallow, rapid breathing with more abdominal movement than chest movement. In all cases, the "look, listen, and feel" steps must be followed, and resuscitation should be started immediately, when necessary. The jaw thrust must be used to establish an opened airway in a victim with a suspected spinal injury. **The head and neck must not be hyperextended.**

During the rescue procedure, treatment of the victim can be improved if additional assistance is available. Additional lifeguards or patrons should be recruited to assist with rescue procedures. In facilities that use only one lifeguard, or in facilities that use a minimum number of lifeguards, this may mean that those who are recruited to assist may have no formal training. To reduce the possibility of this happening and to increase the number of trained people who may be available, these procedures must be included as part of the in-service training program. There should also be patron education demonstrations and seminars conducted in cooperation with local fire and rescue personnel.

OBJECTIVES OF RESCUE TECHNIQUES

As previously stated, all suspected spinal injuries should be considered as fractures and treated accordingly. The rescue technique used may vary, depending on the situation. The technique selected will depend on the lifeguard's ability to perform it with accuracy and competence.

Regardless of which technique is used, the following procedures remain the same:

- **Approach the victim carefully.** Do not jump or dive into a position near the victim. The lifeguard should slip gently into the water. This reduces the possibility of causing any additional movement of the victim.
- **Reduce or eliminate any movement of the victim's spine.** The victim's head, neck, and back must be immobilized. Immobilization is **not** traction. Traction involves the pulling of a muscle in order to bring a fractured or dislocated bone into place. Immobilization prevents movement. This is initially done by the use of the lifeguard's hands, arms, or body, depending on which technique is used.
- **Rotate the victim to a supine position, if necessary.** The victim's face must be kept out of the water to allow the lifeguard to open the airway and begin artificial respiration, if necessary.
- **Move the victim to the surface of the water, if necessary.** A submerged victim must be brought to the surface before first aid can begin.
- **Move the victim to shallow water, if possible.** Immobilization of the victim, proper application of a backboard, and removal of the victim from the water are more easily performed in shallow water. If shallow water is not available (e.g., victim is in a separate diving

well), procedures to provide additional support to the lifeguard and the victim must be established and rehearsed.

- **Maintain an open airway.** If the victim is breathing, the lifeguard must maintain an open airway at all times. If the victim is not breathing, artificial respiration must be started as soon as possible. The procedure for using the modified jaw thrust is described on page 9-42.
- **Position the backboard under the victim.** It is important to position the backboard without any unnecessary jolting of the victim.
- **Secure the victim to the backboard.** As an additional precaution to prevent the victim from sliding or rolling, the victim must be secured to the backboard.
- **Remove the victim from the water, if necessary.** If it is necessary to remove the victim from the water prior to the arrival of emergency medical personnel, the backboard must be kept in a horizontal position. Once on the deck, dock, or shore, the victim should be given first aid for shock. The victim's breathing and circulation must be monitored until emergency personnel arrive.

SPECIFIC RESCUE TECHNIQUES

Several rescue techniques are presented in this chapter. They may be adapted to different situations. Lifeguards should be thoroughly familiar with each technique and should be able to decide which one to use in a particular situation. Some of the steps in a technique may need to be performed simultaneously. The following points must be considered when choosing a technique:

- The buoyancy of the victim
- The buoyancy of the lifeguard
- The victim's size
- The lifeguard's size
- The power of the lifeguard's leg stroke
- The lifeguard's breath-holding capability
- Position of the victim — prone or supine
- Location of the victim — deep or shallow water, on the surface or underwater.
- Wind and water conditions

Head-and-Chin Support Technique
Face-Up Victim

- The lifeguard approaches from either side of the victim (Fig. 9-19).
- The lifeguard places his forearm along the length of the victim's sternum. The hand of the

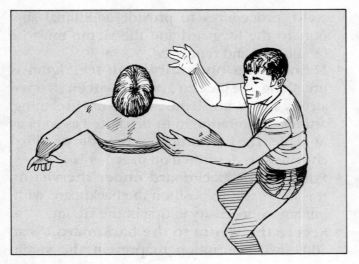

FIG. 9-19

forearm that is against the victim's chest supports the victim's chin. The thumb of that hand is on one side of the victim's chin and the fingers are on the other side (Fig. 9-20).

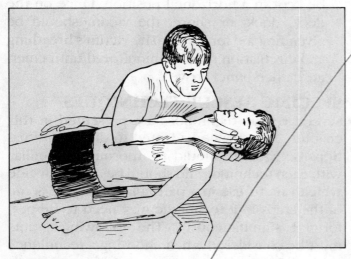

FIG. 9-20

- The lifeguard's other forearm is simultaneously placed along the length of the victim's spine. The hand of this arm supports the victim's head at the base of the skull by using the thumb on one side of the head and the fingers on the other side (Fig. 9-21).
- Both of the lifeguard's wrists are locked and the forearms are squeezed together with inward and upward pressure.
- The victim can be supported or towed to shallow water in this position.

Face-Down Victim
- The lifeguard's approach and hand and arm positioning are identical to the procedure de-

FIG. 9-21

scribed for the victim found in a face-up position (Figs. 9-22, 9-23, and 9-24). It may be necessary to reposition the victim's arm nearest the lifeguard in order to assume the proper hand and arm positions.
- To turn the victim to a face-up position, the victim is rotated toward the lifeguard (Fig. 9-25). The lifeguard submerges during this step and surfaces when the victim is face up in the water.

FIG. 9-22

- This step may be performed while standing in place (Fig. 9-26) or while moving in a headfirst direction (Fig. 9-27).
- This movement must be done slowly to prevent any movement of the lifeguard's arms and hands and also to reduce any drastic twisting of the victim's hips and legs.
- The victim can be supported or towed to shallow water in this position.

The head-and-chin support technique can also be used with a victim who is submerged and who may be lying on the front, back, or side of the body. The steps are performed as described previously, and the victim is brought to the surface. The lifeguard can then tow the victim to shallow water using this technique. However, extreme caution must be exercised when putting either forearm under the victim to prevent any movement of the victim's head or neck.

FIG. 9-23

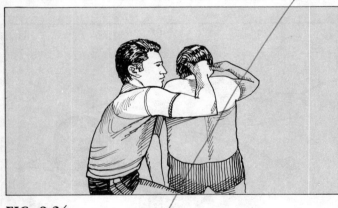

FIG. 9-24

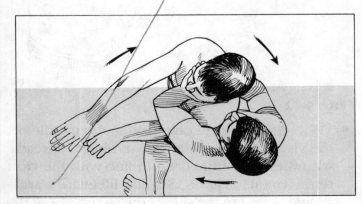

FIG. 9-25

FIG. 9-26

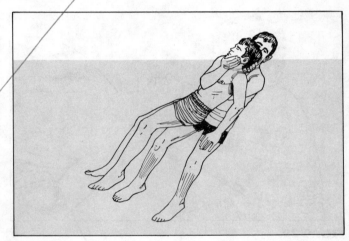

FIG. 9-27

Head-and-Back Support Technique
Face-Up Victim

• The lifeguard approaches the victim from the head (Fig. 9-28).

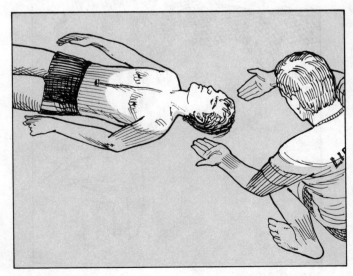

FIG. 9-28

- The lifeguard's shoulders should be at water level or lower.
- The lifeguard places the palm of one hand in the middle of the victim's back. The fingers are spread and the heel of the hand is in line with the victim's armpits.
- The palm of the lifeguard's other hand is placed against the back of the victim's head, at the base of the skull. The fingers are spread, and the thumb and forefinger of this hand are facing toward the victim's shoulder (Fig. 9-29). Figure 9-30 shows the proper hand positioning of the lifeguard.
- The victim can be supported or towed to shallow water in this position.

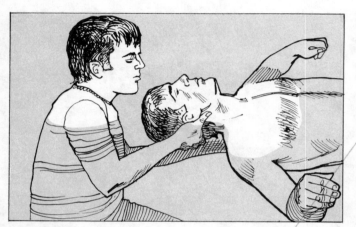

FIG. 9-29

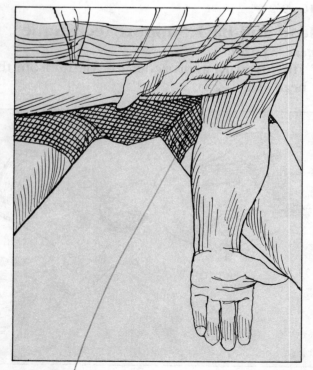

FIG. 9-30

Face-Down Victim

- The lifeguard approaches the victim from the head (Fig. 9-31).

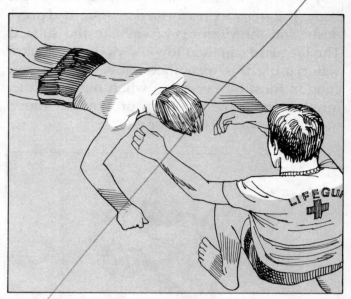

FIG. 9-31

- It may be necessary to place one of the victim's arms alongside his or her body. This will prevent the arm from hitting the lifeguard's body or the bottom during the turn (Fig. 9-32).

FIG. 9-32

- The lifeguard places one hand in the middle of the victim's back, palm down, fingers spread, with the heel of the hand in line with the victim's armpits (Fig. 9-33). The lifeguard's arm should be just to the side of the victim's head to reduce the possibility of flexing the victim's

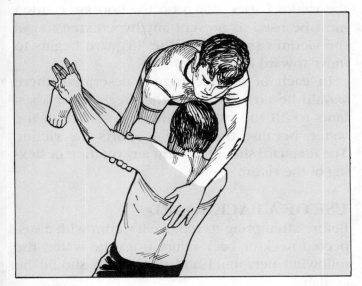

FIG. 9-33

neck. The victim's head should not come into contact with the lifeguard's chest. NOTE. To minimize confusion as to which hand to use, the lifeguard should always use the hand that moved the victim's arm in the previous step.

- The lifeguard places the other hand on the inside of the victim's other arm, midway between the shoulder and the elbow. The thumb and forefinger of this hand should be toward the victim's elbow (Fig. 9-34).

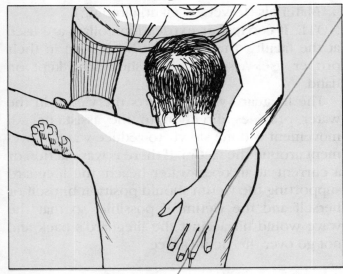

FIG. 9-34

- The lifeguard rotates the victim to a face-up position. All movement must be done slowly. During the rotation, the lifeguard avoids making contact with the victim's face. The lifeguard's elbow is kept high (Figs. 9-35 and 9-36). The lifeguard is also careful not to exert

too much lift on the victim's arm; this will minimize the stress to the victim's spine.

- If there is space available, the lifeguard may move slowly backward during the turn. This will help to align the victim's body properly.

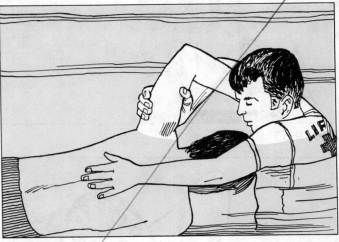

FIG. 9-35

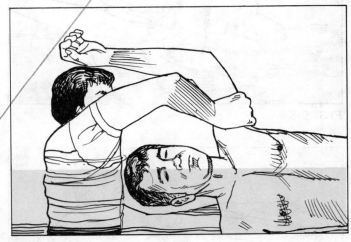

FIG. 9-36

- Once the victim is in a face-up position, the lifeguard places the victim's arm in the water, being careful to avoid any contact with the victim's head (Figs. 9-37 and 9-38).
- The lifeguard removes his or her hand from the victim's arm and places it at the base of the skull. The fingers are spread, and the palm is against the back of the victim's head. The lifeguard's thumb and forefinger should be toward the victim's shoulder. **Caution: Stabilize the victim's head without lifting it (Fig. 9-39).**
- The lifeguard's other arm remains in a position to support the victim's back (Fig. 9-39).
- The victim may be supported or towed to shallow water in this position.

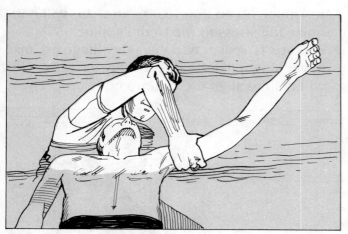

FIG. 9-37

FIG. 9-38

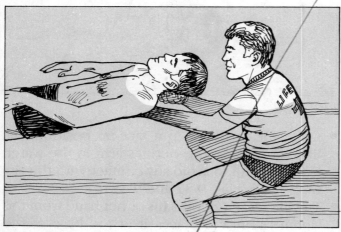

FIG. 9-39

The head-and-back support technique can also be used with a victim who is submerged and who may be lying in any position. The steps are performed as described previously, and the victim is brought to the surface. The lifeguard can then tow the victim to shallow water.

This technique can also be used to recover a victim who is lying on the bottom. However, if the victim is face down on the bottom, caution must be used to prevent any hyperextension of the victim's spine when the lifeguard begins to move toward the surface.

In each of the techniques described, there should be no attempt by the lifeguard or assistants to lift the victim above the surface of the water, because the water supports the victim. The lifeguard should prevent any rotation or flexing of the victim's spine.

USE OF A BACKBOARD

Before attempting to remove a victim with a suspected neck or back injury from the water, the following personnel and equipment should be available:

1. Adequate personnel (minimum of 5 persons in shallow water, a minimum of 7 persons in deep water) to insert the backboard under the victim and maintain it in a horizontal position while the victim is secured to it and then removed from the water.
2. A backboard. Backboard designs are discussed in Chapter 7, "Equipment."
3. At least nine ties for securing the victim to the backboard. Straps or cravat bandages may be used.
4. Materials (towels, blanket, clothing).

NOTE. If cervical or extrication collars are used at the facility, the staff must be trained in their proper use. Assorted sizes should be kept on hand.

The lifeguard who supports the victim in the water provides direction to the assistants. All movement is done slowly to reduce water movement around the victim. If there is wave action or a current at an open-water beach, the lifeguard supporting the victim should position himself or herself and the victim, if possible, so that the wave would hit against the lifeguard's back and not go over the victim's face.

Shallow-Water Procedures

Assistants should bring the backboard and approach the victim from the side (Fig. 9-40). The backboard should be inserted diagonally under the victim from the side, with the foot end of the board going down in the water first (Fig. 9-41). Slide the backboard under the victim until the middle of the board is in line with the victim's

FIG. 9-40

FIG. 9-41

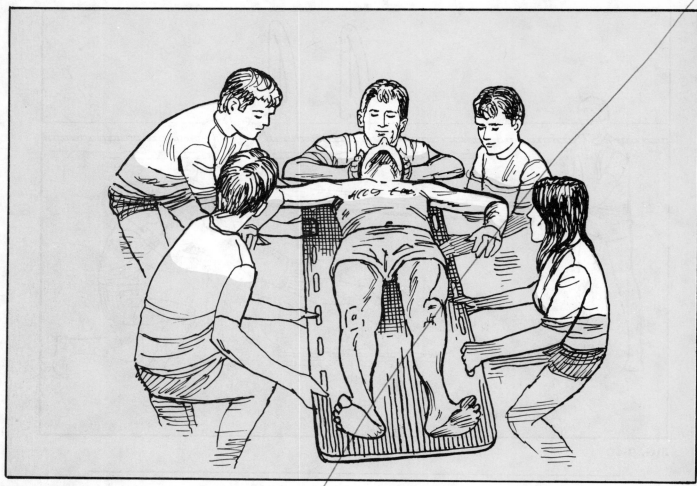

FIG. 9-42

spine and the victim is centered on the board. Allow the board to rise parallel to the victim. At least two assistants should be along each side of the victim to guide the board as it rises to the victim (Fig. 9-42). NOTE. It is important to warn assistants to avoid twisting or bending the victim's body as the board rises. If any adjustment (of the board to the victim) is necessary, the position of the board should be adjusted, not the position of the victim.

As the board rises toward the victim, the lifeguard removes his or her own arm by sliding it between the victim and the board. The lifeguard stabilizes the victim's head by placing his or her own hands against the sides of the victim's head, fingers pointing toward the victim's shoulders (Fig. 9-43). If a cervical or extrication collar is to be used, it should be applied at this time. Great care must be taken to prevent any movement of the victim's head or neck during the application of the collar. It may be necessary to sink the

FIG. 9-43

board a short distance in order to insert the collar between the board and the victim.

Assistants now place the sandbags, or other material to be used, along the sides of the victim's head in order to stabilize it. This is done one side at a time (Fig. 9-44). The lifeguard slides his or

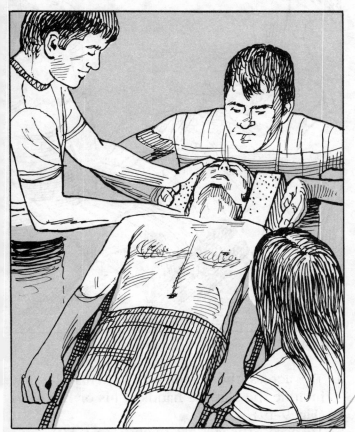

FIG. 9-44

her hand from between the sandbag and the victim's head as the sandbag is being positioned. The lifeguard then resumes the stabilizing position by holding the sandbags to the sides of the victim's head.

Securing the Victim to the Backboard

If cravats are used to tie the victim to the backboard, they should be secured to one side of the board first, then secured to the other side, rather than trying to tie them simultaneously. This will eliminate any unnecessary pulling on the victim. In many facilities, cravats are secured to one side of the board at all times. This allows for a quicker and more efficient tying procedure in an emergency. Straps can be secured to both sides of the board but should not be buckled or fastened when the board is not in use. This minimizes the potential for a strap being left fastened when the

board is inserted under a victim. At facilities where water movement may be strong enough to move the victim's body, it may be necessary to secure the victim's trunk to the board first. This decision will need to be made by the lifeguard prior to beginning the tying sequence.

The following sequence should be followed when tying a victim to a backboard:

1. Tie across the victim's forehead (Fig. 9-45).

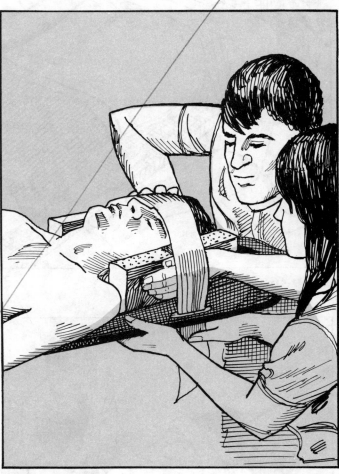

FIG. 9-45

The lifeguard slides his or her hand out from under the tie as the tension from the tie stabilizes the victim's head. The tie should not be tight enough to extend the victim's neck. The lifeguard now helps to support the board and direct the tying process.

2. Tie across the victim's chest, under the armpits (Fig. 9-46).
3. Tie across the victim's chest, to include the arms (Fig. 9-47). The hands may be tied separately (Fig. 9-48).

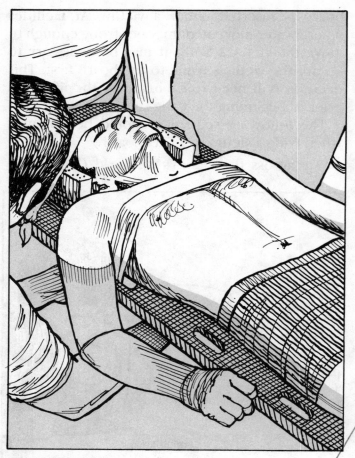

FIG. 9-46

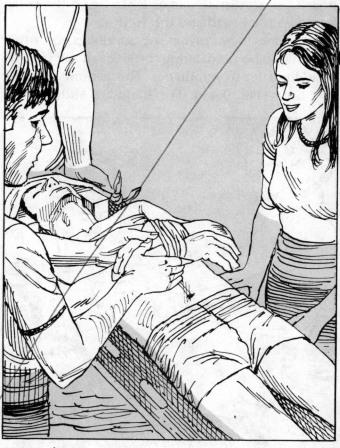

FIG. 9-48

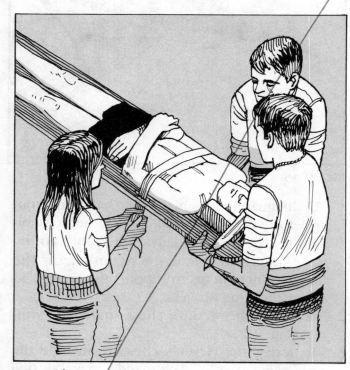

FIG. 9-47

4. Tie across the victim's hips. This tie may include the victim's hands at his or her sides (Fig. 9-49).
5. Tie across the victim's thighs (Fig. 9-50).
6. Tie across the victim's legs, midway between knee and ankle (Fig. 9-51).
7. Tie across the victim's ankles (Fig. 9-52). There are several procedures for securing the feet that will support the victim if the board has to be inclined while being removed from the water (Figs. 9-53 and 9-54). These would be used if there was no footplate that could be attached to the board. NOTE. If a footplate is used, special training is required to ensure proper application and adjustments.

During the tying process, the lifeguard at the head of the victim should constantly monitor the victim's respiration. An assistant at the foot end of the board should ensure that the board remains level at all times.

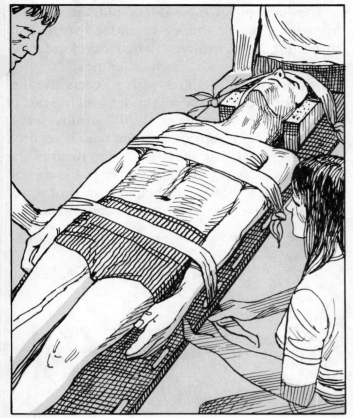

FIG. 9-49

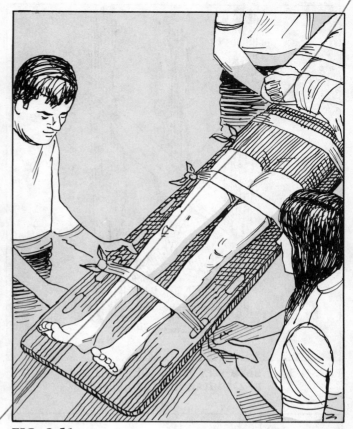

FIG. 9-51

FIG. 9-50

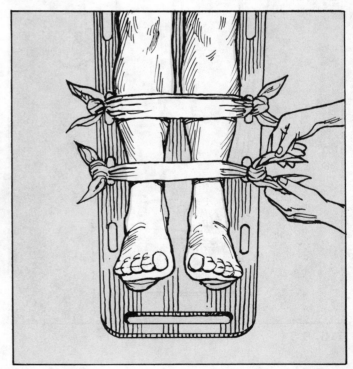

FIG. 9-52

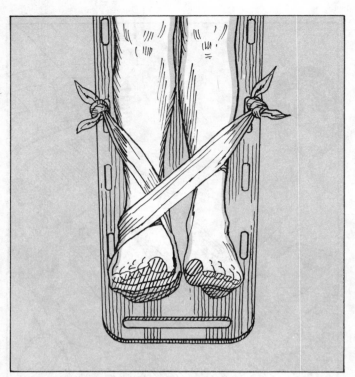

FIG. 9-53   BOTH FEET WOULD BE TIED IN A SIMILAR MANNER

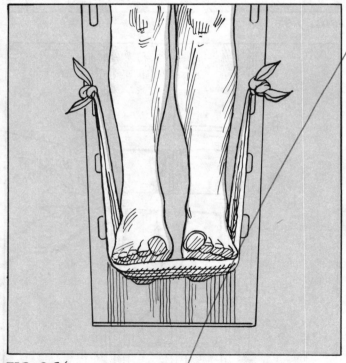

FIG. 9-54

Removing the Victim From the Water

If it is necessary to remove the victim from the water prior to the arrival of emergency medical personnel, the backboard must be kept in a horizontal position as much as possible.

The location of the ladders and the distance from the deck to the water surface are factors that must be considered when developing removal procedures for specific facilities.

At open-water facilities with a beach, the lifeguards can remove the victim by walking out of the water. In swimming pools, the shallow water area is best for removing a victim who is secured to a backboard. The lifeguard at the head of the victim walks backward and the victim is moved headfirst (Fig. 9-55). This helps to prevent water from splashing over the victim's head and face.

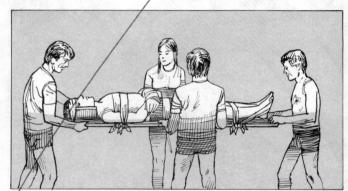

FIG. 9-55

Once the victim is brought to the pool wall, the lifeguard at the head of the board can move to one side of the board to assist in lifting the victim to the deck. At least two persons should be on each side of the board. The victim's head is toward the wall (Fig. 9-56). When preparing to

FIG. 9-56

lift, the lifeguards or assistants should crouch low in the water. Their backs should be straight and their shoulders should be approximately at water level (Fig. 9-56). This will allow them to lift with their legs and not their backs. It may be necessary to break the surface tension under the board prior to lifting. This can be done by lifting the head of the board approximately one inch out of the water.

Keeping the board as level as possible, the lifeguards lift the board by standing up (Fig. 9-57).

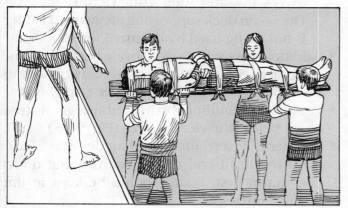

FIG. 9-57

The board is then brought in over the deck. Assistants on the deck should take hold of the board as it comes over the deck (Fig. 9-58). Once

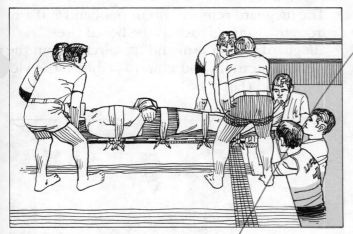

FIG. 9-58

on the deck, dock, or shore, the victim is given first aid for shock and his or her breathing and circulation are monitored until emergency medical personnel arrive (Fig. 9-59).

There may be circumstances, such as excessive bleeding, water that is too cold, or the need to administer CPR, when it is necessary to remove the victim from the water before he or she can be secured to a backboard. In this situation, the lifeguard and assistants must be careful to ensure that the victim does not slide on the board. All movements must be done slowly.

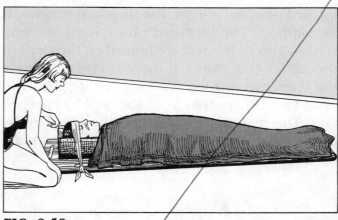

FIG. 9-59

Deep-Water Procedures

The approach and turn for deep water are executed in the same manner as the shallow-water procedure. However, the lifeguard should begin moving the victim toward a corner as soon as possible.

The lifeguard brings the victim into the corner headfirst. The victim's body should bisect the angle of the corner (Fig. 9-60). If there is a ladder

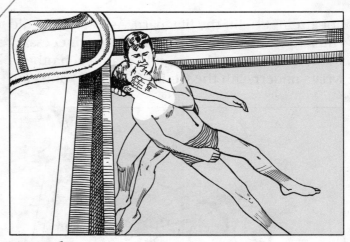

FIG. 9-60

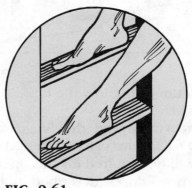

FIG. 9-61

located near the corner, the lifeguard may use it for support. The lifeguard's back is against one wall and his or her feet are braced on the steps of the ladder (Fig. 9-61). If there is no ladder near the corner to provide support, the lifeguard will need to be supported from the wall by an assistant. This assistant should hold the lifeguard by grasping the armpits (Fig. 9-62). He or she should

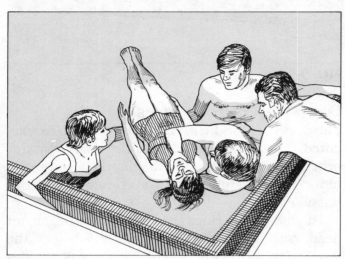

FIG. 9-62

not attempt to lift the lifeguard. Assistants should enter the water slowly to avoid any unnecessary water movement. They should grasp each other's wrists underneath the victim (Fig. 9-63) and sup-

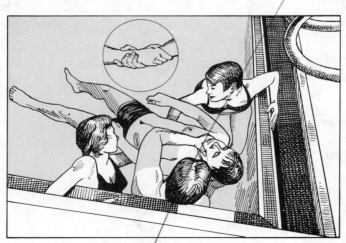

FIG. 9-63

port the victim just below the hips. They do **not** lift the victim.

Once the victim and the lifeguard are supported, the backboard can be inserted. Additional assistants will be required for this operation. The suggested procedures described here may be modified for various facilities.

Head-and-Chin Support

- Lifeguard brings victim to corner as described.
- Assistants support victim and lifeguard as described.
  Number of assistants involved at this time:
  Two — in water supporting victim.
  One — on deck supporting lifeguard, if ladder is not being used by lifeguard for support.
- Additional assistants (two) bring backboard and approach victim from feet, that is, assistants are moving in toward the corner (Fig. 9-64).
- Assistants handling board submerge it to a point below the victim's feet (Fig. 9-65).
- Assistants insert the board under the victim with the head end of the board going under the victim first. Board should be kept in line with victim's spine.
- Assistants supporting victim can guide board under victim.
- The assistants on each side of the board guide it up to the victim's back while keeping the board level.
- The lifeguard removes his or her hand and arm from the victim's back as the board rises.
- Lifeguard's other arm and hand remain on the victim's sternum and chin to stabilize the victim's head (Fig. 9-66).

FIG. 9-64

FIG. 9-65

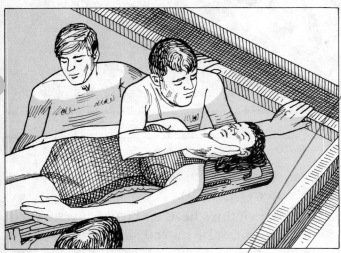

FIG. 9-66

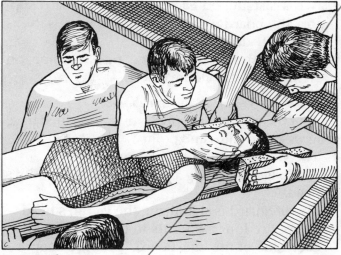

FIG. 9-67

FIG. 9-68

- The four assistants in the water support the board. If the board needs to be repositioned, they submerge the board while the lifeguard maintains stabilization of the victim's head.
- Sandbags should be inserted, one at a time, on each side of the victim's head (Fig. 9-67).

Head-and-Back Support
- Lifeguard brings victim to corner as described.
- Lifeguard either uses a ladder for support or is supported by assistant(s) as described (Fig. 9-68).
- Assistants support victim as described.

- Additional assistants (two) bring board and approach victim from feet as described.
- Assistants submerge board to a point below the victim's feet as described.
- Board is inserted under victim as described.
- As board moves under victim, assistants supporting victim can guide board into position.
- Two assistants on each side of board align board with victim's spine.
- As board is allowed to rise to victim, lifeguard removes his or her hand from victim's back and places that hand alongside the victim's head.
- Once the victim is on the board, the lifeguard removes his or her other hand from behind the victim's head and places it along the other side of the victim's head.

- Two assistants on each side of the board support the board or reposition it, if necessary, as previously described.
- Sandbags should be inserted, one at a time, on each side of the victim's head.

Securing the Victim to the Backboard

Each of the procedures previously described have progressed to the same point:

1. The victim is on the backboard.
2. Sandbags are along each side of the victim's head.
3. The lifeguard is stabilizing the victim's head.
4. There are four assistants in the water, two on each side of the backboard. They are supporting the board with one hand and holding on to the wall with the other hand.
5. The lifeguard is supporting himself or herself on the ladder or he or she is being supported from the deck by an assistant.

Before the victim can be lifted to the deck, he or she must be secured to the backboard. In deep water, it is difficult to completely secure the victim to the backboard as described in the procedure for shallow water. The stability of the backboard and the victim and the area for the assistants to move around the backboard are factors that must be considered during a deep-water procedure.

Additional support for the backboard and the victim can be achieved by inserting flotation devices, such as ring buoys or rescue tubes, under the board. These devices should not be secured to the backboard. They should be held in place by the assistants in the water. This will allow for easy removal and will eliminate the possibility of interference during the lifting process.

The victim's head and trunk must be secured to the board before any movement of the board can be made. This can be done more readily by an assistant on the deck. The following procedure should be used:

1. The first tie goes across the victim's forehead to secure the head between the sandbags (Fig. 9-69). Once the head is secured, the lifeguard may remove his or her hands from the victim's head and assist in supporting the board.
2. The next tie goes across the victim's chest, under the armpits. This secures the victim's trunk to the board and prevents the victim

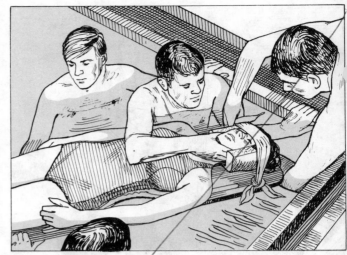

FIG. 9-69

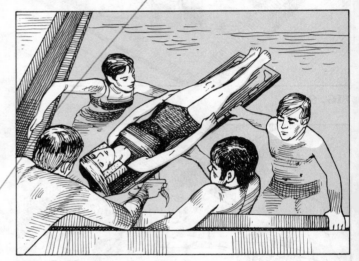

FIG. 9-70

from slipping when the board is lifted out of the water (Fig. 9-70).

3. After the victim's head and trunk are secured, the board must be moved slowly to a position against one wall to allow assistants on the deck to continue to secure the remaining ties.

4. The lifeguard and assistants support the board.

5. Tie across the victim's hips (Fig. 9-71). This tie should also secure the victim's hands.

6. Tie across the victim's legs (Fig. 9-72).

7. Tie either a stirrup or figure eight on the feet (Fig. 9-73) to prevent the victim from slipping when the board is lifted out of the water.

Removing the Victim From the Water

The following procedure for removing the victim from the water may be modified for different

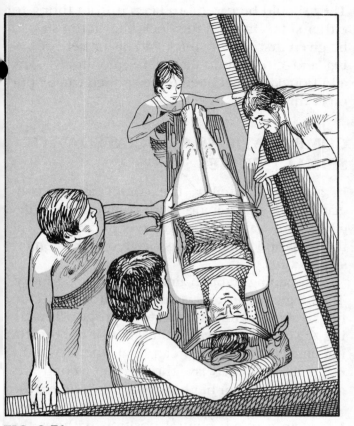

FIG. 9-71

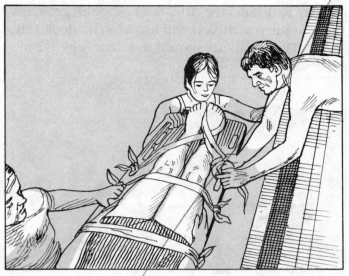

FIG. 9-73

aquatic facilities. Some factors that will determine the procedure to be used are —

- The number of lifeguards and assistants present.
- The design of the pool, for example, the height from the water level and the deck level, the formation of the overflow trough.

To remove the victim there should be at least four assistants on the deck — two on each side of the board as it comes out. Two lifeguards should be in the water — one on each side of the board. Prior to lifting, the board will need to be moved away from the parallel wall to allow one of the lifeguards to get in position for the lift (Fig. 9-74). During the lift, it is important to keep the board from tilting to either side.

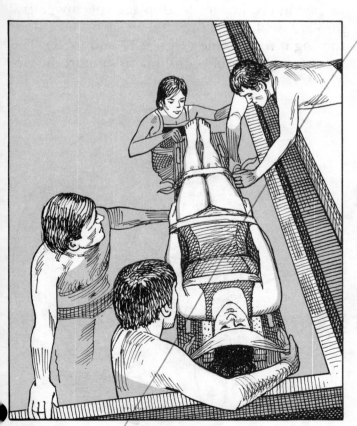

FIG. 9-72

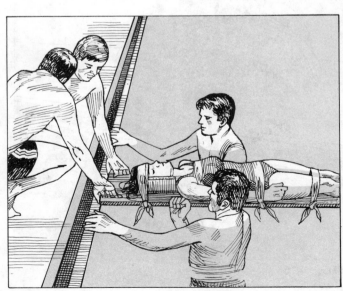

FIG. 9-74

Two assistants on the deck should grab the head of the backboard and lift it to the deck (Fig. 9-75). The assistants should use their legs as their

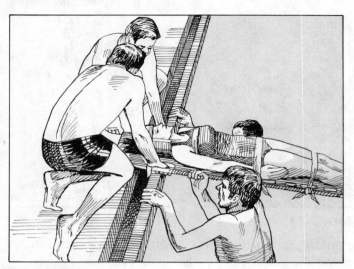

FIG. 9-75

main source of power, not their backs. The lifeguards in the water guide the board as it goes up.

The two assistants at the head of the board begin to move the board away from the edge of the pool. As quickly as they can, the remaining two assistants on the deck should grab hold of the board to help remove it from the water (Fig. 9-76).

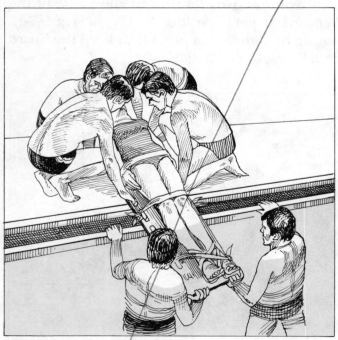

FIG. 9-76

They should be careful to keep it from tilting to either side. Once on the deck, the victim should be given first aid for shock and his or her breathing and circulation should be monitored. Any additional ties that need to be applied can be put on at this time.

COMPLICATIONS ASSOCIATED WITH SPINAL INJURIES

In an aquatic facility, the complications associated with spinal injuries are compounded. Lifeguards must also be able to recognize and treat the signs and symptoms associated with submersion victims.

Maintaining an open airway is always a priority. The lifeguard must constantly monitor the victim for any sign that might indicate stoppage of breathing or a blocked airway. If the victim is not breathing, a second lifeguard can open the airway by using the modified jaw thrust. The second lifeguard places his or her hands on either side of the victim's head. The victim's head must be maintained in a fixed, neutral position without the neck being extended. The lifeguard then uses his or her index fingers to displace the lower jaw forward without tilting the head backward or turning it to the side (Figs. 9-77 and 9-78). The first lifeguard should continue to support the vic-

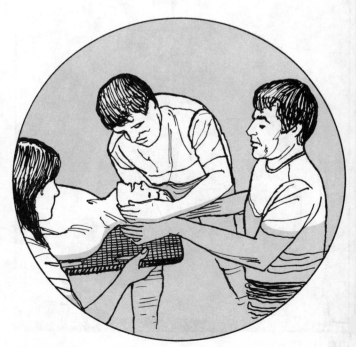

FIG. 9-77

tim's head. Mouth-to-mouth resuscitation can be provided in this position by the second lifeguard, if it is required.

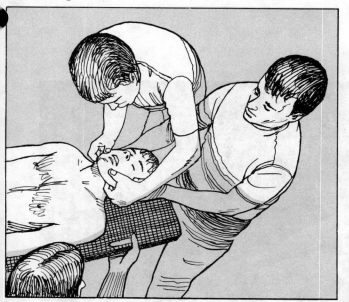

FIG. 9-78

Vomiting and nausea are associated with victims of near-drowning and head injuries. Fluids or mucus may drain from the victim's mouth. If the victim is not yet on a backboard, the head-and-

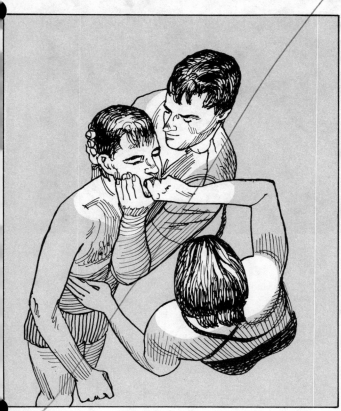

FIG. 9-79

chin support technique can be used to support the victim while an assistant sweeps the victim's mouth (Fig. 9-79). The victim's entire body must be turned as a unit. If the victim is secured to the backboard, the victim and the board can be turned to the side to allow better drainage or to clear the mouth. However, the lifeguard and assistants should hold the victim to prevent any movement when the board is turned (Fig. 9-80). The ties or straps alone should not be trusted to support the victim. Head, neck, and spine alignment must be maintained in the victim.

FIG. 9-80

Head injuries, such as lacerations of the scalp, skull fractures, or direct trauma to the brain, may be associated with spinal injuries. Once an open airway is established and the victim is secured to the backboard, a thorough check of the victim for other injuries should be done.

Research in the handling of spinal injuries is constantly being done. This section reflects the most current information available at the time this book was published. Improvements and developments will be circulated through Red Cross chapters as they become available. It is the responsibility of all lifeguards to continue their training and to be familiar with the rescue equipment that is available at the facility where they are employed. Continued education of the public on diving safety will help to reduce diving injuries. Lifeguards should stress preventive actions by patrons at all times.

9-44

Chapter 10

SEARCH AND RECOVERY OPERATIONS

Every aquatic facility should have procedures established for locating missing persons. All staff members at the facility must be thoroughly trained in these procedures. It must be remembered that time is a critical factor during a search for a missing person. The lifeguard may have little or no idea of how long the person has been missing. Regardless of where the person was last seen, there is always the possibility that the individual is underwater. The missing person must be found as quickly as possible, and artificial respiration or cardiopulmonary resuscitation (CPR) must be started immediately, if necessary.

In recent years, more emphasis has been placed on search and recovery operations because of studies done in the area of cold-water survival. These studies have shown that drowning victims may be revived if given proper treatment in time. Since individual reaction to cold varies according to age and water temperature, it is vital that the individual be found as quickly as possible.

All areas should be searched quickly and thoroughly, using organized search formations and patterns rather than having one or two lifeguards search the areas haphazardly. The following suggested guidelines may be used as a basis for organizing search and recovery operations. These guidelines may be modified to meet the needs of different facilities.

ORGANIZATION AND PLANNING

In the development of plans for search and recovery operations, all possible situations should be considered, such as lost bather, drowning victim, or capsized boat. Procedures should be established for each of these situations. Everyone who will be involved in search and recovery operations must know their responsibilities.

The involvement of additional support personnel, such as police, fire, and rescue departments, should be part of the organization and planning phase. Their assistance will help in the development of effective operations. When they should be called, what should be done before their arrival at the facility, and what type of assistance they will need when they arrive are examples of information these personnel can supply. Another subject that should be discussed and planned for is the involvement of other facility staff, such as park rangers, camp counselors, and maintenance personnel. The recruitment and training of volunteers should also be discussed. The more personnel that are involved with search and recovery operations, the greater the area that can be covered in a shorter period of time.

Communications systems must be established and clearly defined so that there is no delay in an emergency. Communications systems are discussed in Chapter 5, "Emergencies." Calls or signals for communication may be made by whistle, air horn, or announcement over a public address system. Specific signals will be needed for the following situations:

- To indicate that a person has been reported missing
- To summon facility staff to a designated area, such as the office, guard room, or first aid room. (This may not necessarily include lifeguards who are at a guard station.)
- To clear the water of bathers, if necessary
- To summon additional support staff and volunteers
- To sound "all clear" or a signal to indicate that the missing person has been found or that the search is being called off

Crowd control and supervision of bathers are other subjects that must be discussed and planned for during the organizing phase. If they are not controlled, large groups of people can impede operations. Clearing the bathers from the water must be done in a safe and orderly manner. Once out of the water, they must still be supervised to some degree and not allowed to gather in areas where search operations are going on. Because the lifeguards will be involved with the search and rescue operations in the water, crowd control will usually be left to other facility staff, such as locker room attendants or maintenance personnel.

TRAINING

Practice sessions for search and recovery operations should be scheduled on a regular basis for all the staff at an aquatic facility. Volunteers and support personnel should be involved as often as possible. Back-up systems should be established to cover situations such as the use of volunteers during the operations.

Accurate records and evaluations should be kept on all practice sessions. Critiques should be held to discuss all aspects of the operations: procedures, communications, responsibilities, and time frames. Any revisions in the procedures should be made, and repeat drills should be run as soon as possible. To be effective in an emergency, the search and recovery operations must continually be evaluated and improved. That re-

quires the cooperation of all personnel who may be involved.

OPERATIONS

One common type of "missing person" or "lost bather" is the small child who has just wandered off to the bathroom or the snack bar and is reported missing by a parent. The following suggested procedures for a missing person drill may be modified for different aquatic facilities. Factors that must be considered are as follows:

- Size and shape of facility
- Conditions of bottom in water area
- Absence or presence of current
- Number of staff on duty
- Victim's age, skill level, and size
- Length of time person has been missing
- Location where person was last seen
- Number of patrons at facility

SUGGESTED PROCEDURE FOR MISSING-PERSON DRILL

1. A predetermined signal should be given to alert staff when a person is reported missing. All available staff not on duty should report to the office, guard room, or other designated location. A preliminary search of the water area should be made as soon as possible.

2. The person reporting the missing individual should be taken to the same location where the staff is reporting. This person, especially if it is a parent, will usually be very excited and will want to join in the search but should be discouraged from doing so.

   A complete description of the missing person should be given to the staff, such as sex, height, color of hair, skin color, weight, and type of clothing. A relative, parent, or friend should remain at a designated location. Once found, the missing person can then be taken to that location for identification.

3. An announcement over the public address system should be made. This should include a description of the person, the location where he or she was last seen, and the place where the person should be taken, if found.

4. Lifeguards who are not on duty at the time should be assigned to check the swimming area where the person was last seen.

5. At the same time, other lifeguards and facility staff should be assigned to check other areas, such as shallow water, bathrooms, showers, locker rooms, snack bar area, and sunbathing areas.

6. At camp facilities, a staff person should be assigned to check the missing person's cabin.

7. If the person is still missing, personnel should be assigned to check the surrounding areas, such as a playground, campsites, and wooded areas. Facilities that have additional personnel such as park rangers, playground supervisors, camp staff, or maintenance personnel should have some established procedures for calling these people together. They can then be assigned to check the surrounding areas. The aquatic staff should concentrate their search efforts on the water area.

8. The signal should be given to clear the water of all bathers — for example, one long blast on a whistle or an air horn.

9. While bathers are clearing the water, the lifeguards should begin to set the boundary for the area to be searched. If the place where the person was last seen is known, a buoy should be placed in the water at that spot.

10. Volunteers to assist in the search of the shallow-water area should be asked to report to a specific location near the water. One or two lifeguards should be assigned to organize the search teams and to quickly explain the procedures to be followed.

11. While the volunteers are being organized, the remaining lifeguards should begin to check the deep-water area. Depending on the clarity of the water, this can be done by using a short series of dives, or swimming with masks, snorkels, and fins along the surface.

12. At all times during these operations, activities should be directed by only one person, usually the manager or the head lifeguard. This cuts down on confusion and on time that may be wasted.

13. If the person is not found after a thorough search of the swimming area, additional support personnel, from rescue squads or the fire department, should be called in. The swimming area should continue to be searched until these personnel arrive at the scene.

UNDERWATER SEARCH

All available personnel should be used when an immediate search of the underwater area is required. Searchers should be used in water depths that are appropriate to their respective skill levels. The area to be searched first should be the area where the person was last seen. As additional areas are designated, lifeguards should be in charge of each search area. If possible, the areas should be searched simultaneously.

Shallow-Water Areas

Shallow-water areas that have poor-to-no visibility can be searched by having people link arms, or hold hands, and wade in line across the area (Fig. 10-1).

FIG. 10-1

As the line progresses forward slowly, the searchers should gently sweep their feet across the bottom with each step they take. A suggested pattern for shallow-water searchers (Fig. 10-2) covers the entire area. Any person tall enough to stand in the water may be used for this type of search. The searchers should not go beyond chest-deep water, or a depth of more than four feet, since it may be faster to conduct a diving and swimming search in water that is deeper than four feet.

Deep-Water Areas

When a search is made for a lost bather, deep water may be considered to be any depth of water over four feet. The section that follows provides information about some of the search patterns

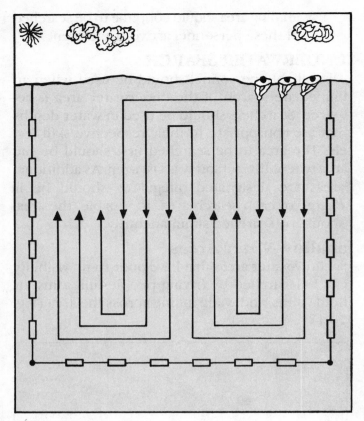

FIG. 10-2

that can be used by lifeguards in deep water. These patterns are used as soon as an individual has been reported missing and cannot be found in shallow water.

Line Search

The searchers line up in a straight line, no more than an arm's length from each other. On command from a lifeguard, they surface dive to the bottom and swim forward a set number of strokes. The searchers' hands touch the bottom lightly as their arms sweep outward from, and then inward toward, the midlines of their bodies. The sweeping actions of the arms are slow and continual (Fig. 10-3). Touching the bottom gently with the

FIG. 10-3

palms of the hands will help to prevent injury to the searchers if they should strike a sharp object. It may be advisable to sweep the hands just above the bottom when the bottom is muddy and when

there is a good chance that disturbing the bottom will create greater visibility problems. The searchers should use the type of kick that is best for them while swimming underwater.

The searchers should swim almost straight up to the surface after completing the designated number of strokes underwater. They then back up about six feet, reform their line, count off to ensure that all of the searchers are accounted for, and repeat the diving sequence (Fig. 10-4). These procedures are repeated until the entire swimming and diving area has been covered in one direction. The searchers should then sweep the area at a 90° angle to the first efforts if the missing person is not located.

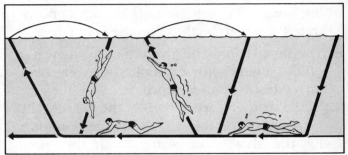

FIG. 10-4

All of the swimming and diving areas should be searched as quickly as possible. The search of adjacent areas must be continued if the missing person has not been found. At waterfront facilities, this includes the area under the docks and outside the swimming area. If there are enough qualified personnel, all of the searches should be done simultaneously. Camp waterfront areas can be divided into separate areas for individuals of different skill levels, such as A for beginners, B for advanced beginners, C for swimmers, and D for swimmers with lifesaving experience (Fig. 10-5). Each section should have a lifeguard in charge of the search in that area.

Circle Search

The circle is another pattern that may be used by searchers. There are two methods of using this type of search pattern:

1. Full circle

   This method can be physically strenuous. Only personnel who are trained in the procedure should be used. A central pivot is set in the approximate area where the missing person was last seen. This can be a boat that is

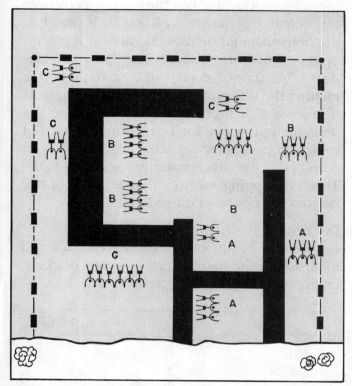

FIG. 10-5

anchored, the corner post of a dock, or even a person who is standing in neck-deep water, if it is possible to do so. A line is tied to, or is held at, the pivot point. It is stretched out and held by the searcher who is the farthest from the pivot point and who remains on the surface. The line should be long enough to accommodate the number of searchers. They align themselves along the stretched line each time they are ready to dive. They use the same procedures for diving, swimming underwater, surfacing, and backing up that were described for the line search pattern. The position of the stretched line is moved each time the divers surface and back up.

2. Half circle

The same procedures as those for the full circle are used for diving, swimming along the bottom, and surfacing in this pattern. The anchor point in this pattern is located on the shore or on the side of a dock (Fig. 10-6).

RECOVERY OPERATIONS
Grappling

There is a remote possibility that grappling equipment could be put into operation in time to save the life of a submerged victim, particularly in cold water. However, because of the time it may

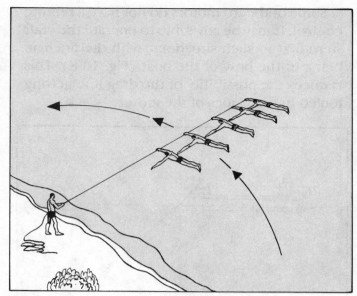

FIG. 10-6

take to assemble the necessary equipment and personnel, the operation usually becomes one of body recovery rather than rescue. A grappling operation must cover the entire area, as is done in a swimming search pattern. The head lifeguard or the facility manager should set the boundaries for each area to be searched. The search pattern is determined by the shape of the area to be searched, the depth of the water, and the nature of the bottom, such as rock, mud, or sand. Other factors, such as currents and the condition of the water and the weather, should also be considered.

The first search efforts should be centered in the area where the missing person was last seen. The following procedures for grappling can be set up quickly and with a minimum of equipment and personnel:

• Single boat

The grappling equipment is usually towed behind a slow-moving rowboat or power craft (Fig. 10-7).

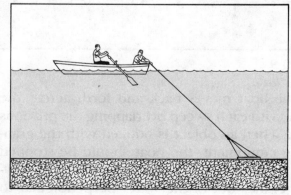

FIG. 10-7

Some outboard motors do not have a remote control. It may be advisable to operate the craft stern-first in such situations, with the lineman being in the bow of the boat (Fig. 10-8). This reduces the possibility of the drag line getting fouled in the blades of the motor.

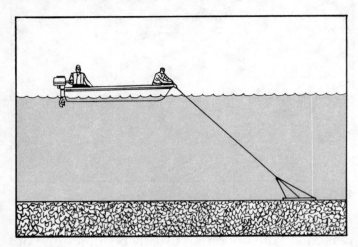

FIG. 10-8

One method of covering an area is shown in Fig. 10-9. Buoys are used to mark the search area.

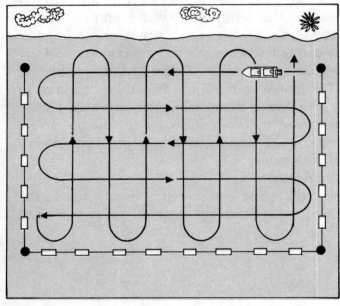

FIG. 10-9

The boat moves back and forth across the area, with each sweep overlapping the previous one. When an object is hooked with the grappling equipment, the boat should be stopped and then moved to a position where the towline comes out of the water perpendicular to the surface. This will put the boat directly over the object that has been hooked. If possible, the object should be raised slowly. If it cannot be raised with the grappling equipment, a lifeguard or a trained diver will have to go down, identify the object, and unhook the equipment if necessary. If there is a need to resume the dragging operation, the boat should be moved back over part of the area that has already been searched before the apparatus is lowered again. This overlapping ensures that an area of the bottom has not been missed.

- Dock to dock
  Grappling equipment can be moved back and forth across the bottom between two docks in enclosed swimming areas (Fig. 10-10).

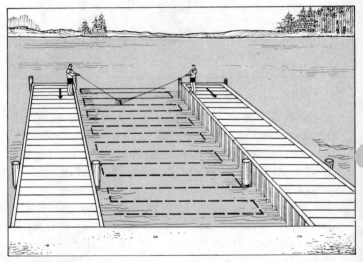

FIG. 10-10

Two lines are attached to the grappling irons, which are pulled across the designated area. After each pass, the searchers move sideways and continue the pattern. Each pass of the equipment should overlap the previous one. The area under the dock can be searched with grappling poles or by divers. In streams where there is a current, the search should start downstream from where the missing person was last seen (Fig. 10-11).

- Boat to shore
  Grappling equipment can be operated between an anchored boat and the shore of a wide river or an open swimming area (Fig. 10-12). If there is a current in the river, the boat heads upstream. The operator on shore moves upstream with each pass of the equip-

FIG. 10-11

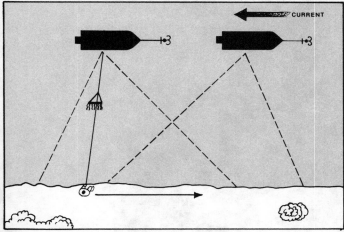

FIG. 10-12

ment. Once a designated area has been searched, the boat moves upstream parallel to shore. A new search area is established with some overlap of the previous area.

Scuba

All personnel who will use scuba equipment during recovery operations should first be trained and certified by a nationally recognized organization and have additional training in scuba search and recovery operations.

Scuba divers can use the same types of search patterns that have been discussed previously in this chapter. They may also use other types of patterns because of their ability to remain underwater for longer periods of time than divers without scuba equipment.

Chapter 11

WEATHER AND ENVIRONMENTAL CONDITIONS

Weather conditions in outdoor aquatic facilities such as lakes, rivers, and swimming pools are directly related to the safety of the bathers. These conditions will vary greatly in different parts of the United States. This chapter deals with the basic knowledge needed by lifeguards to evaluate certain weather or environmental conditions that may exist or occur, in order to make decisions relating to the bathers' safety.

WEATHER AND ENVIRONMENTAL AGENCIES

A lifeguard's personal knowledge of weather and environmental conditions may be limited to knowing which agencies can supply information concerning the safety of aquatic activities. Many state and local weather bureaus provide 24-hour telephone service for weather reports. Their telephone numbers should be included on the list of emergency telephone numbers at all aquatic facilities. Local weather conditions may change quickly and drastically. A call to these agencies two or three times daily can prevent patrons in the facility from getting caught in unexpected storms.

Local radio stations broadcast weather reports throughout the day. In remote areas, additional weather information can be received by means of CB radios and scanners.

WEATHER SIGNS

The following are examples of different cloud formations that can assist lifeguards in predicting weather changes:

- Clouds that are high and hazy will usually form a halo around the sun or moon. These clouds indicate that a bad storm may arrive within hours (Fig. 11-1).

FIG. 11-1

- Large clouds with hard, cauliflower-like tops indicate an eminent thunderstorm. When they become active, the tops will form anvil-like structures, and they will look dark and heavy from below (Fig. 11-2).
- Rolling dark clouds indicate that bad weather can arrive within minutes (Fig. 11-3).
- Fleecy white clouds indicate that good weather is ahead (Fig. 11-4).

FIG. 11-2

FIG. 11-3

FIG. 11-4

Once bad weather is predicted, staff members should be on the alert for further signs such as thunder and lightning. Precautionary measures should be taken if lightning is observed. Estimating the distance to the storm is relatively easy. When lightning is seen, begin counting seconds. Continue to count until you hear the thunder. Light travels approximately 186,000 miles per second (300,000 kilometers). Sound travels about 1,100 feet per second (330 meters). Divide the number of seconds between the lightning and the thunder by five to estimate the distance to the storm in miles. Divide the number of seconds by three to obtain the distance in kilometers. For example:

1. Lightning is seen.
2. Begin counting—one thousand one, one thousand two, one thousand three, and so on.
3. Thunder is heard.
4. Stop counting. Six seconds have been counted.
5. Divide by five to determine the distance in miles. The storm is approximately 1.2 miles away.
6. Divide by three to find the distance in kilometers. The storm is approximately two kilometers away.

There are no defined guidelines for determining exactly when the water should be cleared of bathers. Since sound travels slower than light, it would be a safe practice to clear all personnel from the water at the first sound of thunder. Guidelines for responding to lightning and thunder should be established and put in writing at each facility, since the frequency and duration of storms and the speed at which they travel will vary in different locations. It is helpful to get advice from the local weather bureau when establishing policies relating to weather.

CLEARING THE WATER OF BATHERS

Procedures for clearing the water of bathers because of an impending storm should be specifically outlined. Once the decision has been made by the manager or the head lifeguard to clear the water, an appropriate signal should be given by all lifeguards. This signal may be a long blast of a whistle or some other prearranged signal. Bathers should be warned about the storm and directed to shelter. Patrons should not congregate under umbrellas, trees, or other tall objects that attract lightning. Some suggestions for further protection are as follows:

- Get inside a large building.
- Stay away from metal pipes, metal railings, wire fences, or other metal objects that may carry lightning. This includes bicycles, motorcycles, and golf carts.
- Avoid using the telephone, unless it is an emergency.

- Do not stay in structures that are in open areas, such as picnic shelters.
- Stay away from heights, beaches, and fields.
- Get down from lifeguard chairs as soon as possible.
- Do not use the showers.

After all the patrons are supposed to be out of the water, lifeguards should check the swimming area for possible stragglers, secure the area, and then report to the office or the guard room for further instructions. Assistance may be needed to maintain order and discipline in locker rooms or other safe areas where patrons have congregated. In camp situations, campers should be told to report to a central location or to their counselors, depending on the procedures of the facility.

A suggested guideline for determining when to allow patrons to return to the water is to wait for 15 minutes after the last visible sign or sound of the storm. However, continual observations should be made, and weather forecasts should be monitored on the radio.

WEATHER HAZARDS

HEAVY RAIN AND HAIL

Heavy rain and hailstorms can cause dangerous conditions. Patrons should be cleared from the water and directed to take shelter as soon as either of these conditions occurs. The same precautions should be followed as for thunder and lightning. Heavy rains can also cause changes in the clarity and depth of the water.

TORNADOES

Aquatic facilities should monitor all weather forecasts in areas that are prone to tornadoes. A "tornado watch" indicates that tornadoes and thunderstorms are possible. A "tornado warning" means that a tornado has been sighted and that people should take shelter immediately. Additional safety tips are as follows:

- Stay away from all windows, doors, and outside walls.
- Go to the basement of a building or to the interior parts at the lowest level. Go to a pre-designated shelter if time permits.
- If there is no shelter nearby, lie flat in the nearest ditch, culvert, or ravine. Cover your head with your hands.

HIGH TEMPERATURE AND SUN

Another weather condition that should be closely monitored is high temperature. At outdoor facilities, high temperature can cause more people to be in the water, and consequently, overcrowding may result. Lifeguards should attempt to disperse crowds if this happens.

Sunburn, heatstroke, and heat exhaustion more commonly occur to patrons who stay out of the water, for example, a parent who has been watching a child in the wading pool. A lifeguard or other staff member should periodically check the patrons in the water, as well as in the sunbathing areas, for these possibilities. Lifeguards must also take personal precautions to guard against these conditions.

Sunburn

The most effective form of sunburn prevention is the limiting of exposure time, especially for individuals who are sun sensitive. Sunburn may develop following exposure, even on a cloudy day. Some facilities require lifeguards to wear hats, jackets, pants, and, in some cases, socks, for protection.

An advisory panel of the U.S. Food and Drug Administration concluded that liberal and regular use of a sunscreen may help to reduce the chances of skin cancer as a result of long-term overexposure to the sun.

Commercial preparations for sunburn protection vary in their effects. Most preparations contain oils to keep the skin from drying because of exposure to heat, wind, and water. Some have hardly any protection effects. Others are highly effective but may be more expensive. Some preparations may cause allergic reactions in individual cases. A small sample should be tested on the skin before liberal amounts are applied. Preparations that protect against ultraviolet rays should be reapplied after swimming.

The eyes should also be protected, either by shade or by sunglasses, from overexposure to the glare of sun, sand, and water.

Heatstroke

The main signs of heatstroke are as follows:
- Hot, dry skin, although the person may have been sweating earlier
- Redness of light skin

- Extremely high body temperature, sometimes about 106°F (41°C)
- Possible dizziness, nausea, headache, rapid pulse, and unconsciousness

Heat Exhaustion
The main signs of heat exhaustion are cool, clammy skin, and a great deal of perspiration, but normal body temperature.

Drinking large amounts of water may help to avoid heat illness. Using large quantities of salt or salt tablets should be discouraged. Wearing loose-fitting and light-colored clothing in hot, sunny weather helps to lower the incidence of heat reaction.

HIGH WIND
High wind can cause hazardous conditions at outdoor aquatic facilities. Wind may cause wave actions that can reduce visibility and can influence currents. Wind may also create potential hypothermia conditions on cool days, especially for small children and elderly people. Lifeguards must be alert to these conditions. They should take whatever steps are necessary to protect the patrons. At waterfronts, the wind may also affect the stationing of rescue boats. Procedures to be followed for windy days should be established. Lifeguards should protect themselves from the effects of wind.

FOG
Fog is a condition that can create problems in open-water areas. Fog can occur at any time of the day and is caused when certain weather conditions occur, such as the approach of a cold front. The facility should be closed or no one should be allowed into the water if the fog limits good visibility.

ENVIRONMENTAL CONDITIONS

Environmental conditions may exist that can be hazardous to patrons. Such things as weeds, rocks, tree stumps, or erosion should be taken care of before opening the facility to the public. These hazards may be found either in the water or on land. They should be removed, if possible, or clearly marked to warn patrons of their existence.

Any changes in water conditions, such as discoloration, excessive turbidity, or dead fish or waterfowl, should be immediately reported to the local board of health or to other environmental regulation agencies. Lifeguards should clear the facility of patrons if there is any possibility that unsafe conditions exist.

Some facilities are subject to changes in shoreline and bottom conditions because of currents. Daily inspections should be conducted to verify the depth of the water in certain areas. Also, any debris or obstacles that may have been brought into the swimming area should be removed.

Lifeguards should be aware of beds of underwater weeds that may be in or near the swimming area. If possible, these beds should be removed before the facility opens for the season. If it is necessary to enter one of these beds to assist a distressed or drowning victim, the lifeguards must remember that all movements should be slow and careful. This will help to prevent their arms and legs from getting entangled in the weeds. If the victim is conscious, attempts should be made to calm the person down in order to prevent any further entanglement. Once calmed down, the victim can be slowly assisted out of the weed bed.

The information in this chapter does not cover all the types of weather and environmental conditions that can affect the safe operation of an aquatic facility. However, this information can serve as a guide and an incentive to lifeguards, owners, and operators of aquatic facilities for seeking out and developing local resources that can provide the information and training needed in these areas.

Chapter 12

WATERFRONT AREAS

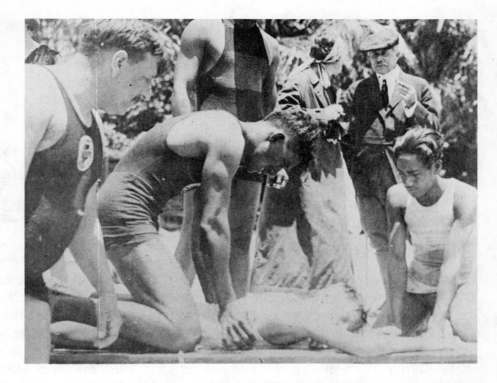

Open-water, nonsurf beach areas are a large segment of the increasing number of recreational aquatic facilities used by the public. These facilities are found at private camps, inland lake areas, state parks, resorts, trailer parks, wilderness areas, and playgrounds. They may be used by patrons for short terms (daily) or for long terms (seasonal). They may be man-made lakes, natural spring-fed lakes, bays in ocean areas, or part of a river system. Like swimming pools, each of these facilities will have its own characteristics, such as water clarity, currents, or beach areas, that lifeguards must deal with while supervising the patrons.

When operational procedures are being established for a waterfront facility, certain factors must be taken into consideration, such as the following:

- Natural features of areas
  Knowing the source of the water, such as a river or a natural spring, can give information on approximate temperatures. This helps when scheduling classes or recreational swims.
- Water characteristics
  If the waterfront is part of a river system, currents have to be considered. Also, the staff has to be aware of debris and any other hazards that currents may bring into the swimming areas.
- Vantage points
  The best locations for lifeguard stations may

change throughout the day because of variable winds and sun glare.
- Types of activity to be conducted
  Classes, recreational swims, boating and canoeing, scuba diving, water skiing, and springboard diving are examples of waterfront activities. Coordinating these activities to use all available space and still provide proper supervision is an important aspect of waterfront operations.
- Communications
  Effective communications systems between facility staff, with other camp staff, and with emergency personnel should be established before opening the waterfront. Lifeguard chairs should be equipped with a communications system such as a telephone, bullhorn, or two-way radio.
- Types and numbers of people to use the facility
  A capacity limit should be established for each area of the facility: nonswimmer, swimmer, and boating areas. A system should be established for testing swimming skill levels or for designating skill levels for admission to certain areas.
- Times of peak activity
  Peak activity times should be identified on the daily schedules and should be considered in the scheduling of lifeguards and other staff members.
- Availability of additional personnel
  Waterfront staff may need support personnel,

such as camp counselors, to assist as lookouts during recreational swims. Many of these personnel could be trained as instructor aides to assist with classes.

Almost all of the information in this textbook can be modified and applied to the safe operation of an open-water, nonsurf beach. The following section deals with specific conditions and areas that will need additional attention from lifeguards at a waterfront facility.

GENERAL CHARACTERISTICS OF WATERFRONT AREAS

BOTTOM

The bottom should have a gentle slope from the shallow-water area to the deeper-water area. There should be no holes or sudden drop-offs. All underwater obstructions, such as tree stumps or rocks, should be removed from the swimming and diving areas. They should be clearly marked in areas that are provided for boating if they cannot be removed.

SWIMMING AREAS

Separate swimming areas should be designated for different levels of swimming ability, such as nonswimmer, beginner, and swimmer. Buoyed lines or docks should be placed between each of these areas to help prevent patrons from straying into areas beyond their respective skill levels.

SMALL CRAFT AREA

An area designated for small craft activity should be separated from the swimming area. Small craft areas should have separate lifeguards and lookouts, if possible. Additional information on small craft areas is discussed later in this chapter.

SCUBA AREA

If scuba diving is allowed at a facility, it should be restricted to a clearly defined area and should be marked with a diver's flag (Fig. 12-1). The area should also be marked with signs under the water, if possible or practical, to prevent divers from straying into a boating area. No small craft should be allowed in the scuba area, except for a safety boat.

DIVING AREAS

All diving should be restricted to areas having a water depth greater than nine feet. Competitive

FIG. 12-1

diving organizations such as U.S. Diving and the National Collegiate Athletic Association (NCAA) recommend that the minimum depth of water should be 12 feet under a 1-meter board and 13 feet under a 3-meter board. The length and width of the area should be defined with lifelines. Because of the limited visibility of the water at most facilities, no diver should be allowed to dive until the preceding diver has surfaced and has moved out of the way. Further information on diving boards and towers is in Chapter 4, "Preventive Lifeguarding."

BEACH AREA

The beach area should be raked daily to remove glass, rocks, sharp objects, or trash. All holes should be filled immediately.

DOCKS AND RAFTS

Docks, piers, rafts, and other platforms should be anchored securely or attached to pilings to prevent shifting due to winds or currents. There should be a daily inspection to look for rotting wood, protruding nails, and weak or frayed anchor cables or lines. **No one should be allowed to swim under docks, rafts, or platforms.** All rafts and platforms with diving boards must be strongly anchored and stable enough to prevent tilting when dives are executed. There should be no movement of the diving platform from actions of the wind or waves.

BATHHOUSE

The bathhouse should be located near the waterfront. There should be a daily inspection of the shower rooms, the restrooms, and the locker areas. Water should not be allowed to stand on any floors. (Refer to Chapter 8, "Health and Sanitation," for further information on shower water temperature.)

LIFEGUARD STATIONS

Towers

Lifeguard towers should be placed in positions that permit clear and elevated views of the entire swimming area. There should be a lookout in each tower at all times. Lookouts are useful in directing lifeguards to trouble spots.

Chairs or Stands

Locations of chairs or stands determine the lifeguard's area of responsibility. A piece of rescue equipment, such as a rescue tube or a ring buoy, should be stationed on each chair or stand. If there is a diving platform that is separate from the main diving area, there should be a lifeguard chair on it that provides a clear view of the entire diving area.

Further information on lifeguard stations is in Chapter 4, "Preventive Lifeguarding."

Rescue Boat

A separate rescue boat should be assigned to patrol the small craft area. Further information on rescue boat operations is presented later in this chapter.

FIRST AID STATION

The first aid station should be clearly identified and should be located close to the swimming area. The equipment maintained in the first aid station will depend on such things as the management policy, the medical personnel on the staff, the level of first aid training of the lifeguards, and the response time of EMS personnel.

COUNSELORS AND LOOKOUTS

Additional safety personnel should be assigned whenever there is a large number of patrons in the facility. This can be done by utilizing counselors or advanced swimmers as lookouts. These people must be instructed to use only elementary forms of rescue in emergencies, such as reaching and throwing assists, or to direct a lifeguard to the trouble spot.

CLASSIFICATION OF BATHERS AND BOATERS

Whenever possible, all patrons participating in any aquatic activity should be given a skill-screening examination to determine their respective swimming ability. At residential and day camps, this should be done on the first day after the health examination and before the patrons are allowed to participate in any aquatic activity. At open waterfront areas, such as state parks or campgrounds, swimming areas should be clearly marked for various skill levels. A sign describing each area's skill requirements and limitations should be posted where everyone entering the area can see it. If a lifeguard has any doubts about a patron's swimming ability, that patron should be cautioned and, if possible, screened before being allowed to enter the water or to use small craft.

CONTOUR AND TERRAIN CHART (MAP)

Waterfront shorelines and underwater contours are subject to changes from erosion and from wind and wave actions. There is also an influence from currents in facilities that are part of a river system. A map or chart, showing the contour and physical arrangements of the facility, should be available and should be maintained and updated as needed. The chart should indicate water depths, drop-offs, holes, rocks, logs, tree stumps, and any other underwater obstructions. It should also indicate all construction such as docks, rafts, diving platforms, pilings, anchors, and lifeguard stations. All lifeguards should be familiar with the facility, its hazards, and its changing environment (Fig. 12-2).

SMALL CRAFT SAFETY

The small craft area should be separated from the swimming area. If possible, there should be separate docking facilities for each type of craft, such as rowboats, canoes, sailboats, and powerboats. This allows for safer maneuvering of the craft while leaving and approaching the dock. A personal flotation device (PFD) is required by the U.S. Coast Guard for each person on board a small craft. Nonswimmers should wear a properly fitted

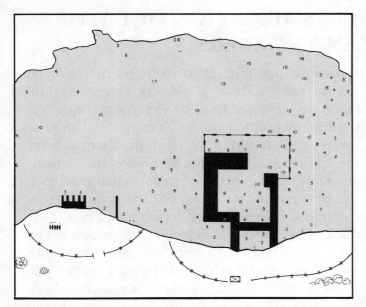

FIG. 12-2

PFD at all times while in the craft. Everyone should be required to wear a properly fitted PFD when using small craft at residential and day camps. This rule also applies to the facility staff.

SIGNAL FLAGS

Signal flags should be positioned so that they can be seen from anywhere in the small craft area (Fig. 12-3). A sign should be posted that identifies the flags. Patrons should be instructed to keep a watch on the flags on shore, as well as the flags on the rescue boat and the guard tower, for warnings of changing weather or water conditions.

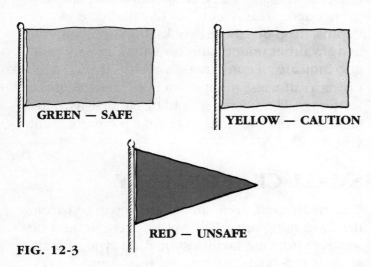

GREEN — SAFE

YELLOW — CAUTION

RED — UNSAFE

FIG. 12-3

CARE OF EQUIPMENT

All small craft should be moored or docked correctly at the end of each day. Canoes should be removed from the water and put on racks or

secured for the night. All equipment, such as oars, paddles, PFDs, and sails, should be stored away in a well-ventilated place.

Boat motors should be checked and serviced once a week during the season. Small outboard motors should be removed from the boats at night. Large motors should be tilted up and locked, with the propeller out of the water. Gasoline should be stored in a cool, dry place.

DOCK FORMATIONS AND RESCUE-BOAT LOCATIONS

A waterfront area should have docks designed for the needs of that facility, especially at camps. Some camps may have younger children who have little or no swimming skills. These camps will require a different dock formation from a camp that has older patrons with better swimming skills. The following dock formations (Figs. 12-4 through 12-10) are common and can be adapted to different facilities.

The locations for rescue boats will depend on such things as the number of bathers in each area, water currents, dominant wind direction, and the type of craft used, for example, canoe, rowboat, or power craft.

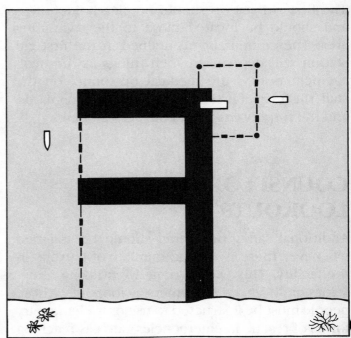

FIG. 12-4

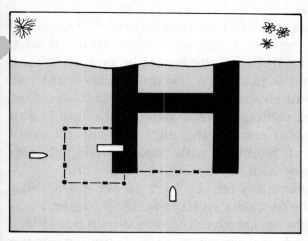

FIG. 12-5

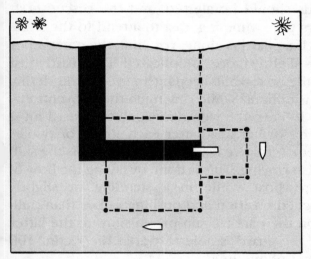

FIG. 12-6

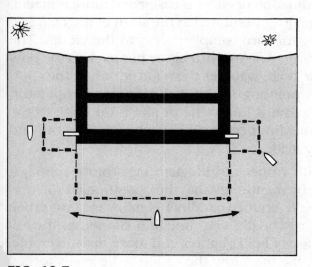

FIG. 12-7

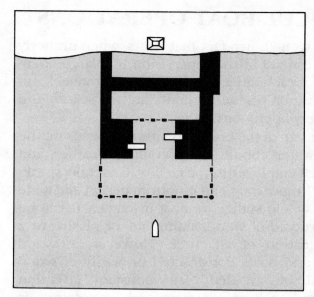

FIG. 12-8

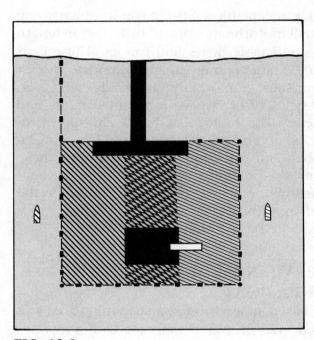

FIG. 12-9

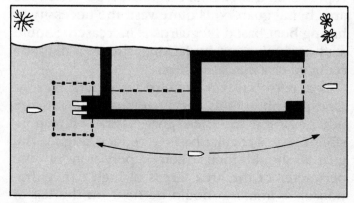

FIG. 12-10

RESCUE-BOAT OPERATIONS

It is a well-known fact that boats, when properly used, can aid in the supervision of a large open-water beach area. They can be invaluable in open-water rescue attempts and in search and recovery operations.

The size of the boat to be used depends on the area, water conditions, prevailing weather, and the staff employed at the facility. Generally speaking, a 14-foot boat of flat-bottom design and wide beam would suffice in most instances. It can be constructed of wood, aluminum, or plastic, or a combination of all three. However, all-wood boats and boats constructed primarily of wood should be avoided. The constant attention required to keep them properly maintained is often prohibitive.

Other acceptable craft for use in lifeguarding are small motorboats from 16 to 18 feet in length or less, inflatable boats, and canoes. These craft should be large enough to accommodate at least two persons comfortably and safely. However, these types of craft have inherent dangers and problems. The motorboat has a churning propeller, an air cell may be punctured in an inflatable boat, and the canoe is unstable. For these reasons, this section will deal with the rowboat primarily as a rescue boat. The differences in the use of motorboats, inflatable craft, and canoes will be noted where appropriate.

SUPERVISING A BEACH AREA USING A BOAT

Shore-based supervision of a swimming area at a beach or waterfront is paramount. Only when sufficient staffing and equipment permit should supervision from a boat be considered. When the area being guarded is quite vast, the necessity of having boat-based lifeguards is increased. Should staff or equipment be lacking, the area must be reduced to a manageable size.

Boat patrols usually require a two-person crew. One person acts as the boat operator and the other as a spotter. These guards trade off responsibilities on a regular basis to reduce fatigue. The guards should focus their supervision on the perimeter of the area. Areas of high concentration of swimmers should be next on the list of priorities. Lone swimmers should be encouraged to return to shore or swim with at least one other person.

When the craft remains stationary, one guard can supervise an area that covers 40 to 50 yards from each side of the boat. The craft should be moored in place by some quick-release method. A slip-hitch through a ring on an anchored float should suffice. A quick yank on the line causes immediate release. This method avoids the problems of fumbling with less-than-optimal snap hooks or with other methods of mooring.

The stability offered by a proper rescue boat permits the guard to stand securely to gain a better sight perspective. The oars should be in place and ready for immediate use at all times while the guard and craft are on station.

Once an emergency situation is detected, other guards should be alerted, and the rescue craft enters the swimming area to attend to the situation. If a guard is alone, reaching the emergency site is slightly more complicated. The guard must row the boat while keeping an eye on the victim. This is difficult while rowing in the conventional way. To keep the victim in sight, the guard must turn his or her head after each stroke or two. A better alternative used by many guards is the skill of push rowing. This is done by facing the bow of the rowboat while in a standing or slightly crouched position and pushing rather than pulling on the oars to gain propulsion. In the latter case, the guard is able to watch the victim 100 percent of the time.

If a two-person craft is moved into action, the coordination of effort is easier and more efficient. The spotter, stationed in the stern of the craft and facing forward, simply points to the victim. The operator, rowing with his or her back to the bow of the boat, watches the spotter. When the spotter is pointing in the direction of the operator, the operator knows he or she is on track to the victim. Minor course corrections are obvious and easily made.

With respect to lifeguarding from a canoe, it must be mentioned that the operational skill level of the operator (paddler) is more exacting than for a rowboat. Even though a canoe has the advantage of being lighter and more maneuverable, these factors allow the canoe to be easily forced off course and out of position by wave and wind action. The properly trained lifeguard must possess a high degree of canoeing skill to be able to guard any swimming area with a canoe.

As with a rowboat, the canoe can be used to patrol an area or can be stationed at a particular location. The canoe has an added advantage of being light enough to be brought out of the water aboard a raft or other such platform. This has the benefit of affording the lifeguard a higher, more stable vantage point. The canoe can also be easily and quickly launched in response to an emergency. Since the canoe is less stable than a rowboat, the most stable position for the lifeguard to take while in a canoe is kneeling while resting gently against a seat or thwart. This precludes standing and crouching as was recommended for the rowboat.

The safe operation of a canoe by one or two lifeguards is accomplished from the kneeling position only. Getting to the victim is straightforward, since the lifeguards are facing the victim all of the time. Rowboats and canoes will slide easily across most lifelines that mark the perimeter of the swimming area.

Outboard motorboats have an obvious problem where entry into a swimming area is concerned, when the area is marked with lifelines. However, there are three acceptable methods for crossing the perimeter of a swimming area. First, the boat operator and crew can lift the lifeline up and over the motorboat as it passes beneath. Second, special openings in the perimeter can allow the motorboat, with its motor shaft and propeller, to pass. Third, and perhaps more desirable with an outboard motorboat, the motor shaft and propeller can be tilted out of the water while the craft slides across the lifeline, as would a rowboat or canoe.

Motorboats are normally used to patrol a perimeter or a specific area. Rarely, if ever, are they used as a stationary platform or observation point. Long-term stationary use of the motorboat requires that the motor be shut down. This can cause many problems in an emergency situation, such as the inability to get the motor started.

Proceeding to an emergency situation in a motorboat should be carried out with extreme caution. The spinning propeller, with its sharp blades, can cause severe bodily injury.

USING A BOAT FOR RESCUE

When using a rowboat to rescue a person in distress, the lifeguard rows the boat to the victim and permits the victim to grab the boat. Caution should be exercised in approaching the victim, to avoid striking the victim with an oar or with the boat itself. Words of encouragement should be given to the victim. The lifeguard should give directions to the victim on exactly what to do.

Most rowboats are quite stable. There is little hazard associated with permitting a single victim to grasp the bow, stern, or side (gunwale) of the boat. However, multiple victims must be dealt with one at a time. This is accomplished by tossing some sort of flotation device to each victim, then picking the victims up one at a time. If there is danger of overloading the boat, other craft must be summoned immediately. An experienced lifeguard should be able to size up a distress situation early enough to call for appropriate assistance before reaching the victims.

When using a canoe to rescue a distressed swimmer, the lifeguard should paddle close enough to the victim to be heard clearly. The lifeguard then gives instructions to the victim to grab the bow of the canoe. (**Never** permit a victim to grab the gunwale of the canoe. A canoe can be capsized easily.) The victim can then be towed to shallow water while hanging on to the bow. Also, an unpanicked victim can be brought to the center of the canoe and assisted into the craft by various rescue techniques.

Approaching a victim with an outboard motorboat must be done with great care. The spinning propeller is capable of causing severe injury. It is for this reason that the following procedure is recommended:

1. Approach the victim slowly from the leeward side (side opposite the wind).
2. When the boat is within three boat lengths of the victim, **shut down** the engine (turn it off).
3. Coast or paddle to the victim.
4. If the engine is to be restarted, bring the victim aboard first.

The above procedures are for approaching and contacting swimmers in distress, when it is the victim who grabs the rescue craft. Things are reversed in a drowning situation. Since a drowning person is quite unlikely to be aware of what is happening around him or her and is usually in a state of panic (if active), it is the lifeguard who must grab the victim. This is done **from the craft.** The lifeguard should enter the water from the rescue craft only if the victim is passive and out of reach, or if a second lifeguard is in the craft and can maneuver it to assist the lifeguard who enters the water.

The lifeguard maneuvers the rescue craft close to the victim and takes the most appropriate opportunity to grab the victim. Once supported with the face out of the water, an actively drowning person will usually calm down quickly and may then be reasoned with. From this point on, the rescue procedures are the same as for a distress situation.

In the above situations, an inflatable craft can be powered either by an outboard engine or manually and is handled exactly as a rowboat or motorboat. The only difference is the difficulty in getting victims aboard some inflatable crafts. The material itself often tends to "grab" the victim or the victim's clothing. This makes if difficult to slide the victim up and across the air cell into the boat. Simply wetting the air cell can make the rescue easier.

It is imperative that any rescue boat be properly equipped. The following lists are prepared as a guide for normal circumstances. The lists are essentially the same. They differ only in the quantity of items to be carried, based on the capacity of the boat. Remember, the boat must be capable of carrying two lifeguards, the required equipment, and the victims that are rescued.

EQUIPMENT LISTS

Rowboat	Motorboat	Canoe
Oars	Outboard motor and gas tank	Paddles
Extra oar	Paddles or oars	Extra paddle
PFD for each crew member	PFD for each crew member	PFD for each crew member
Two extra PFDs	Three extra PFDs	One extra PFD
Line for extension	Line for extension	Line for extension
Anchor (medium to large) and line	Anchor (large) and line	Anchor (small) and line
Extra line for towing	Extra line for towing	Extra line for towing
Marker buoys (three minimum)	Marker buoys (three minimum)	Marker buoys (three minimum)
Rescue buoy	Rescue buoy	Rescue buoy
Reaching pole	Reaching pole	Reaching pole
Bailer	Bailer	Bailer
First aid kit	First aid kit	First aid kit

SUMMARY

To guard a waterfront or a small craft area with any kind of small boat requires practice in handling the particular craft being used. Without this, the asset of having rescue craft for guarding purposes can quickly become a liability in an emergency situation. To become proficient, it takes hours of practice in the use of rescue craft, especially in the rescue and retrieval of victims from the water. Every possible emergency situation should be practiced repeatedly and regularly throughout the season.

Appendixes

CHAIN OF COMMAND

SWIM OR RACQUET CLUB

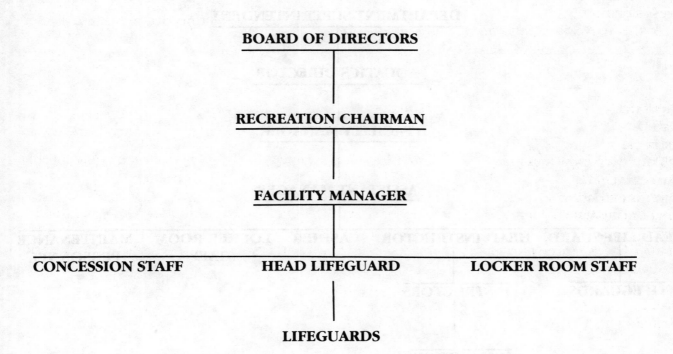

BOARD OF DIRECTORS

RECREATION CHAIRMAN

FACILITY MANAGER

CONCESSION STAFF   **HEAD LIFEGUARD**   **LOCKER ROOM STAFF**

LIFEGUARDS

CHAIN OF COMMAND

LARGE CITY

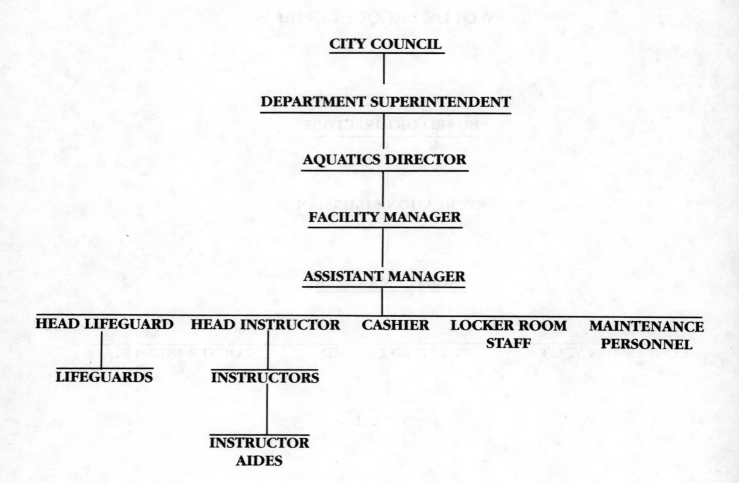

CITY COUNCIL

DEPARTMENT SUPERINTENDENT

AQUATICS DIRECTOR

FACILITY MANAGER

ASSISTANT MANAGER

HEAD LIFEGUARD   HEAD INSTRUCTOR   CASHIER   LOCKER ROOM STAFF   MAINTENANCE PERSONNEL

LIFEGUARDS   INSTRUCTORS

INSTRUCTOR AIDES

CHAIN OF COMMAND

SMALL TOWN

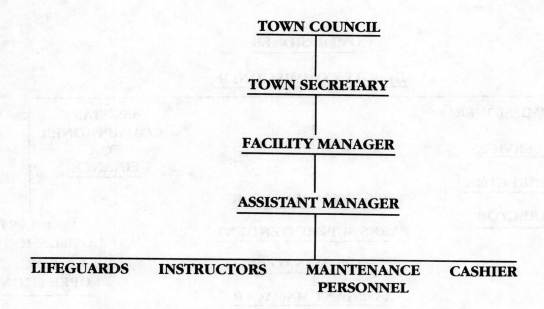

TOWN COUNCIL

TOWN SECRETARY

FACILITY MANAGER

ASSISTANT MANAGER

LIFEGUARDS   INSTRUCTORS   MAINTENANCE   CASHIER
PERSONNEL

CHAIN OF COMMAND

COUNTY OR STATE RECREATION DEPARTMENT

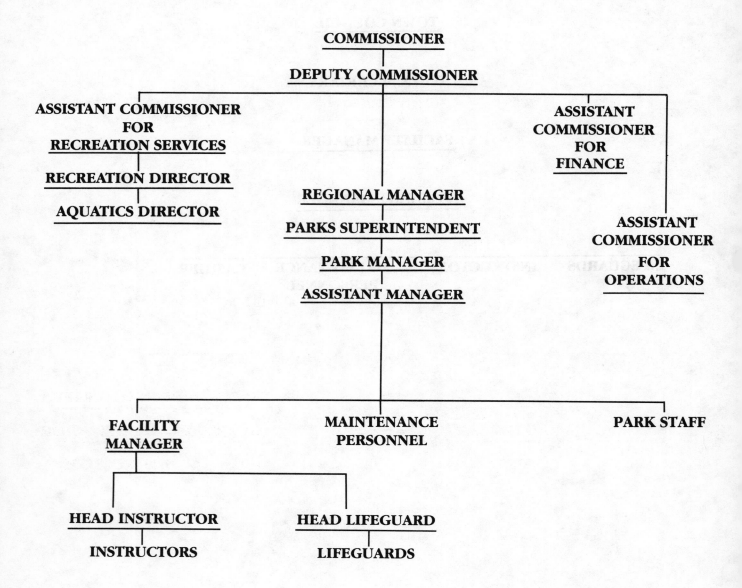

CHAIN OF COMMAND

CAMP (AGENCY OR PRIVATE)

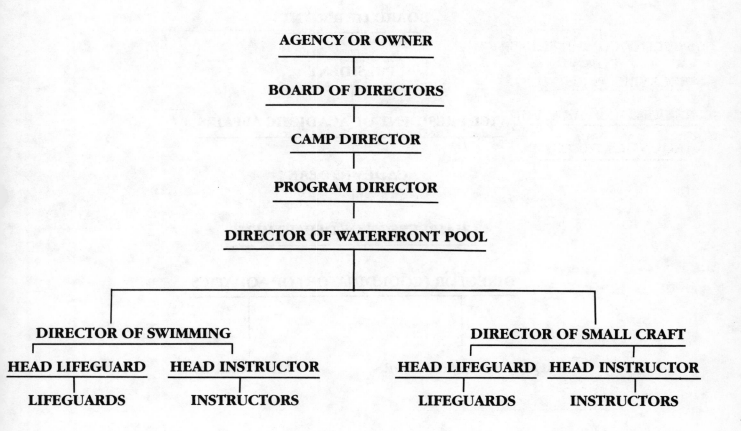

AGENCY OR OWNER

BOARD OF DIRECTORS

CAMP DIRECTOR

PROGRAM DIRECTOR

DIRECTOR OF WATERFRONT POOL

DIRECTOR OF SWIMMING

HEAD LIFEGUARD   HEAD INSTRUCTOR

LIFEGUARDS   INSTRUCTORS

DIRECTOR OF SMALL CRAFT

HEAD LIFEGUARD   HEAD INSTRUCTOR

LIFEGUARDS   INSTRUCTORS

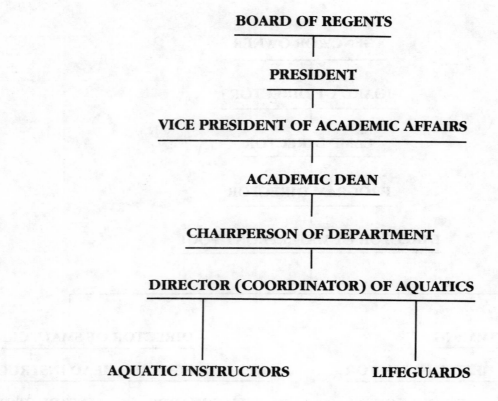

CHAIN OF COMMAND

COLLEGE OR UNIVERSITY

BOARD OF REGENTS

PRESIDENT

VICE PRESIDENT OF ACADEMIC AFFAIRS

ACADEMIC DEAN

CHAIRPERSON OF DEPARTMENT

DIRECTOR (COORDINATOR) OF AQUATICS

AQUATIC INSTRUCTORS   LIFEGUARDS

APPENDIX B

MINOR ACCIDENT AND FIRST AID TREATMENT RECORDS
(Sample)

Name of Facility _____

Manager _____

Date/Time	Name and Address of Person Treated	Type of Injury	Treatment	Lifeguard's Initials

INJURY LOG
(Sample)

Date	Hour	Name and Address	Age	Nature or Extent of Injury	Where and What Happened	Action Taken

ACCIDENT REPORT
(Sample)

Name of injured party _____
Address _____
Where did accident occur? (Be specific.) _____
When did accident occur? Date and time: _____
In what class did accident occur? Check one.
    ____ General program   ____ Professional program
    ____ Intramural activity   ____ Other—please indicate: _____
In what activity was person participating when accident occurred? _____
_____

What piece of equipment, if any, was involved in accident? _____
_____

Was there supervision at time of accident? ____ Yes ____ No
By whom? _____
What part of body was injured? _____
What type of injury (e.g., bruise, laceration) was sustained? _____
Physician's diagnosis _____
Exactly how did accident occur? Describe what happened. _____
_____

What was cause of accident?
    ____ Participating in unsafe act   ____ Lack of knowledge or skill
    ____ Defective facilities or equipment
    ____ Personal factors (overaggressive, nervous, shy)
    ____ Other—please indicate: _____
Was first aid administered?   Yes ____   No ____   By whom? _____

Was injured party referred to medical assistance?   ____ Yes   ____ No
Did injured party need help in going to medical assistance?
    ____ Yes   ____ No
Name of person who accompanied injured person to medical assistance
_____

How could this accident have been prevented? _____
_____
_____
_____

Names, addresses, and telephone numbers of witnesses
    1. _____
    2. _____
    3. _____
Name of person filling out report _____
Signature _____
Date report was filled out _____

ACCIDENT REPORT
(Sample)

Date _____ Fatality ____ Personal injury ____

_____

Personal data—injured party
Name _____ Age ____ Sex ____
Address (street and number) _____
City, town _____ State_____ Zip code_____
Country _____ Home telephone_____ Work telephone_____

_____

Type of injury   Area of injury
    ____ Fracture   ____ Head   ____ Trunk
    ____ Burn   ____ Neck   ____ Leg
    ____ Sprain/abrasion   ____ Arm   ____ Foot
    ____ Dislocation   ____ Hand   ____ Multiple
    ____ Drowning   ____ Unknown
    ____ Other (specify)

Accident Data
Date and day of week _____ Time of day _____
Name of facility _____ Address of facility _____
Weather conditions: Air temperature ____ Clear ____ Cloudy ____ Fair ____ Poor ____
Wind conditions: Wind direction ____ Light winds ____ Moderate winds ____ Strong winds ____
Water conditions: Calm ____ Choppy ____ Small waves ____ Whitecaps ____
Moving turbidity: Clear ____ Fair ____ Poor ____
Water temperature _____ Depth of water at point of accident _____

REPORT FOR ALL INJURY AND SUBMERSION CASES
(Sample)

Give the following information as accurately as possible:

1. Names, titles, employment histories, and locations of all facility employees involved.

2. Dates, types, and amounts of training and experience in lifeguarding and first aid techniques of all employees involved.

3. Time and location of injury or submersion.

4. Names, addresses, and ages of all persons involved in injury or submersion.

5. Description of water and weather temperatures and conditions at time of accident.

6. Number of patrons at beach or pool at time of accident.

7. How did involved facility employees first become aware of accident? (Include **exact** time.)

8. In rescues only:
   a. How far did employee(s) have to swim to victim? _____
   b. How far to safety did rescuer have to swim with victim? _____
   c. What assistance was given to rescuer? _____
   d. Were there any impediments to rescue? Describe them.
   e. How much time elapsed before and during rescue? _____
   f. Specify any equipment that was used in rescue.
   g. What steps, if any, were taken to revive victim? Describe in detail.
   h. Was artificial respiration required? Yes ____ No ____ CPR? Yes ____ No ____
   i. Give names of rescuers and duration of rescue efforts.

9. Was injured person identified? By whom?

10. What was victim doing at time of accident?

11. Was victim a nonswimmer? ____ Poor swimmer? ____ Good swimmer? ____

12. Did victim disregard any pool or facility rules or specific instructions by guard?

13. Were police, ambulance, rescue squad, or doctor called? By whom? How long did it take them to respond? What action did they take? Was first aid given? By whom? Describe. Did doctor arrive? Did doctor make any statements as to victim's condition? If so, what? Was victim removed from premises? By whom? Under what conditions?

14. Give additional pertinent details (including sketch of facility, if desirable).

ACCIDENT REPORT
(Sample)

Check one: Rescue ____
            First aid ____
            Other (Specify) ____

Name of victim _____ Address _____

Age ____ Sex ____ Date of accident _____ Time _____

Site of occurrence: Beach ____ Pool ____ Waterfront ____ In swimming area ____

Witnesses: Names, addresses, and telephone numbers
1. _____
2. _____
3. _____

Cause of accident _____

Condition of water: Rough ____ Mild ____ Calm ____

Equipment used in rescue _____

Description of accident and treatment (print or write clearly) _____

Lifeguard who made rescue _____ Lifeguard's signature _____
Other guards on duty _____

ACCIDENT REPORT
(Sample)

Date of accident _____ Time of accident _____

Name of injured person _____ Age _____ Sex _____

Address _____ Telephone number _____

Location of accident _____

What was injured person doing when hurt? _____

Number of persons involved _____ Names _____

_____

Water conditions _____ Weather conditions _____

Number of patrons at beach/pool at time of accident _____

Swimming ability of injured person _____

Did victim disregard rules or orders of lifeguard? Yes _____   No _____

Explain: _____

_____

Was artificial respiration used? _____ How long? _____ What type? _____

Was mechanical resuscitator used? _____ How long? _____

Was cardiopulmonary resuscitation (CPR) used? _____ How long? _____

Where was injured person taken after accident? _____

Name of doctor attending victim _____

Were police or rescue squad called? _____ Time called _____

Time of arrival _____ Action taken _____

Name of lifeguard making rescue _____ Position _____

Number of seasons (years/months) employed as lifeguard _____

Location of assignment (station) _____

List of witnesses (names, addresses, and telephone numbers) _____

_____

_____

General comments of staff _____

_____

_____

Sketch the accident area, showing unusual conditions and positions of personnel

RESCUE REPORT

(Sample)

(Required for each rescue at wave pools)

Date _____

Time _____

Position of lifeguard making rescue _____

Were waves on? Yes _____ No _____

If so, who pushed button? _____

Was victim sent to nurse? Yes _____ No _____

Was ambulance called? Yes _____ No _____

Remarks _____

Signature of person making report _____